# Functional Skills
# English Level 2

# Summative Assessment Papers, Marking Scheme and Tutors' Guide

## Roslyn Whitley Willis

# Lexden Publishing Ltd
www.lexden-publishing.co.uk

First Published in 2010 by Lexden Publishing Ltd.

ISBN:  978-1-9049955-5-5

eBook ISBN: 978-1-9049955-6-2

Lexden Publishing Ltd
14 Morant Road
Colchester
Essex
CO1 2JA

**Web:** www.lexden-publishing.co.uk
**Email:** info@lexden-publishing.co.uk

Printed in by Lightning Source

# CONTENTS

# What are Functional Skills?

Functional Skills are a new type of qualification being developed as part of the Government's reforms in education for 14 –19 year olds in England. Their aim is to improve standards in literacy, numeracy and ICT and encourage the level of competence necessary to function in learning, work and life.

There are three Functional Skills which aim to develop the skills seen as essential. These are literacy (Functional English), numeracy (Functional Mathematics), and ICT (Functional ICT).

It is intended that Functional Skills will reach a broader range of learners than is currently achieved by the Key Skills and the Adult Literacy and Adult Numeracy qualifications.

At the time of writing, the Qualifications and Curriculum Development Agency (QCDA) intends the following for Functional Skills:

1. They will be constituent qualifications of new Foundation, Higher and Advanced Diplomas and feature within each of the four qualification routes for 14–19 year olds.

2. From September 2010, the new GCSEs in Maths, English and ICT are expected to provide for the achievement of higher grades and demonstrate competence equivalent to Functional Skills at Level 2. In the new GCSEs in English, Mathematics and ICT, taught first in September 2010, the skills will also be assessed. Students will be encouraged to take the stand-alone Functional Skills qualifications in addition to these GCSEs and this is even more important if these GCSEs are not part of their study programme.

3. Functional Skills qualifications are a compulsory part of the new 14–19 Diplomas. Pre-16 learners are likely to have Functional Skills developed in an embedded capacity in English, Mathematics and ICT classes, whilst post-16 learners are likely to have both discrete (stand alone) and embedded Functional Skills in their Diploma studies.

4. It was announced in July 2010 that the inclusion of Key Skills in the apprenticeship frameworks would be extended until March 2011. Thus, Apprenticeship providers have flexibility of choice and can offer either Functional Skills or Key Skills to learners until 31 March 2011. With effect from April 2011, when the new apprenticeship frameworks will come into force, Functional Skills only will be available to apprenticeships.

5. Key Skills in the Adult Literacy and Adult Numeracy (ALAN) qualifications will gradually be replaced by Functional Skills.

The following web links have useful up-to-date information to expand on the above points:

www.qcda.gov.uk  (and search for "Functional Skills")

www.dcsf.gov.uk/14-19/index.cfm?go=site.home&sid=3&pid=225&lid=658&l4id=308&ptype=Single&ctype=FAQ

---

**Note:** the last registration for Key Skills is expected to be 2010 with the exception of the Wider Key Skills qualifications which will still be available to candidates for registration until August 2012 and awarded until August 2014.

---

1

## Functional Skills Points for Assessment and Attainment Tables

Level 2*  =  23 points

Level 1*  =  12.5 points

Entry 1   =  5 points

Entry 2   =  6 points

Entry 3   =  7 points

* The points for these Levels are in addition to points allocated for other qualifications such as GCSEs and Adult Literacy/Numeracy.

## Stand-alone Functions Skills Qualifications

As detailed in points 1–5 on *Page 1,* it is currently intended that Functional Skills will form an integrated part of several qualifications. However, they can also be stand-alone qualifications. The recommended guided learning is 30–45 hours, which is considered an appropriate period to give learners the opportunity to improve and develop their knowledge of, and competence in, each of the Functional Skill's requirements. Learners do not have to do every Functional Skill if they are working towards separate Functional Skills qualifications. Students will be able to work towards the most appropriate qualification for their individual needs or, particularly in the case of Apprenticeships, at the level determined by the individual apprenticeship programme.

## How are Functional Skills Assessed?

### Final Assessment

Unlike Key Skills, there is no Portfolio of Evidence requirement for Functional Skills. Rather the learner undertakes a supervised assessment. The topics are general and not related to specific employment sectors. The assessment approach will be primarily task-based scenario questions.

There is a final assessment (summative assessment) and at present each Awarding Body has adopted a slightly different assessment method.

It must be stressed that when your learners undertake Functional Skills it is important to check your Centre's Awarding Body's website for up-to-date information on this evolving qualification.

Some Awarding Bodies allow the assessment material to be available "on demand".

The work may have to be marked in the Centre or may be marked by the Awarding Body's panel of markers and the results communicated to the Centre. Check the system used by your Centre's Awarding Body along with their timetable of assessment and for the notification dates of results.

In order to ensure that tutors become familiar with producing formal assessment evidence, forms designed to enable the tutor to give feedback to learners on the assessments they complete have been included in this resource.

It is important to give written feedback to the learner so they are aware of their strengths and weaknesses. The front cover of each sample assessment paper allows the assessor to record the marks gained for each of the activities, together with allowing for the calculation of a percentage total translating to a pass or fail. By formalising the process in this way it indicates to the learner the importance of the tasks and is a recognition of their efforts.

## Explaining the Summative Assessment Papers in this book

### The Awarding Bodies' different approaches to summative assessment

At the time of writing the Awarding Bodies each have different approaches to their assessment of the Functional Skills. These variations include the length of the assessment and the type of questions and criteria covered.

Some Awarding Bodies allow that if the Centre considers the assessment paper to be too long for learners, the assessment can take place during a number of sessions. The current indication seems to be up to two sessions for Functional English.

It is deemed acceptable for Centres to use different Awarding Bodies for different Functional Skills.

Some Awarding Body assessments cover Reading, Writing and Speaking, others Reading and Writing. Understanding the source documents (reading) can be tested by the learner answering multiple-choice questions, **and** writing responses in the form of opinions to show an understanding of the source document(s). Other assessments might be scenario-based and require the writing of structured, formal documents such as letters, articles, handouts, **and** include a demonstration of competence in speaking in the form of making a presentation and/or discussion.

Until, and if, QCDA decides upon a definitive method of assessment, the practice papers in this book vary but they collectively cover the activities of Reading and Writing, **and** Speaking and Listening. There are a range of contexts, and each paper is scenario-based with linked activities. Each of the 16 sample Assessment Papers in this resource have a number of sections, some have suggested timings but others, particularly those involving research, have no suggested timing. Centres can split the assessment material into a number of sessions as they wish. It must be emphasised, again, that Centres should check with their Awarding Body what is acceptable in terms of the summative assessment.

Some activities are time-constrained to help learners prepare for this aspect of their real, Award-Body-based assessment. Those which involve research or the writing of extended documents and making a presentation or taking part in a discussion/exchange are not time-constrained. It is up to tutors to determine timings for such tasks taking into account the available equipment, the number of learners involved in the activities and the length of their classroom sessions.

## Assessment Evidence

I anticipate that the good practice of providing assessment evidence of the Key Skills Portfolio work will continue to be a requirement with the summative assessment of Functional Skills.

With this in mind, each assessment paper has a front sheet which shows the marks allocated to each question, with an additional sheet allowing assessors to record feedback.

As each aspect of the assessment should be evidenced, an Assessor Observation Sheet related to Taking Part in a Discussion/Exchange is included (*Page 9*). It can be completed by tutors to record the outcome of each learner's participation in Speaking and Listening, clearly indicating to the learner and verifier that the learner was assessed against the criteria as set out in the Standards and what the learner did, or did not do, in order to meet the Standard.

## Assessment Achievement Record Keeping

There are 16 sample summative assessment papers in this book and tutors using them with groups will need to keep track of individual learner achievement. A Student Achievement Assessment Tracking Sheet can be found on *Page 8* which may prove a useful method of recording this information.

# Explaining the Functional Skills English Level 2 Standards

There are three components to Functional Skills English at Level 2:

1    Speaking and Listening (SL);

2    Reading (R);

3    Writing (W).

Standards for all Functional Skills can be found at:
www.ofqual.gov.uk/files/QCA-07-3472-functional-skills_standards.pdf.

An explanation of the Standards appears on *Page 4* to *Page 7*. This explanation has been directed towards the learners so they can better understand what they are expected to achieve, although the information should also be useful for tutors.

# The Functional Skills English Level 2 Standards explained

## SPEAKING AND LISTENING

| WHAT YOU MUST BE ABLE TO DO | WHAT SKILLS ARE INVOLVED |
|---|---|
| SL2　Make a range of contributions to discussions.<br><br>**What and who is involved**<br><br>In a wide range of contexts, including those that involve others who are unfamiliar. | SL2.1　listen to complex information and give a relevant, cogent response in appropriate language<br><br>SL2.2　present information and ideas clearly and persuasively to others<br><br>SL2.3　adapt contributions in discussions to suit audience, purpose and situation<br><br>SL2.4　make significant contributions to discussions, taking a range of roles and helping to move discussion forward to reach decisions |

| WHAT THIS MEANS YOU MAY HAVE TO DO WHEN YOU ARE INVOLVED IN A DISCUSSION OR A PRESENTATION | |
|---|---|
| SL2.1 | You will show that you can listen to what others say and show that you are listening to their contribution by your body language, through questioning them and responding politely.<br><br>You will show that you can do each of the following:<br>- respond to the speaker (perhaps giving an answer to a question or agreeing with what the speaker is saying or asking you);<br>- respond to a question from someone listening to you;<br>- summarise the comments of others (perhaps making sure everyone involved understands the discussion and their roles and responsibilities);<br>- encourage others to contribute to the discussion. |
| SL2.2 | You will sometimes need to persuade listeners of your point of view/ideas and you will need to choose carefully what you say in order to convince the listeners of the points you make. You can use documents (perhaps that include one or more images) which support your points and this may involve research into the topic. You will be able to decide on the degree of formality or informality suitable for the audience and the context.<br><br>When involved in an exchange, or in making a presentation, you will show you can structure your points and arguments so the audience finds it easy to follow and understand what you say and is persuaded to agree with you. |
| SL2.3 | You will be involved in discussions with different people on different topics and must show you can adapt what you say and how you say it to the people involved. For example, a discussion with members of your class group (peers) might be more informal and friendly than a discussion with teachers or people at work, and people you have not met before.<br><br>Your audience will be different probably on each occasion you have a discussion or make an effective presentation and you will need to prepare what you say so you do not confuse the listener(s). You should do this by preparing your thoughts and making notes, perhaps finding evidence to support what you say and saying things in a way which the listeners can understand.<br><br>Your listeners will range in their age, experience and understanding of the topic and you might have to explain some technical terms to them. Always adapt your exchange/presentation to meet the needs of the audience.<br><br>Make responses to people giving complex information through discussion and make sure what you say is logical and relevant to the subject and the topic. |

| SL2.4 | Help to move the discussion forward so that decisions can be made. |
|---|---|
| | You might do this in any of the following ways: |

- ask questions of the speaker to make sure you have understood what is being said;
- ask the speaker to explain facts offered;
- ask the speaker to explain their point of view/opinion;
- offer a different point of view to challenge the speaker;
- repeat what has been said to show you have understood the points and ideas;
- introduce your ideas which might be different from what has been said and changes the focus of the discussion;
- offer a summary of what has been said and establish agreement by suggesting what happens next as a result of the discussion.

## READING

| WHAT YOU MUST BE ABLE TO DO | | WHAT SKILLS ARE INVOLVED | |
|---|---|---|---|
| R2 | Compare, select, read and understand texts and use them to gather information, ideas, arguments and opinions. | R2.1 | select and use different types of texts to obtain relevant information |
| | | R2.2 | read and summarise succinctly information/ideas from different sources |
| **What kind of texts and from where** | | R2.3 | identify the purposes of texts and comment on how effectively meaning is conveyed |
| In a wide range of texts for different purposes, on paper and on screen. | | R2.4 | detect points of view, implicit meaning and/or bias |
| | | R2.5 | read and actively respond to different texts (for example, reply to each point in a letter of complaint) |

| WHAT THIS MEANS YOU MAY HAVE TO DO WHEN SELECTING AND READING TEXT | |
|---|---|
| R2.1 | You will show that you understand what information you need to find and be able to decide where to look for the information appropriate to the topic and be able to select different types of text to meet the purpose/activity. |
| | You will find information from paper-based sources (for example, a newspaper article; a letter; a report; a graph or chart; an instruction manual), and electronic sources (for example, a website; a CD-ROM; or a document, spreadsheet or database stored electronically). |
| R2.2 | Use the information you find to write a document which summarises this information and shows that you understand what is written in the document. |
| | The documents will vary in purpose and display, for instance an accident report or a table of text, or a chart/graph containing statistics. |
| | You will sometimes be expected to find information which offers different points of view on the same topic, and to summarise both points of view in either a written form or in the spoken form. |
| | In a written summary you will show that you have understood the text by expressing the ideas/ facts in your own words and perhaps offering your own point of view. |
| R2.3 | You will have to identify the purpose of texts by recognising the style and aim of the document (for example, a letter which states facts; an advertisement containing a mixture of fact and opinion; a memo which contains instructions) and be able to judge how effectively the ideas and facts are expressed. For example, did you understand the point made, or have you changed your opinion on the topic as a result of reading the text? |
| R2.4 | You will have to show that you have understood the points of view put forward in the document. For example, whether they represent opinion or fact; whether they put forward a balanced argument for and against the topic, whether the information is biased towards one point of view, whether the information is humorous or serious and whether the meaning of the document is able to be understood. |
| | You should be able to recognise whether the way in which the document is laid out helps the reader to understand what it contains (for instance, have headings and sub-headings been used which effectively draw the reader's attention to main points; is there a summary to the document perhaps; is there a logical sequence to the ideas presented?). |
| R2.5 | You will usually have to write, and read, a document as a result of your research and from the document(s) you find and you must show you can pick out the important main points and respond to them appropriately. |
| | If appropriate, you will show you can follow instructions contained in a document, or respond to part of a document, for instance a letter asking for a reply to certain questions, or a set of instructions to be followed. |

## WRITING

| WHAT YOU MUST BE ABLE TO DO | | WHAT SKILLS ARE INVOLVED | |
|---|---|---|---|
| W2 | Write documents, including extended written pieces, communicating information, ideas and opinions, effectively and persuasively.<br><br>**What kind of documents and in what format**<br><br>In a wide range of documents on paper and on screen (handwritten and computer-generated). | W2.1 | present information/ideas concisely, logically and persuasively |
| | | W2.2 | present information on complex subjects concisely and clearly |
| | | W2.3 | use a range of different styles of writing for different purposes |
| | | W2.4 | use a range of sentence structures, including complex sentences |
| | | W2.5 | punctuate accurately using commas, apostrophes and inverted commas |
| | | W2.6 | ensure written work has accurate grammar, punctuation and spelling and the meaning is clear |

| WHAT THIS MEANS YOU MAY HAVE TO DO WHEN WRITING TEXT | |
|---|---|
| W2.1 | You will be able to write documents which express information clearly and which is relevant to the topic (or the talk you will give), making sure there is a logical order and a clear introduction and conclusion.<br><br>Documents will range in purpose, for instance explaining, instructing, advising etc.<br><br>The documents you write can be in handwritten form, or can be computer-generated. |
| W2.2 | Some of the documents you write will refer to complex subjects perhaps produced as a result of reading complex material.<br><br>Your documents will be written so the meaning is clear to the reader.<br><br>You will write documents which convey the meaning to the intended audience (familiar or unfamiliar with the topic/situation) in a way which is to the point, avoiding unnecessary repetition of points.<br><br>You must be able to select an appropriate format for the documents you write. For instance a business letter, a report, a fax, and decide on the degree of formality required. |
| W2.3 | You will be able to write a range of documents each of which will be suited to the purpose and the audience (for example, writing a letter to ask for information; writing a report to give information to people not familiar with the subject; writing an advertisement to persuade people to buy something).<br><br>The documents you write will be displayed correctly and contain all the necessary information and sections. For example, a business letter will have a date, a name and address of the recipient, the salutation and complimentary close will match correctly; a report will have the standard headings and include a date). |
| W2.4 | Your writing will show you can use sentences formed correctly with accurate spelling and punctuation and using correct joining of sentences with such words as and/but. |
| W2.5 | Your writing will show you can use punctuation accurately, including commas, apostrophes and inverted commas. You will know the implication of writing a document which is not correct in this aspect, i.e. giving a poor reputation to your company because of errors in the letter you write and sign; the unlikelihood of your getting an interview for a job when your letter of application and CV has spelling and punctuation errors in it. |
| W2.6 | Your written work will be accurate and the meaning will be clear to the reader even if they are unfamiliar with the topic.<br><br>To help the reader understand your written work another important aspect is the layout. You will use sub-headings and paragraphs to help the reader select and understand the main points and ideas which you present, whether you are putting forward facts, opinions or ideas. |

# FUNCTIONAL ENGLISH LEVEL 2  STUDENT ACHIEVEMENT ASSESSMENT TRACKING SHEET:

## FUNCTIONAL ENGLISH LEVEL 2 STUDENT ACHIEVEMENT ASSESSMENT TRACKING SHEET

**GROUP**

| Name | Assessment Title | | | | | | | | | | | | | | |
|---|---|---|---|---|---|---|---|---|---|---|---|---|---|---|---|
| | | | | | | | | | | | | | | | |
| | | | | | | | | | | | | | | | |
| | | | | | | | | | | | | | | | |
| | | | | | | | | | | | | | | | |
| | | | | | | | | | | | | | | | |
| | | | | | | | | | | | | | | | |
| | | | | | | | | | | | | | | | |
| | | | | | | | | | | | | | | | |
| | | | | | | | | | | | | | | | |
| | | | | | | | | | | | | | | | |
| | | | | | | | | | | | | | | | |
| | | | | | | | | | | | | | | | |
| Date | | | | | | | | | | | | | | | |

Functional Skills English Level 2  Summative Assessment Papers, Marking Scheme, and Tutors' Guide – ISBN: 978-1-9049955-5-5

# Functional Skills English Level 2: Taking Part in a Discussion/Exchange

## Observation Sheet

### SL2.1 – 2.4 Speaking and Listening

| Student's Name | | Date of Discussion Exchange | |
|---|---|---|---|

| Assessment Title | |
|---|---|

| Names of Group Members | |
|---|---|

| Topic of Discussion | |
|---|---|

| Criteria | Achieved (✓) | Assessor's Comments |
|---|---|---|
| **SL2.1** <br><br> Listen to complex information and give a relevant, cogent response in appropriate language | | |
| **SL2.2** <br><br> Present information and ideas clearly and persuasively to others | | |
| **SL2.3** <br><br> Adapt contributions in discussions to suit audience, purpose and situation | | |
| **SL2.4** <br><br> Make significant contributions to discussions, taking a range of roles and helping to move discussions forward to reach decisions | | |

| Assessor's Signature | | Date | |
|---|---|---|---|

Functional Skills English Level 2  Summative Assessment Papers, Marking Scheme,  and Tutors' Guide – ISBN:  978-1-9049955-5-5

# Using ICT equipment in Functional English

**Research** Students should be encouraged to use both ICT- and paper-based resources wherever possible.

**Producing the work** Students should be encouraged to produce their work in a range of contexts. This is likely to involve using a computer to produce some work, particularly that which includes illustrations or images. However, do not assess the student's ICT skills when considering their completed Functional English documents. Clearly, some work should be handwritten.

**The "Pass" mark**

Each of these assessment papers has 50 marks allocated. The mark the student gains should be doubled so it represents a percentage.

Until, and if, QCDA publishes a "pass mark" I advise tutors to work on the principle of 75 per cent. At present, Awarding Bodies allocate different pass marks to the various sections of Functional English so it is important that Centres find out this information from their Awarding Body.

At present, as with the structure and content of the assessments set by different Award Bodies, the pass marks vary from section to section, paper to paper, series to series and Award Body to Award Body. My advice is to assess higher rather than lower because it better prepares the student as it allows for some "slippage" in the real Summative Assessment.

# Number of Words in the written work

Until, and if, QCDA makes a decision on the recommended number of words which a student needs to include in an extended piece of writing, the guidelines for Key Skills Communication Level 2 are mostly assumed, i.e. a minimum of 500 words. There are exceptions, notably when the student is required to produce a Fact Sheet or presentation notes, but some of the assessment opportunities in this resource provide the opportunity to write 500 words. Centres can adjust this if required to do so by their Functional Skills Awarding Body.

# Dictionaries

Students are allowed to use a dictionary in the Summative Assessment so this should be encouraged as they work through the papers in this book.

# Reflective Statement

Although I have not included this necessity in the individual Assessment Papers, it is good practice to encourage the learner to reflect upon and review their planning and achievements upon completion of a structured piece of work.

A learner's ability to recognise their strengths and their weaknesses, and to be able to articulate how they overcame any problems, together with how the assessment experience has highlighted areas which they need to improve or revise, is one which helps the learner to better achieve expected outcomes in the future. This necessity is required both in the world of work and day-to-day life.

Whether you wish to include this reflective process in all, most, or none of the Assessment Papers, is your decision. A sample reflective statement is included on *Page 11 – Page 16*.

# REFLECTIVE STATEMENT

In any learning or assessment activity it is important to reflect upon your approach and your achievements. It is only by going through this process that you can be aware of what you have done well and are happy with and, equally importantly, what you need to improve through practice and revision.

The questions on the following pages are designed to help you in this process.

There are four categories of reflection:

1   **preparing** for the assessment – your planning process;

2   **describing** your method of working – showing you know what you are required to do and describing your approach to the work;

3   **reviewing** your work and methods of working – reflecting on how you worked and the quality of what you produced;

4   **grading** your handling of the assessment and the quality of the work you produced.

# PREPARING FOR THE ASSESSMENT

It is always important to read the material thoroughly before you begin work. By doing this you will better be able to:

1      understand what you are expected to do;

2      plan how best to achieve what is required; and

3      understand the type of work you are expected to produce and the standard to which you must work.

---

Describe what you were expected to achieve in this assessment

and

describe how thoroughly reading the paper prepared you for the tasks you had to complete.

# DESCRIBING MY METHOD OF WORKING

When you understand what you are required to produce in the assessment, it is important to plan how you will complete the tasks and work to the required standard.

Describe what you had to produce for the tasks in the assessment

and

describe how you prepared for each task in the assessment, making sure you could do what was required, and describing your approach to the activities.

Functional Skills English Level 2 Summative Assessment Papers, Marking Scheme, and Tutors' Guide – ISBN: 978-1-9049955-5-5

# REVIEWING MY WORK AND MY METHODS OF WORKING

After completing an assessment, it is important to reflect upon the experience. In this way you will be able to recognise your achievements, your strengths and your weaknesses and plan how to overcome your weaknesses so you are better prepared for future tasks.

Reflect on each of the following:

- the quality of the work you produced;

- the advantages of working in the way you did;

- the problems you encountered and how you solved them;

- what you have learnt as a result of completing the assessment.

Describe the quality of the work you produced. For instance, does it meet the requirements of each activity; are there things you would wish to improve, and if so, what are they and why do you think this?

And

say whether you think the way in which you planned and worked during the assessment helped you complete the work, or would you have done anything differently, and if so, what and why

and

describe any problems you had whilst doing the assessment and how you overcame them

and

state what you have learnt by doing the assessment, including details of your strengths and weaknesses, and how you aim to turn your weaknesses into strengths for the future.

Functional Skills English Level 2 Summative Assessment Papers, Marking Scheme, and Tutors' Guide – ISBN: 978-1-9049955-5-5

Functional Skills English Level 2  Summative Assessment Papers, Marking Scheme, and Tutors' Guide – ISBN:  978-1-9049955-5-5

# FINALLY, RATE YOURSELF ON EACH OF THE FOLLOWING CATEGORIES

Tick (✓) one answer for each category.  Be honest: you will have to justify what you say!

| Category | Very Good | Good | Satisfactory | Not good enough |
|---|---|---|---|---|
| 1   My ability to understand what I was required to achieve. | | | | |
| 2   My ability to plan successfully for what I was required to achieve. | | | | |
| 3   My ability to overcome difficulties. | | | | |
| 4   What I feel is the standard of work in my completed assessment. | | | | |
| 5   My understanding of my strengths. | | | | |
| 6   My understanding of my weaknesses. | | | | |
| 7   My ability to know how to change my weaknesses into strengths – from whom to seek help; what I need to practise/revise. | | | | |

Write a statement justifying the grades you have attached to each of the above seven categories.

Functional Skills English Level 2  Summative Assessment Papers, Marking Scheme, and Tutors' Guide – ISBN: 978-1-9049955-5-5

# PRACTICE ASSESSMENT MATERIAL

## Practice Assessments Coverage Grid

| Assessment Title | Activity 1 | Activity 2 | Activity 3 | Activity 4 |
|---|---|---|---|---|
| 1 The Blue Flag Scheme | Reading and writing | Reading and writing | Writing a business letter | Researching and writing a handout<br><br>Making a presentation |
| 2 National Blood Service | Reading | Researching and writing a fact sheet | Researching and making a presentation | |
| 3 A Holiday in Budapest | Reading | Reading and writing | Speaking (telephone call) and writing a personal letter | |
| 4 Buying Safely Online | Reading | Reading and writing | Reading and writing | Researching and writing a fact sheet and a personal letter |
| 5 Trinity House | Reading and writing | Reading and writing | Researching and writing a fact sheet and an invitation | |
| 6 Climate Change | Reading and writing | Reading and writing | Researching and writing two illustrated articles | Researching and making a presentation |
| 7 The Yorkshire Three Peaks Challenge Walk | Reading | Reading and writing | Reading and speaking (telephone call) | Researching and writing a business letter |
| 8 Swim Better – Feel Fitter | Reading and writing | Reading and writing | Researching and writing a report | |
| 9 Think about Recycling | Reading and writing | Reading and writing | Reading | Researching and writing a promotional leaflet |
| 10 Binge Drinking | Reading and writing | Reading | Reading and writing | Researching and writing a report |
| 11 5-A-Day | Reading and writing | Reading and writing | Researching and writing a newsletter and a memo | |
| 12 No Messin' | Reading and writing | Reading and writing | Reading and writing | Researching and writing an information booklet |
| 13 The Cost of Being a Football Fan | Reading | Reading and writing | Researching and writing a summary sheet and making a presentation | |
| 14 Travel Safely Abroad | Reading and writing | Reading and writing | Researching and writing a personal letter | |
| 15 Sunbed Safety | Reading and writing | Reading and writing | Researching and writing an information booklet | |
| 16 Waste Battery Recycling and Disposal | Reading and writing | Reading and writing | Researching and designing an illustrated poster and writing a memo | |

# CRITERIA COVERED IN EACH SAMPLE ASSESSMENT PAPER

**Assessment Title and Number**

| No. | Assessment Title |
|---|---|
| 1 | The Blue Flag Scheme |
| 2 | National Blood Service |
| 3 | A Holiday in Budapest |
| 4 | Buying Safely Online |
| 5 | Trinity House |
| 6 | Climate Change |
| 7 | The Yorkshire Three Peaks Challenge Walk |
| 8 | Swim Better Feel Fitter |
| 9 | Think about Recycling |
| 10 | Binge Drinking |
| 11 | 5-A-Day |
| 12 | No Messin'? |
| 13 | The Cost of Being a Football Fan |
| 14 | Travel Safely Abroad |
| 15 | Sunbed Safety |
| 16 | Waste Battery Recycling and Disposal |

| Criteria | 1 | 2 | 3 | 4 | 5 | 6 | 7 | 8 | 9 | 10 | 11 | 12 | 13 | 14 | 15 | 16 |
|---|---|---|---|---|---|---|---|---|---|---|---|---|---|---|---|---|
| **Reading** | | | | | | | | | | | | | | | | |
| R2.1 | ✓ | ✓ | ✓ | ✓ | ✓ | ✓ | ✓ | ✓ | ✓ | ✓ | ✓ | ✓ | ✓ | ✓ | ✓ | ✓ |
| R2.2 | ✓ | ✓ | ✓ | ✓ | ✓ | ✓ | ✓ | ✓ | ✓ | ✓ | ✓ | ✓ | ✓ | ✓ | ✓ | ✓ |
| R2.3 | ✓ | ✓ | ✓ |  | ✓ | ✓ | ✓ |  | ✓ | ✓ |  | ✓ | ✓ | ✓ | ✓ | ✓ |
| R2.4 |  | ✓ | ✓ |  |  |  | ✓ |  | ✓ | ✓ |  |  | ✓ | ✓ | ✓ | ✓ |
| R2.5 |  |  | ✓ | ✓ | ✓ | ✓ |  |  | ✓ | ✓ | ✓ | ✓ | ✓ | ✓ | ✓ | ✓ |
| **Writing** | | | | | | | | | | | | | | | | |
| W2.1 | ✓ | ✓ | ✓ | ✓ | ✓ | ✓ | ✓ | ✓ | ✓ | ✓ | ✓ | ✓ | ✓ | ✓ | ✓ | ✓ |
| W2.2 | ✓ | ✓ | ✓ | ✓ | ✓ | ✓ | ✓ | ✓ | ✓ | ✓ | ✓ | ✓ | ✓ | ✓ | ✓ | ✓ |
| W2.3 | ✓ | ✓ | ✓ | ✓ | ✓ | ✓ | ✓ | ✓ | ✓ | ✓ | ✓ | ✓ | ✓ | ✓ | ✓ | ✓ |
| W2.4 | ✓ | ✓ | ✓ | ✓ | ✓ | ✓ | ✓ | ✓ | ✓ | ✓ | ✓ | ✓ | ✓ | ✓ | ✓ | ✓ |
| W2.5 | ✓ | ✓ | ✓ | ✓ | ✓ | ✓ | ✓ | ✓ | ✓ | ✓ | ✓ | ✓ | ✓ | ✓ | ✓ | ✓ |
| W2.6 | ✓ | ✓ | ✓ | ✓ | ✓ | ✓ | ✓ | ✓ | ✓ | ✓ | ✓ | ✓ | ✓ | ✓ | ✓ | ✓ |
| **Speaking and Listening** | | | | | | | | | | | | | | | | |
| SL2.1 | ✓ |  | ✓ |  |  |  | ✓ |  |  |  |  |  | ✓ |  |  |  |
| SL2.2 | ✓ | ✓ | ✓ |  |  | ✓ |  |  |  |  |  |  | ✓ |  |  |  |
| SL2.3 | ✓ | ✓ | ✓ |  |  | ✓ | ✓ |  |  |  |  |  | ✓ |  |  |  |
| SL2.4 |  |  | ✓ |  |  |  | ✓ |  |  |  |  |  |  |  |  |  |

The criteria R2.4 is included in the activities because the learner has to understand the research documents' content and any possible bias in order to adapt the information for a specific purpose in their written work. In some assessments this requirement is more overt.

# GUIDANCE RELATED TO THE IMPORTANT ASSESSMENT POINTS

## Written response guidance

The suggested assessment points (See *Page 308* to *Page 336*) for the written responses do not represent an exhaustive list. Learners will possibly offer additional points which the tutor may consider to be valid and appropriate. In some cases learners may offer alternative choices, but their reasons for must be valid.

If learners have failed to put text into their own words, and have just copied the wording from the source documents, using that as their answer, the allocated marks should not be awarded. Writing tasks test the learner's ability to write cogent statements which show they have understood what they have read.

When the task requires the learner to produce a formal document, the standard conventions of display need to be followed and all the standard text should be included.

The wording and layout of all documents must be appropriate for the context, purpose and the audience.

## Research Guidance

Tutors should look for evidence the learner has put information from the source documents into their own words and shown an understanding of what has been read.

Learners should be encouraged to find and use a range of suitable documents from both paper- and computer-based sources.

Learners must show evidence of going some way towards annotating the source documents to indicate that which they deem useful to amend/adapt/include into their written document(s). This helps focus their attention and it also aids your assessment process!

## Presentation Guidance

Tutors should look for learners to make presentations, and engage in discussions and exchanges, with increasing confidence and competence as they practise the assessment tasks.

Any illustrations/images used should be appropriate and used to enhance the topic under discussion and/or the audience's understanding.

The presentation content must be structured logically. There should be an introduction and a close.

The content and style of the presentation must be appropriate for the audience and the situation.

On at least one occasion the learner should ask for questions from the audience and be able to deal with responding to such questions competently, demonstrating an ease with the audience and knowledge of the topic under discussion.

---

### IMPORTANT NOTE ABOUT THE BLANK PAGES INCLUDED IN EACH SAMPLE SUMMATIVE ASSESSMENT PAPER

Blank pages, appropriately headed, have been included in each assessment paper to enable the learner to draft and plan documents, exchanges or presentation notes. In each instance, only one such page is included for each type of document as this enables you, the tutor/assessor, to decide how many such sheets to give to each learner.

---

## Functional Skills English Level 2 Assessment Paper

Student's Name

Paper's Title

**THE BLUE FLAG SCHEME**

Date Set

Hand-in Date

| Activity | Possible Marks | | Marks Awarded | Totals |
|---|---|---|---|---|
| 1  Reading and Writing | Q1 | 1 | | |
| | Q2 | 2 | | |
| | Q3 | 2 | | |
| | Q4 | 2 | | |
| | Q5 | 2 | | |
| | Q6 | 3 | | |
| | | | Activity 1 | |
| 2  Reading and Writing | Q1 | 1 | | |
| | Q2 | 2 | | |
| | Q3 | 1 | | |
| | Q4 | 1 | | |
| | Q5 | 1 | | |
| | Q6 | 1 | | |
| | Q7 | 1 | | |
| | | | Activity 2 | |
| 3  Writing | Q1 | 10 | | |
| | | | Activity 3 | |
| 4  Researching, Writing and Making a Presentation | Q1 | 6 | | |
| | Q2 | 14 | | |
| | | | Activity 4 | |
| | | | PAPER TOTAL | |
| | | | **PERCENTAGE** | |

**Result**

Circle the appropriate result

**PASS**

**FAIL**

Assessor's Signature ......................................................... Date ...........................

Functional Skills English Level 2  Summative Assessment Papers, Marking Scheme,  and Tutors' Guide – ISBN:  978-1-9049955-5-5

# THE BLUE FLAG SCHEME

## Assessor's Comments

| Activity | Comments |
|---|---|
| 1 | |
| 2 | |
| 3 | |
| 4 | See also my comments on the Speaking and Listening Observation Sheet |

Functional Skills English Level 2 Summative Assessment Papers, Marking Scheme, and Tutors' Guide – ISBN: 978-1-9049955-5-5

# THE BLUE FLAG SCHEME

This paper has 4 sections:

| | |
|---|---|
| Sections 1 and 2 | involve reading and writing |
| Section 3 | involves writing a business letter |
| Section 4 | involves researching, writing a handout and making a presentation |

There are **two** documents for you to read.

Read both documents **before** you begin to answer the questions and keep referring to them when you work through the sections.

You are reminded that clear written and spoken English and correct spelling and punctuation are important, together with presenting work neatly and making sure it is suitable for the purpose and the audience.

Functional Skills English Level 2 Summative Assessment Papers, Marking Scheme, and Tutors' Guide – ISBN: 978-1-9049955-5-5

# THE BLUE FLAG SCHEME

ACTIVITY 1 — Reading and Writing

You will be assessed on the following:

— reading, finding and summarising facts and ideas from text;

— identifying the purpose and effectiveness of texts;

— presenting your work and ideas clearly and logically;

— using a range of sentence structures, including complex sentences;

— using spelling, grammar and punctuation accurately and correctly.

Read **Document 1** then answer the following questions.

You should spend no longer than 20 minutes on questions 1 — 6.


1    Tick (✓) the option which **best** describes the main purpose of Document 1?
     **1 mark**

     A    to advertise                              ☐

     B    to inform                                 ☐

     C    to encourage a course of action           ☐

     D    to offer advice                           ☐

Referring to **Document 1**, answer the following questions

2    Describe **two** ways in which you think the writer successfully described the
     purpose of the Scheme. Give examples for each point you make. **2 marks**

     _____

     _____

     _____

     _____

     _____

     _____

3    What were the intentions of the Blue Flag scheme when it began in 1985?
     **2 marks**

_____

_____

_____

_____

4    How has the scheme developed since 1985?  **2 marks**

_____

_____

_____

_____

5    Explain what the BMC is and what it does.  **2 marks**

_____

_____

_____

_____

6    Related to safety, what must at least one Blue Flag beach have in any area?
     **3 marks**

_____

_____

_____

_____

Functional Skills English Level 2  Summative Assessment Papers, Marking Scheme, and Tutors' Guide – ISBN: 978-1-9049955-5-5

# THE BLUE FLAG SCHEME

ACTIVITY 2 — Reading and Writing

You will be assessed on the following:

— reading, finding and summarising facts and ideas from different types of document;

— identifying the purpose of text;

— presenting your work and ideas clearly using a range of sentence structures, including complex sentences;

— using spelling, grammar and punctuation accurately and correctly.

**Document 2** is written by Blue Flag and includes an invitation for the reader to send for an Information Pack and application form. Read the document, then answer the following questions.

You should spend no longer than 15 minutes on questions 1 — 7.

1    Tick (✓) the option which **best** describes the main purpose of Document 2?
    **1 mark**

    A    to encourage a course of action    ☐

    B    to encourage a purchase    ☐

    C    to provide information    ☐

    D    to request assistance    ☐

2    The document says being a member "can boost the local economy by encouraging tourists to the area". Explain why this might occur. **2 marks**

    _____

    _____

    _____

    _____

    _____

For questions 3 — 7 choose one answer, A, B, C or D, and put a ✓ (tick) in the box.

1 mark is awarded for each correct answer.

3 Looking at the graph, select the correct statement from the following.

A Scotland has the fewest marinas but the most beaches ☐

B Wales has twice as many beaches as marinas ☐

C Croatia has the fewest marinas and Spain the most ☐
beaches

D Spain and France have an equal number of marinas and ☐
Spain has approximately twice as many beaches as
France

4 Who makes the decision about whether a beach and/or marina can be included in the Blue Flag scheme?

A Blue Flag ☐

B the FEE ☐

C an International Jury ☐

D the Local Council ☐

5 Looking at the document in general, and the graph in particular, which of the following statements is correct?

A only 8 countries belong to the Blue Flag scheme ☐

B countries from around the world are members of the ☐
Blue Flag scheme but the graph shows only details of a
few

C 2633 countries belong to the Blue Flag scheme and the ☐
graph shows details of 12 of the marinas

D where the 620 marinas are located is illustrated on the ☐
graph

26

Functional Skills English Level 2 Summative Assessment Papers, Marking Scheme, and Tutors' Guide – ISBN: 978-1-9049955-5-5

6    Which South American countries are interested in applying to Blue Flag for recognition?

    A      Chile and Brazil ☐

    B      Argentina and Ecuador ☐

    C      Chile and Ecuador ☐

    D      Brazil, Ecuador and Argentina ☐

7    What is significant about Canada?

    A      it has been successful in joining the Blue Flag Scheme ☐

    B      it is working towards becoming a Blue Flag member ☐

    C      it recently lost its membership to the Blue Flag Scheme ☐

    D      it has been a member of the Blue Flag scheme since 2001 ☐

Functional Skills English Level 2  Summative Assessment Papers, Marking Scheme, and Tutors' Guide – ISBN:  978-1-9049955-5-5

# THE BLUE FLAG SCHEME

ACTIVITY 3 — Writing

## Writing a business letter

You will be assessed on the following:

— presenting your written work clearly and logically;

— using a style of writing suited to the situation and the audience;

— using a range of sentence structures, including complex sentences;

— using spelling, grammar and punctuation accurately and correctly.

**There are no suggested timings for this activity.**

## Scenario

You work for Shorefield-on-Sea District Council which has completed the application form to become a member of the Blue Flag scheme.

As your Application Form was sent in seven weeks ago and you have not heard anything, you must now write to the Blue Flag Association, using the address shown in **Document 2.**

## 1    Business Letter    10 marks

The aim of your letter is to ask if the Association has received your Application Form – numbered AP338/662909 which was posted on (give a date seven weeks ago).  If they have not received the form you will need to ask if a photocopy of the copy you kept can be submitted rather than having to complete the five pages all over again.

You also want to know, once the form is received, what is the next stage in the process. You understand it to be a visit to the beaches/marinas listed on the application form but want to know if someone from your department in the Council will be able to be present during the inspection visit.

Ask your Tutor for a Council letter heading on which to write your letter which Sevendilho Porec, the Senior Environmental Officer, will sign.

Your letter should contain no fewer than 150 words.

If you wish to do so, you can plan your work on the blank pages your tutor will hand you.

Functional Skills English Level 2  Summative Assessment Papers, Marking Scheme,  and Tutors' Guide – ISBN:  978-1-9049955-5-5

# Business Letter

---

Functional Skills English Level 2  Summative Assessment Papers, Marking Scheme,  and Tutors' Guide – ISBN:  978-1-9049955-5-5

Functional Skills English Level 2 Summative Assessment Papers, Marking Scheme, and Tutors' Guide – ISBN: 978-1-9049955-5-5

# THE BLUE FLAG SCHEME

ACTIVITY 4 – Researching, Writing and Making a Presentation

## Preparing an audience handout and making a presentation

You will be assessed on the following:

— locating relevant information from research;

— summarising the research documents and the information and ideas they contain;

— adapting researched information to prepare documents, suitably illustrated if appropriate;

— presenting information and ideas clearly and persuasively to the audience;

— using spelling, grammar and punctuation accurately and correctly;

— making contributions which suit the audience, the purpose and the situation.

**There are no suggested timings for this activity.**

## Scenario

(Select an area of the country which is included in the Blue Flag scheme and assume Shorefield-on-Sea is in that area.)

Shorefield-on-Sea District Council's area of responsibility covers an area of 304 square miles which has land on the coast and in the surrounding countryside. As part of your Council's application to have some beaches and marinas included in the Blue Flag scheme, you have to present information about the scheme to an audience from your Environment Department. The aim of the presentation is to:

— inform the audience, briefly, about the work of the Blue Flag and assume they know little, or nothing, of the scheme;

— produce a handout to explain one point;

— mention beaches/marinas in your area of the country which are already part of the Blue Flag scheme;

— encourage understanding of, and enthusiasm for, the Blue Flag scheme.

Carry out the necessary research and keep copies of your research documents to hand in with your work.

If you wish to do so, you can plan your work on the blank pages your tutor will hand you.

# Research Notes/Findings

Functional Skills English Level 2  Summative Assessment Papers, Marking Scheme,  and Tutors' Guide – ISBN:  978-1-9049955-5-5

## 1    Audience Handout    6 marks

You must produce a handout on the four criteria necessary for the receipt of an award. These were mentioned in **Document 1** but the information included in the four points did not represent the **complete** list. Conduct some research so you can prepare a handout which includes **all** the information on each point.

You can illustrate the handout, appropriately, if you wish to do so.

If you wish to do so, you can plan your work on the blank pages your tutor will hand you.

## 2    Presentation    14 marks

Your presentation must cover the points listed in "Scenario" and you will need to conduct research to find relevant information.

When you are ready to do so, make your presentation to your audience, which should last no fewer than four minutes and no more than six minutes.

If you wish to do so, you can plan your work on the blank pages your tutor will hand you.

Functional Skills English Level 2  Summative Assessment Papers, Marking Scheme, and Tutors' Guide – ISBN: 978-1-9049955-5-5

# Audience Handout

Functional Skills English Level 2  Summative Assessment Papers, Marking Scheme, and Tutors' Guide – ISBN:  978-1-9049955-5-5

# Presentation Notes

Functional Skills English Level 2 Summative Assessment Papers, Marking Scheme, and Tutors' Guide – ISBN: 978-1-9049955-5-5

# SHOREFIELD ON SEA DISTRICT COUNCIL

Shorefield

EX27 4MK

www.shorefielddc.gov.uk

0800 709 2346

Functional Skills English Level 2  Summative Assessment Papers, Marking Scheme,  and Tutors' Guide – ISBN:  978-1-9049955-5-5

## THE BLUE FLAG SCHEME

## BLUE FLAG BEACHES

**The Blue Flag** scheme began in France in 1985 and originally the flag was awarded if the area met criteria covering sewage treatment and bathing water quality. It has since been developed, and has become an international award scheme which indicates to visitors and residents near beaches and marinas that the site has achieved the highest quality in a number of criteria.

### The Criteria for receiving an Award

There are 29 criteria with which a beach or marina must comply in order to receive a Blue Flag award.

The following are aspects which are taken into account :

1    Environmental education and information;

2    Water quality;

3    Environmental management;

4    Safety and services.

Some criteria are known as **imperative** (necessary) whilst others are only guidelines. The Blue Flag is only awarded for one season at a time. If some of the **imperative** criteria are not fulfilled during the season, or the conditions change, the Blue Flag will be withdrawn during the season.

### Some requirements for Point 1

● Information about ecosystems and natural, sensitive areas in the zone must be displayed.

● Information about bathing water quality must be displayed.

● Information about the Blue Flag scheme must be displayed.

● Code of conduct for the beach area must be visible.

Functional Skills English Level 2 Summative Assessment Papers, Marking Scheme, and Tutors' Guide – ISBN: 978-1-9049955-5-5

## Some requirements for Point 2

- The standards for excellent bathing water quality must be met.

- No industrial or sewage related discharges may affect the beach area.

## Some requirements for Point 3

- There must be a Beach Management Committee which is in charge of environmental management systems.

- This BMC must carry out regular environmental inspections of the beach.

- The beach must be clean.

- Waste disposal bins/receptacles must be available on or by the beach in adequate numbers and they must be regularly maintained and emptied.

## Some requirements for Point 4

- An adequate number of lifeguards and/or lifesaving equipment must be available at the beach.

- There must be safe access to the beach.

- The beach area must be patrolled.

- A minimum of one Blue Flag beach in each municipality must have access and toilet facilities provided for disabled persons.

- Map of the beach showing different facilities must be displayed.

# GET INVOLVED

**The Blue Flag scheme** considers applications for membership from boroughs in the United Kingdom, and countries around the world, every year.

Being a member helps the environment and the people who use the facilities and can boost the local economy by encouraging tourists to the area.

It's not an exclusive club, anyone can apply to join.

# Blue Flag Beaches and Marinas Around the World

Blue Flag Beaches and Marinas exist in not only European countries, but countries around the world, as far away as New Zealand and Canada.

At present there are 2,633 awarded beaches and 620 awarded marinas.

The graph below shows an **extract** of Blue Flag areas for 2008/2009. The full list is updated each year after consideration of an International Jury.

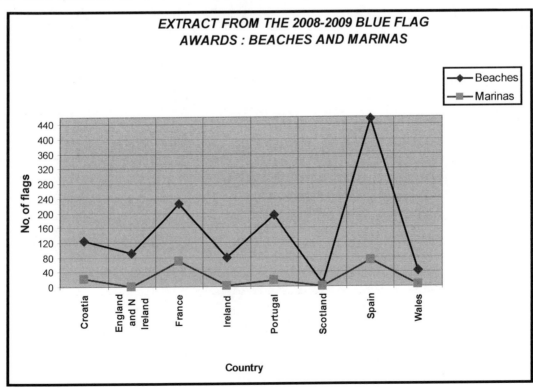

Functional Skills English Level 2 Summative Assessment Papers, Marking Scheme, and Tutors' Guide – ISBN: 978-1-9049955-5-5

## The Foundation for Environmental Education (FEE) and the Blue Flag scheme outside Europe

In 2001 the FEE decided to become a world-wide organisation. Since that date many countries outside Europe have made an application to join the organisation, and be considered for the Blue Flag scheme. Countries that have been successful include the Republic of South Africa, Morocco, Canada, New Zealand and several countries in the Caribbean region.

Chile, in South America, is working towards acceptance on the Blue Flag scheme and interest has been expressed by three other South American countries — Argentina, Brazil and Ecuador — and the United Arab Emirates and some countries in South East Africa.

# Why don't **YOU** apply to join

# our ever-growing scheme

# **TODAY?**

### **Complete the tear-off form and return to us and we'll send you details**

### **WELCOME TO THE CLUB**

...................................................................................................................

**To: The Blue Flag Association**     Floor 2, Countisbury House, 18 Lynmouth Road, Penzance, Cornwall   PZ1 5BF

Please send me an Information Pack and an application form **Today**

Name _____  Title _____

Name of Council _____

Address _____

_____

_____ Post Code_____

Telephone Number and Extension Number _____

Email Address _____

Functional Skills English Level 2  Summative Assessment Papers, Marking Scheme,  and Tutors' Guide – ISBN:  978-1-9049955-5-5

# Functional Skills English Level 2 Assessment Paper

Student's Name

Paper's Title

**NATIONAL BLOOD SERVICE**

Date Set

Hand-in Date

| Activity | Possible Marks | | Marks Awarded | Totals |
|---|---|---|---|---|
| 1   Reading | Q1 | 1 | | |
| | Q2 | 1 | | |
| | Q3 | 1 | | |
| | Q4 | 1 | | |
| | Q5 | 1 | | |
| | Q6 | 1 | | |
| | Q7 | 1 | | |
| | Q8 | 1 | | |
| | Q9 | 1 | | |
| | Q10 | 1 | | |
| | | | Activity 1 | |
| 2   Researching and Writing a Fact Sheet | Q1 | 15 | | |
| | | | Activity 2 | |
| 3   Researching and Making a Presentation | Q1 | 25 | | |
| | | | Activity 3 | |
| | | | PAPER TOTAL | |
| | | | **PERCENTAGE** | |

**Result**

Circle the appropriate result

**PASS**

**FAIL**

Assessor's Signature ................................................................................ Date ...........................

Functional Skills English Level 2  Summative Assessment Papers, Marking Scheme,  and Tutors' Guide – ISBN:  978-1-9049955-5-5

# NATIONAL BLOOD SERVICE

## Assessor's Comments

| Activity | Comments |
|---|---|
| 1 | |
| 2 | |
| 3 | See also my comments on the Speaking and Listening Observation Sheet |

Functional Skills English Level 2 Summative Assessment Papers, Marking Scheme, and Tutors' Guide – ISBN: 978-1-9049955-5-5

## NATIONAL BLOOD SERVICE

This paper has **three** sections:

Section 1              involves reading

Section 2              involves researching and writing a fact sheet

Section 3              involves researching and making a presentation

There are **two** documents for you to read.

Read both documents **before** you begin to answer the questions and keep referring to them when you work through the sections.

You are reminded that clear written and spoken English and correct spelling and punctuation are important, together with presenting work neatly and making sure it is suitable for the purpose and the audience.

Functional Skills English Level 2 Summative Assessment Papers, Marking Scheme, and Tutors' Guide – ISBN: 978-1-9049955-5-5

# NATIONAL BLOOD SERVICE

ACTIVITY 1 — Reading

You will be assessed on the following:

— reading, finding and summarising information and ideas from different types of document.

## Scenario

You work in the Health Promotion Department of Shorefield-on-Sea District Council. Your work involves the Council's partnership with the National Blood Service.

**Document 1** is an email which was recently sent to all employees.

Read this document then answer the following questions.

You should spend no longer than 20 minutes on questions 1 — 10.

For each question choose one answer, A, B, C or D and put a ✓ (tick) in the box.

1 mark is awarded for each correct answer.

1     What is the document about?

     A     statistics on available stocks of blood in the UK     ☐

     B     how donated blood saves lives     ☐

     C     an invitation to a presentation about the work of the National Blood Service     ☐

     D     a request to donate blood, some facts about blood supplies and an invitation to learn about blood donor procedures     ☐

2     Select the option which **best** describes the main purpose of Document 1?

     A     to persuade     ☐

     B     to inform     ☐

     C     to encourage and inform     ☐

     D     to advertise a product     ☐

43

3    What is going to happen in the Education Committee Room No 1?

   A    a presentation ☐

   B    a donor session on 4th February ☐

   C    a registration session ☐

   D    a donor session on 15th February ☐

4    How many centres hold blood stocks?

   A    21 ☐

   B    16 ☐

   C    15 ☐

   D    25 ☐

5    Where are the National Blood Service centres situated?

   A    in hospitals ☐

   B    in hospitals and clinics ☐

   C    in England and Wales ☐

   D    in England and North Wales ☐

6    How many blood donor sessions are planned by Shorefield-on-Sea District Council?

   A    2 ☐

   B    3 ☐

   C    15 ☐

   D    1 ☐

7    What is the purpose of the event on 16th January?

   A    to provide leaflets on the National Blood Service ☐

   B    to hold a blood donor session ☐

   C    to provide information about blood donor session procedures ☐

   D    to take names of people wishing to donate blood on 15th February ☐

44

Functional Skills English Level 2 Summative Assessment Papers, Marking Scheme, and Tutors' Guide – ISBN: 978-1-9049955-5-5

8    Looking at **Graph 1** which of the following statements is true?

    A      there are equal stocks of groups B positive and O   ☐
negative

    B      in all pairs of groups, there are fewer stocks of the   ☐
negative blood type

    C      in all pairs of groups, there are greater stocks of the   ☐
negative blood type

    D      there are identical stocks of B negative and AB   ☐
negative

9    Looking at **Graph 2** which blood group will be available for the most number of
days?

    A      A negative   ☐

    B      A positive   ☐

    C      AB positive   ☐

    D      B positive   ☐

10    Looking at **Graph 2** which of the following statement is true?

    A      there are 10 days' stock of AB negative and 5 of B   ☐
negative

    B      the blood group of which there is the most number   ☐
of days' supply is AB positive, whilst B negative and O
negative have the lowest supply

    C      supplies of B negative and A negative are equal   ☐

    D      A positive and AB positive have an equal number of   ☐
days' supply

# NATIONAL BLOOD SERVICE

ACTIVITY 2 — Researching and Writing

## Writing a Fact Sheet

You will be assessed on the following:

— locating relevant information from research;

— summarising the research documents and the information/ideas they contain;

— adapting research information to prepare documents;

— using a style of writing and presentation suited to the situation and the audience;

— presenting your work clearly, including appropriate illustration(s);

— using spelling, grammar and punctuation accurately and correctly.

**There are no suggested timings for this activity.**

## Scenario

Your Department — Health Promotion — is making a presentation on 16 January about what happens during a blood donor session.   You are the speaker and know it is the Department's intention to produce a Fact Sheet which will be available to those attending the presentation and which will also be made available to every Council employee.

## 1    Fact Sheet    15 marks

**Document 2** has been put together by a colleague who has gone on annual leave and you must now finish it by carrying out research to locate additional information to include.

The aim of the Fact Sheet is to inform readers of the valuable work of the NBS and you have been asked to include additional information on the following points:

● How frequently someone can donate blood.

● How blood is used.

● The four components which make up blood.

● Any interesting stories about the topic.

● Anything else you think will be interesting to the reader, who will know little or nothing about the topic.

Functional Skills English Level 2  Summative Assessment Papers, Marking Scheme, and Tutors' Guide – ISBN: 978-1-9049955-5-5

Decide where to include your information in the existing document, what headings to use and how you will best display your information. You should write a minimum of 300 words.

If you wish to do so, you can plan your Fact Sheet and/or make rough notes about your research on the blank pages your tutor will hand you.

Keep copies of your research documents to hand in with your work.

# Fact Sheet Plan and Research Notes/Findings

Functional Skills English Level 2  Summative Assessment Papers, Marking Scheme,  and Tutors' Guide – ISBN:  978-1-9049955-5-5

# NATIONAL BLOOD SERVICE

ACTIVITY 3 — Researching and Making a Presentation

## Writing Presentation Notes and Making a Presentation

You will be assessed on the following:

— locating relevant information from research;

— summarising the research documents and the information and ideas they contain;

— making a presentation suitable for the audience and the situation;

— presenting ideas and information clearly and persuasively to the audience;

— presenting work clearly, perhaps including appropriate illustration(s).

**There are no suggested timings for this activity.**

## Scenario

You know the subject of the presentation on 16th January — who can donate blood and what happens during a blood donor session — and must now research these topics so you can talk about them.

## 1    Research and Presentation    25 marks

When you have completed your research you must put together your presentation notes. (There is no need to produce a handout for the audience as you have already produced a Fact Sheet which will be available at the event.)

Your talk should last no fewer than four minutes and no longer than eight minutes.

Hand in the documents from your research.

If you wish to do so, you can plan your work on the blank pages your tutor will hand you.

# Research Notes/Presentation Plan

Functional Skills English Level 2 Summative Assessment Papers, Marking Scheme, and Tutors' Guide – ISBN: 978-1-9049955-5-5

Functional Skills English Level 2 Summative Assessment Papers, Marking Scheme, and Tutors' Guide – ISBN: 978-1-9049955-5-5

**Document 1**

| | |
|---|---|
| From: | Health Promotion Department |
| Sent: | 10 January 2010  10:09 |
| To: | All Staff |
| Subject: | SHOREFIELD-ON-SEA DISTRICT COUNCIL WORKING WITH THE NATIONAL BLOOD SERVICE |

# SHOREFIELD-ON-SEA DISTRICT COUNCIL

# IN PARTNERSHIP WITH

# THE NATIONAL BLOOD SERVICE

## SESSION REMINDERS

**Please don't forget that we have our very first in-house sessions coming up next month on:**

**4ᵀᴴ FEBRUARY**

**IN**

**LAW AND DEMOCRACY COMMITTEE ROOM 2**

**FLOOR 3**

**(fully booked)**

**AND**

**15ᵗʰ FEBRUARY**

**IN**

**EDUCATION COMMITTEE ROOM 1**

**FLOOR 2**

**(places still available)**

Everyone who has already booked an appointment to donate on 4th February should by now have received a reminder from the Blood Service.

Please ensure you turn up so that we can show our commitment to this invaluable service and help to save some lives.

For further information

or to find why donating blood is so important

visit

the National Blood Service at:

www.blood.co.uk

To encourage you of the importance of donating blood the graphs on the next page illustrate the blood stocks which are held TODAY in the NBS 15 blood centres* in England and North Wales and shows the number of days stocks which are left in these centres.

IF YOU ARE NOT SURE YOU CAN DONATE BLOOD

OR WANT TO KNOW WHAT HAPPENS IN A

DONOR SESSION

COME ALONG TO THE PRESENTATION WHICH WILL TAKE PLACE

ON

16TH JANUARY

AT 1600 HOURS

IN COMMITTEE ROOM 2

HOUSING DEPARTMENT

FLOOR 4

EVERYONE IS WELCOME

(NO BLOOD WILL BE TAKEN AT THE EVENT,

BUT WE HOPE YOU WILL

DECIDE TO DONATE SOME WILLINGLY ON

15TH FEBRUARY!)

* The figures do not include blood held in hospitals

Functional Skills English Level 2 Summative Assessment Papers, Marking Scheme, and Tutors' Guide – ISBN: 978-1-9049955-5-5

## GRAPH 1

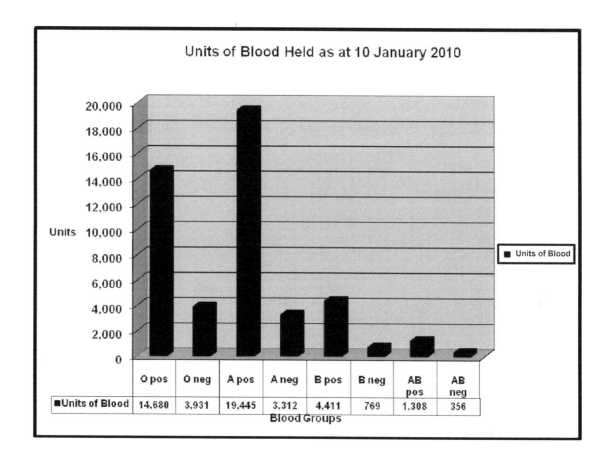

**Units of Blood Held as at 10 January 2010**

| | O pos | O neg | A pos | A neg | B pos | B neg | AB pos | AB neg |
|---|---|---|---|---|---|---|---|---|
| ■ Units of Blood | 14,680 | 3,931 | 19,445 | 3,312 | 4,411 | 769 | 1,308 | 356 |

Blood Groups

## GRAPH 2

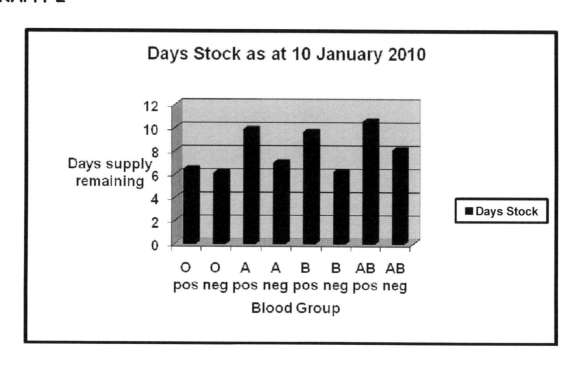

**Days Stock as at 10 January 2010**

Blood Group

Functional Skills English Level 2 Summative Assessment Papers, Marking Scheme, and Tutors' Guide – ISBN: 978-1-9049955-5-5

## What is the National Blood Service?

The National Blood Service (NBS) guarantees to deliver blood, blood components, blood products and tissues to anywhere in England and North Wales.

The blood is tested, processed, stored and issued. The NBS receives 2.1 million blood donations each year from the general public.

### Research is important too

The NBS is not just concerned with blood donations, it carries out research into improving the safety of blood, and investigates new ways in which the precious liquid can be used to help save more lives. A single donation of blood can save up to three lives.

### The aims and intentions of the NBS

1. To save patients' lives.

2. To improve patients' lives.

3. To deliver a world-class service.

4. To build partnerships with donors and the National Health Service.

### How is the donated blood mostly used?

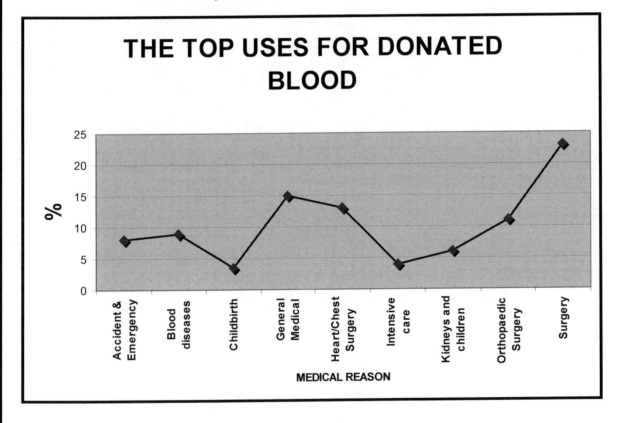

THE TOP USES FOR DONATED BLOOD

Functional Skills English Level 2 Summative Assessment Papers, Marking Scheme, and Tutors' Guide – ISBN: 978-1-9049955-5-5

How popular is each blood group in the UK population?

| Group | Positive % of UK population | Negative % of UK population |
|---|---|---|
| O+ | 37% | |
| O- | | 7% |
| TOTAL BLOOD TYPE "O" | 44% of the UK population | |
| A+ | 35% | |
| A- | | 7% |
| TOTAL BLOOD TYPE "A" | 42% | |
| B+ | 8% | |
| B- | | 2% |
| TOTAL BLOOD TYPE "B" | 10% of the UK population | |
| AB+ | 3% | |
| AB- | | 1% |
| TOTAL BLOOD TYPE "AB" | 4% of the UK population | |
| TOTAL % IN POSITIVE BLOOD GROUPS | 83% | |
| TOTAL % IN NEGATIVE BLOOD GROUPS | | 17% |

If you don't already know, but would wish to know, your blood group, and/or give blood, the NBS will help you.

Functional Skills English Level 2 Summative Assessment Papers, Marking Scheme, and Tutors' Guide – ISBN: 978-1-9049955-5-5

# Functional Skills English Level 2 Assessment Paper

Student's Name

Paper's Title

**A HOLIDAY IN BUDAPEST**

Date Set

Hand-in Date

| Activity | Possible Marks | | Marks Awarded | Totals |
|---|---|---|---|---|
| 1 Reading | Q1 | 1 | | |
| | Q2 | 1 | | |
| | Q3 | 1 | | |
| | Q4 | 1 | | |
| | Q5 | 1 | | |
| | Q6 | 1 | | |
| | Q7 | 1 | | |
| | Q8 | 1 | | |
| | Q9 | 1 | | |
| | Q10 | 1 | | |
| | Q11 | 1 | | |
| | Q12 | 1 | | |
| | Q13 | 1 | | |
| | | | Activity 1 | |
| 2 Reading and Writing | Q1 | 4 | | |
| | Q2 | 3 | | |
| | Q3 | 2 | | |
| | Q4 | 3 | | |
| | | | Activity 2 | |
| 3 Speaking and Writing | Q1 | 10 | | |
| | Q2 | 15 | | |
| | | | Activity 3 | |
| | | | PAPER TOTAL | |
| | | | **PERCENTAGE** | |

**Result**

Circle the appropriate result

**PASS**

**FAIL**

Assessor's Signature .................................................... Date ............................

Functional Skills English Level 2 Summative Assessment Papers, Marking Scheme, and Tutors' Guide – ISBN: 978-1-9049955-5-5

# A HOLIDAY IN BUDAPEST

## Assessor's Comments

| Activity | Comments |
|---|---|
| 1 | |
| 2 | |
| 3 | See also my comments on the Speaking and Listening Observation Sheet |

Functional Skills English Level 2  Summative Assessment Papers, Marking Scheme, and Tutors' Guide – ISBN:  978-1-9049955-5-5

# A HOLIDAY IN BUDAPEST

This paper has **three** sections:

Section 1          involves reading

Section 2          involves reading and writing

Section 3          involves taking part in a telephone call and writing a personal letter

There is **one** multi-page document for you to read.

Read the document **before** you begin to answer the questions and keep referring to it when you work through the sections.

You are reminded that clear written and spoken English and correct spelling and punctuation are important, together with presenting work neatly and making sure it is suitable for the purpose and the audience.

Functional Skills English Level 2  Summative Assessment Papers, Marking Scheme, and Tutors' Guide – ISBN: 978-1-9049955-5-5

# A HOLIDAY IN BUDAPEST

ACTIVITY 1 — Reading

The questions in this section assess your reading skills.

You will be assessed on the following

— reading, finding and summarising facts and ideas from different types of document.

Read **Document 1** which comprises:

— an extract from **Cities and Flights** website;

— details of the hotels included on the cities and flights website; and

— flight details included on the website.

Then answer the following questions.

You should spend no longer than 25 minutes on questions 1 — 13.

For each question choose one answer, A, B, C or D and put a ✓ (tick) in the box.

1 mark is awarded for each correct answer.

1    How many steps are involved when a user wants to find out flight details?

    A    1    ☐

    B    2    ☐

    C    3    ☐

    D    4    ☐

2    On what dates is the traveller planning to fly?

    A    12th August and 17th August    ☐

    B    Any time    ☐

    C    7th August and 12th August    ☐

    D    2nd August and 12th August    ☐

3    How many four star (4*) hotels are described in the document?

    A    3    ☐

    B    5    ☐

    C    2    ☐

    D    4    ☐

4    What is the **main** purpose of the hotel descriptions?

    A    to encourage visitors to Budapest                                              ☐

    B    to promote the hotels of Budapest                                              ☐

    C    to inform the reader about the city of Budapest                          ☐

    D    to give information  about each hotel and encourage a           ☐
        booking

5    Looking at the information on the Marco Polo Hotel, choose the correct
    statement from this list.

    A    it offers luxury, has 181 bedrooms and is close to the          ☐
        River Danube

    B    it has an indoor swimming pool and the hotel is close to      ☐
        theatres

    C    the hotel was renovated in 2002 and its facilities                 ☐
        include cable television

    D    it was renovated in 2002,  is furnished traditionally          ☐
        and comfortably, has a library and is close to a metro
        station

6    According to the text describing the Hotel Danube Park, where is the hotel
    situated?

    A    close to a park                                                                          ☐

    B    close to the River Danube                                                        ☐

    C    a 20-minute walk from Gelert Hill                                          ☐

    D    in the heart of the shopping and business district of         ☐
        Gelert Hill

7    Which hotel(s) have air conditioning?

    A    Marco Polo and Astoria Park                                                   ☐

    B    Budapest City, Marco Polo and Astoria Park                        ☐

    C    Astoria Park and Danube Park                                              ☐

    D    Budapest City, Danube Park and Dominica                          ☐

Functional Skills English Level 2  Summative Assessment Papers, Marking Scheme,  and Tutors' Guide – ISBN:  978-1-9049955-5-5

8    Looking at the description of the Astoria Park Hotel, what is specifically mentioned about the Wi-Fi, the Theatre Reservation service and the Spa Treatment?

  A    they are available 24-hours a day                                              ☐

  B    the guest will have to pay extra for these facilities/ services                ☐

  C    guests have to reserve these services 24 hours in advance                      ☐

  D    the Concierge will arrange these facilities for the guest   ☐

9    From which UK Airport would the customer fly from and return to?

  A    Belfast International                                                          ☐

  B    Bristol International                                                          ☐

  C    Birmingham International                                                       ☐

  D    Bournemouth International                                                      ☐

10   How many non-direct flights are available **to** Budapest?

  A    3                                                                              ☐

  B    4                                                                              ☐

  C    6                                                                              ☐

  D    7                                                                              ☐

11   What is the flight number of the journey which takes the **longest** time to fly to Budapest?

  A    BNL4462                                                                        ☐

  B    KLM832                                                                         ☐

  C    AF836                                                                          ☐

  D    S772                                                                           ☐

12   Looking at the **whole** table, how many flights, prefixed KLM, are direct flights?

  A    4                                                                              ☐

  B    3                                                                              ☐

  C    2                                                                              ☐

  D    1                                                                              ☐

13    What, in your opinion, is missing from the hotel and flight information which will help a reader decide where to stay and at what time to fly?

    A    details of attractions close to the hotel and the type of plan used   ☐

    B    the accommodation availability and the type of plan used   ☐

    C    the cost of the accommodation and the luggage allowance   ☐

    D    the cost of both the accommodation and the flights   ☐

Functional Skills English Level 2  Summative Assessment Papers, Marking Scheme,  and Tutors' Guide – ISBN:  978-1-9049955-5-5

## A HOLIDAY IN BUDAPEST

ACTIVITY 2 — Reading and Writing

In this section you are expected to **write** sentences reflecting your opinion and giving reasons for those opinions.

You will be assessed on the following:

— reading, finding and summarising facts and ideas from different types of document;

— presenting your work and ideas clearly and logically;

— identifying the purpose of the text and the style of writing;

— using a range of sentence structures, including complex sentences;

— using spelling, grammar and punctuation accurately and correctly.

You should spend no longer than 20 minutes on questions 1 — 4.

1    Your family comprises yourself, your parents, a brother two years younger than you and a sister aged three.  Thinking about you and your family taking this short holiday, which hotel would you be **most likely** to book?  Give reasons for your choice.
     **4 marks**

_____

_____

_____

_____

_____

_____

_____

_____

Functional Skills English Level 2  Summative Assessment Papers, Marking Scheme, and Tutors' Guide – ISBN: 978-1-9049955-5-5

2     Related to your choice of hotel selected in Question 1, list what other information you think should have been included in order to help the traveller make a decision on which accommodation to select. Give reasons for your comments. **3 marks**

_____

_____

_____

_____

_____

_____

3     This question is about the language used to describe your chosen hotel and its facilities. Describe what it was about the language in the description which attracted you. **2 marks**

_____

_____

_____

_____

Functional Skills English Level 2 Summative Assessment Papers, Marking Scheme, and Tutors' Guide – ISBN: 978-1-9049655-5-5

4      From the language used for your chosen hotel, what impression do you get about what to expect when staying there?  Give reasons for your comments.  **3 marks**

_____

_____

_____

_____

_____

_____

Functional Skills English Level 2  Summative Assessment Papers, Marking Scheme,  and Tutors' Guide – ISBN:  978-1-9049955-5-5

# A HOLIDAY IN BUDAPEST

ACTIVITY 3 — Speaking and Writing

**Taking part in a Telephone Call and Writing a Business Letter**

In this section you are expected to **take part in a telephone call and write a business letter** following the discussion on the telephone.

You will be assessed on the following:

— speaking clearly so that others understand your contribution;

— speaking in a way which suits the situation and the purpose;

— showing you are listening and responding to what is said to you;

— making contributions to the discussion and closing the discussion;

— presenting your written work and ideas clearly and logically;

— using a style of writing suited to the situation and the audience;

— using a range of sentence structures, including complex sentences;

— using spelling, grammar and punctuation accurately and correctly.

**There are no suggested timings for this activity.**

## Scenario

Your family has decided on the hotel in which it wishes to stay and you must now decide the accommodation you will need and the flights you wish to book. You will then telephone "Cities and Flights" and make the booking requests. Once you have done this you will write a letter confirming the bookings.

## 1    Telephone Call    10 marks

With your tutor taking the part of the member of staff from "Cities and Flights", telephone and make your reservation. Be clear about:

— the number in your party (you will probably be asked for names because these will be required on the flight tickets);

— the date you will be travelling;

— the airport in the UK;

— the flight times you require;

— the hotel you require;

— the accommodation you wish to book in the hotel.

Functional Skills English Level 2 Summative Assessment Papers, Marking Scheme, and Tutors' Guide – ISBN: 978-1-9049955-5-5

You can ask for any additional information. For instance, you might want to know the baggage allowance per person, or the arrangements for getting from the airport in Budapest to the hotel. Make notes of the details you receive because you have to confirm these in the letter you write.

If you wish to do so, you can plan your work on the blank pages your tutor will hand you.

## 2 Letter confirming your booking as a result of the telephone call 15 marks

As a result of making the telephone booking for your family's short holiday, you must now write to "Cities and Flights" confirming the arrangements.

The letter is a business letter written from your personal address (make one up) to be sent to:

The Reservations Manager, Cities and Flights, Suite 12,

Birchtree Buildings, Tavistock, Devon TK5 4JJ

You should write no fewer than 150 words.

If you wish to do so, you can plan your work on the blank pages your tutor will hand you.

## Telephone Call Plan

Functional Skills English Level 2 Summative Assessment Papers, Marking Scheme, and Tutors' Guide – ISBN: 978-1-9049955-5-5

# Business Letter Plan

**DOCUMENT 1**

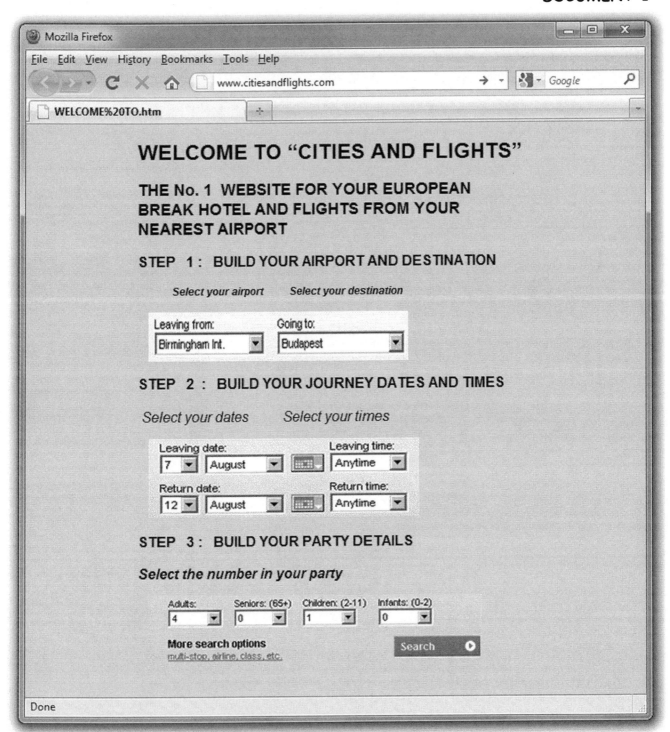

Functional Skills English Level 2 Summative Assessment Papers, Marking Scheme, and Tutors' Guide – ISBN: 978-1-9049955-5-5

# Hotel : Budapest City  4*

The Budapest City Hotel towers at the foot of Castle Hill, within a five minute walk from the city.

The Budapest City Hotel offers panoramic views of the town, and offers a wide range of services to its guests.

The hotel is good value for money.  It offers elegance with style and its staff is professional and friendly.

## The facilities include:

### Hotel Facilities

Room service

3 Restaurants

3 Lifts

Air conditioning

Concierge

Laundry

Night Porter

Safety deposit boxes

Wi-Fi

Currency exchange facilities

Car rental desk

Gardens

### Facilities for Children

Baby-sitting service

Cots/cribs

High chairs

Children's menu in all the restaurants

### Leisure Facilities

Pool

Sauna

Steam room

### Room Facilities

Air conditioning

Alarm clock

Direct dial telephone

Private bathroom

Climate control

Satellite television

Wi-Fi

Hairdryer

Trouser Press

Minibar

Functional Skills English Level 2  Summative Assessment Papers, Marking Scheme,  and Tutors' Guide – ISBN:  978-1-9049955-5-5

# Hotel : Marco Polo Hotel  3*+

The Marco Polo Hotel is a building which prides itself on its architectural grandeur.  The hotel, and its facilities, are sophisticated, stylish and luxurious.

The hotel, which was renovated in 2002, is close to the Opera House and the metro station in Deak Ferenc Square.

Each of its 118 bedrooms is furnished in traditional style with comfortable furnishings and Internet access.

# The facilities include:

## Hotel Facilities

24-hour room service

3 Restaurants

Air conditioning

2 Lifts

Laundry and dry cleaning facilities

Night porter

Safety deposit boxes

Library

Games room

Wi-Fi*

Currency exchange facilities

24-hour concierge service

Early check-out facilities

Car rental desk

Underground garage

Gift shop

## Room Facilities

Air conditioning

Complimentary toiletries

Alarm clock

Direct dial telephone with voice mail

Private bathroom

Climate control

Satellite television

Wi-Fi*

Hairdryer

Minibar

Free daily newspaper

## Leisure Facilities

Indoor swimming pool

Sauna

Steam room

Spa treatments*

Hairdresser*

Beauty salon*

**The hotel accepts payment by all major Credit and Debit cards**

\* There is a small additional charge for these facilities

Functional Skills English Level 2  Summative Assessment Papers, Marking Scheme,  and Tutors' Guide – ISBN:  978-1-9049955-5-5

# Hotel : Astoria Park Hotel   3*+

The Astoria Park Hotel is a new hotel located in the centre of Budapest. Newly built to blend ultra-modern facilities and stylish interior design, this hotel is in the heart of Budapest, suitable for business travellers, families or groups.

The city's shopping areas, theatres, tourist attractions, restaurants and cafes are within walking distance, and Buda Castle is only 3km away. This hotel provides an oasis of peace in the busy heart of the city and the professional and efficient staff will do everything to make a guest's stay happy and memorable.

# The facilities include:

## Hotel Facilities

2 Restaurants

3 Lifts

Dry cleaning facilities

Night porter

Games room

Wi-Fi*

Currency exchange facilities

24-hour concierge service

Theatre reservations*

Car rental desk

Underground garage

## Leisure Facilities

Indoor swimming pool

Sauna

Steam room

Spa treatments*

Hairdresser*

Beauty salon*

Gym*

## Children's Facilities

Child minding service* (make your reservation through the concierge)

Children's menu in both restaurants

Baby-sitting service between 1900 and 2300 hours daily*

Cots available on request

## Room Facilities

Complimentary toiletries

Alarm clock

Direct dial telephone with voice mail

Private bathroom with either a bath or a shower

Satellite television

Air conditioning

Wi-Fi*

Hairdryer

Minibar

Trouser press

Safe

* There is an extra fee chargeable for these services

Functional Skills English Level 2 Summative Assessment Papers, Marking Scheme, and Tutors' Guide – ISBN: 978-1-9049955-5-5

# Hotel Dominica   4*

The Hotel Dominica is situated in the heart of the city of Budapest and is convenient for tourists and business travellers because it is within walking distance of the main city sights and its business centre.

The hotel underwent refurbishment 18 months ago and offers 40 luxuriously-appointed guest bedrooms, each with en suite facilities.

# THE FACILITIES WE OFFER

### In The Hotel

2 Restaurants

Concierge

Laundry

Safety deposit boxes

Wi-Fi*

Car rental desk

### For The Visiting Children

Cots/cribs

High chairs

Baby-sitting service*

Children's menu in both restaurants

Room service between 4pm and 7pm daily

### In Your Room

Private bathroom with either shower or tub

Direct dial telephone

Cable television

Hairdryer

Minibar

Tea and coffee making facilities

Refrigerator

* an hourly fee is payable for this service

Functional Skills English Level 2 Summative Assessment Papers, Marking Scheme, and Tutors' Guide – ISBN: 978-1-9049955-5-5

# Hotel Danube Park  4*

The Hotel Danube Park (the front of which is seen in the picture to the left of the bridge) is situated only a ten minute walk from the business and shopping districts of the city. It is a short walk from Gellert Hill.

The hotel is set in a beautiful park located on the Buda side of the Danube with breathtaking views of the river and its grounds which stretch beyond the back of the hotel.

The rooms are luxurious, the perfect place to relax after a busy day in Budapest. The hotel's staff are attentive to a guest's every need and the services of the hotel are second to none.

## The facilities include:

### Hotel Facilities

4 Restaurants
4 Lifts
24-hour room service
24-hour Concierge service
Laundry facilities
Dry cleaning facilities
Wi-Fi*
Car rental desk
Theatre reservations
Restaurant reservations
Taxi reservations
Boat trip reservations (from the hotel's private water-side quay)
Parking
Luggage Room
Gift shops
Conference facilities
Photocopying and fax facilities*

### Room Facilities

Private bathroom
Flat screen LCD TV
CD player
Modem access*
Direct dial telephone with voice mail
Satellite television
Hairdryer
Trouser press
Minibar
Tea and coffee making facilities
Complimentary daily newspapers

### Facilities For Children

All children welcome
Cots/cribs
High chairs
Baby-sitting service
Children's menu in all the restaurants
Kids' club activity centre
Room Service for tea between 5pm and 7pm

### Leisure Facilities

2 indoor pools
Sauna
Steam room
Gym*
Beautician*
Health spa*

* an hourly fee is payable for this service

Functional Skills English Level 2  Summative Assessment Papers, Marking Scheme, and Tutors' Guide – ISBN: 978-1-9049955-5-5

# FLIGHT DETAILS
## ~Daily from 30 September to 31 March~

| OUTWARD FLIGHTS | | |
|---|---|---|
| **Birmingham International (BHX) Departure** | | **Budapest (BUD) Arrival** |
| BNL4462 | 0630 | 1300 |
| LH3556* | 0700 | 1215 |
| TAP407* | 0800 | 1315 |
| KLM832 | 0945 | 1550 |
| AF836 | 1050 | 1600 |
| S772* | 1200 | 1700 |
| KLM607* | 1300 | 1755 |

| RETURN FLIGHTS | | |
|---|---|---|
| **Budapest (BUD) Departure** | | **Birmingham International (BHX) Arrival** |
| KLM800* | 0650 | 1145 |
| AF832 | 0740 | 1325 |
| S736 | 0900 | 1535 |
| AF988* | 1200 | 1650 |
| LH3357 | 1400 | 2000 |
| KLM610* | 1530 | 2000 |
| AF9832* | 1800 | 2245 |

* Direct flights (all other flights involve a flight change at Frankfurt or Paris)

Functional Skills English Level 2 Summative Assessment Papers, Marking Scheme, and Tutors' Guide – ISBN: 978-1-9049955-5-5

# Functional Skills English Level 2 Assessment Paper

Student's Name

Paper's Title

**BUYING SAFELY ONLINE**

Date Set

Hand-in Date

| Activity | Possible Marks | | Marks Awarded | Totals |
|---|---|---|---|---|
| 1  Reading | Q1 | 1 | | |
| | Q2 | 1 | | |
| | Q3 | 1 | | |
| | Q4 | 1 | | |
| | Q5 | 1 | | |
| | | | Activity 1 | |
| 2  Reading and Writing | Q1 | 5 | | |
| | Q2 | 3 | | |
| | Q3 | 3 | | |
| | | | Activity 2 | |
| 3  Reading and Writing | Q1 | 1 | | |
| | Q2 | 1 | | |
| | Q3 | 1 | | |
| | Q4 | 8 | | |
| | | | Activity 3 | |
| 4  Researching and Writing | Q1 | 14 | | |
| | Q2 | 9 | | |
| | | | Activity 4 | |
| | | | PAPER TOTAL | |
| | | | **PERCENTAGE** | |

| Result | | PASS |
|---|---|---|
| Circle the appropriate result | | FAIL |

Assessor's Signature ................................................................. Date ...............................

Functional Skills English Level 2  Summative Assessment Papers, Marking Scheme, and Tutors' Guide – ISBN: 978-1-9049955-5-5

## BUYING SAFELY ONLINE

Assessor's Comments

| Activity | Comments |
|----------|----------|
| 1 | |
| 2 | |
| 3 | |
| 4 | |

Functional Skills English Level 2 Summative Assessment Papers, Marking Scheme, and Tutors' Guide – ISBN: 978-1-9049955-5-5

## BUYING SAFELY ONLINE

This paper has **4** sections:

Sections 1, 2 and 3    involve reading and writing

Section 4                involves researching and writing a fact sheet and a personal letter

There are **two** documents for you to read.

Read both documents **before** you begin to answer the questions and keep referring to them when you work through the sections.

You are reminded that clear written English and correct spelling and punctuation are important, together with presenting work neatly and making sure it is suitable for the purpose and the audience.

Functional Skills English Level 2  Summative Assessment Papers, Marking Scheme, and Tutors' Guide – ISBN:  978-1-9049955-5-5

## BUYING SAFELY ONLINE

ACTIVITY 1 — Reading

You will be assessed on the following:

— reading, finding and summarising facts and ideas from text;

— identifying the purpose and effectiveness of text.

Read **Document 1** then answer the following questions.

You should spend no longer than 15 minutes on questions 1 — 5.

For each question choose one answer, A, B, C or D and put a ✓ (tick) in the box.

1 mark is awarded for each correct answer.

1    Select the option which **best** describes the main purpose of Document 1?

    A    to advertise    ☐

    B    to frighten the reader    ☐

    C    to give facts    ☐

    D    to give facts and offer advice    ☐

2    How many people in the UK made purchases on the Internet in 2007?

    A    over 21 billion    ☐

    B    21 million    ☐

    C    1000 million    ☐

    D    over 20 million    ☐

3    What fraction of the Internet customers bought goods valued at **more than** £1000?

    A    two-thirds    ☐

    B    half    ☐

    C    one-third    ☐

    D    three-fifths    ☐

Functional Skills English Level 2 Summative Assessment Papers, Marking Scheme, and Tutors' Guide – ISBN: 978-1-9049955-5-5

4    According to the text, which of the following is the correct statement?

   A    if a purchaser uses a credit card to buy goods          ☐
         they will be protected under the Distance Selling
         Regulations

   B    a purchaser must spend over £100 to be able to use     ☐
         a credit card for an Internet purchase

   C    a purchaser, spending over £100 and using a credit      ☐
         card, may be protected by the Consumer Credit Act

   D    if a purchaser pays by credit card for goods valued     ☐
         at over £100 they will definitely have protection
         under the Consumer Credit Act


5    What type of purchaser is not covered under the Distance Selling Regulations?

   A    one using a debit card                                  ☐

   B    a business                                              ☐

   C    one using a credit card for goods worth less than       ☐
         £1000

   D    a business using a debit card                           ☐

## BUYING SAFELY ONLINE

ACTIVITY 2 — Reading and Writing

In this section you are expected to write sentences which show you have understood the content of **Document 1**.

You will be assessed on the following:

— reading, finding and summarising facts and ideas from text;

— presenting your work and ideas clearly and logically;

— using a range of sentence structures, including complex sentences;

— using spelling, grammar and punctuation accurately and correctly.

Referring to **Document 1**, answer the following questions.

You should spend no longer than 20 minutes on questions 1 — 3.

1       The reader is advised, under certain circumstances, to pay for goods using a credit card.  Explain the circumstances when this is advisable and of benefit to the customer.  **5 marks**

_____

_____

_____

_____

_____

2       The document mentions a "cooling-off" period of seven working days.  Explain what this means.  **3 marks**

_____

_____

_____

_____

82

3    Point 4 in the **Safe Internet Banking and Buying Goods via the Internet**
     section advises the reader not to buy goods over the Internet unless they are
     using their own PC. Explain why you think this is important security advice.

     **3 marks**

     _____

     _____

     _____

     _____

     _____

# BUYING SAFELY ONLINE

ACTIVITY 3 — Reading and Writing

In this section you are expected to answer questions **and** write sentences that show you have understood the content of **Document 2.**

You will be assessed on the following:

— reading, finding and summarising facts and ideas from different types of document;

— presenting your work and ideas clearly and logically;

— using a range of sentence structures, including complex sentences;

— using spelling, grammar and punctuation accurately and correctly.

**Document 2** is an extract from a web page of a direct mail watch retailer in the United Kingdom.

You should spend no longer than 20 minutes on questions 1 — 4.

1 mark is awarded for each correct answer to questions 1 — 3.

1    What do watch numbers **RW73**, **RW987** and **RW983A** have in common?

    A    they have leather straps    ☐

    B    they each have a calendar on the watch face    ☐

    C    they are ladies' watches    ☐

    D    they have black faces    ☐

2    Which style has eight diamonds on its face?

    A    RW738    ☐

    B    RW983    ☐

    C    RW73    ☐

    D    RW983A    ☐

3    If you wanted to buy a gent's watch with a stainless steel strap, from which style(s) could you choose?

    A    RW51 and RW738    ☐

    B    RW51    ☐

    C    RW983 and RW738    ☐

    D    RW738    ☐

84

Functional Skills English Level 2  Summative Assessment Papers, Marking Scheme, and Tutors' Guide – ISBN:  978-1-9049955-5-5

4    Looking at the advertisement extract **and** the information in **Document 1** about what a business must tell a purchaser when distance selling is involved, describe whether Relogio Watches meets all the criteria. Remember this is an **extract** from the website so you might want to word your answer to outline which criteria this page meets, and then say what the following pages will need to display as the customer progresses through the order process.

Give reasons for everything you write. **8 marks**

_____

_____

_____

_____

_____

_____

_____

_____

_____

_____

# BUYING SAFELY ONLINE

ACTIVITY 4 — Researching and Writing

**Producing a Fact Sheet and Writing a Personal Letter**

You will be assessed on the following:

— locating the relevant information from research;

— summarising the research documents and the information and ideas they contain;

— adapting researched information to prepare documents;

— producing work which is suitable for the purpose and the audience;

— presenting your work clearly;

— using a range of writing styles for different purposes;

— using a range of sentence structures ensuring the meaning is clear;

— using spelling, grammar and punctuation accurately and correctly.

**There are no suggested timings for this activity.**

## Scenario

You have several family members and friends who buy goods on Internet auction sites. As you have become more knowledgeable about purchasing goods or services on the Internet you decide to look into this aspect of buying by auction, so you can advise your friends on their rights (if any) and give them some tips on the subject so they can adopt a safe approach to buying.

## Researching the topic

Carry out some research into the topic of "Safe Trading when buying on Internet Auctions". You might visit www.oft.gov.uk as a starting point. Use the results of your research to help you produce your Fact Sheet.

Keep copies of your research documents to hand in with your work.

If you wish to do so, you can plan your work on the blank pages your tutor will hand you.

Functional Skills English Level 2 Summative Assessment Papers, Marking Scheme, and Tutors' Guide – ISBN: 978-1-9049955-5-5

# Research Notes

87

Functional Skills English Level 2  Summative Assessment Papers, Marking Scheme,  and Tutors' Guide – ISBN:  978-1-9049955-5-5

# 1    Fact Sheet   14 marks

The aim of the Fact Sheet is to draw attention to the key facts and summarise your findings in a way which is easily understood by the reader.  You should consider your readers will have little, if any, knowledge of their rights and obligations related to buying on Internet auction sites.

Your Fact Sheet should contain no fewer than 500 words.

If you wish to do so, you can plan your work on the blank pages your tutor will hand you.

# 2    Personal Letter   9 marks

Having produced your Fact Sheet you decide to send it to one of your friends who regularly buys goods on Internet-based auction sites.

Make up an address for yourself and your friend and write a brief letter which says why you are sending the Fact Sheet and that you hope it will be of interest and help next time they are bidding on an auction site.

Your letter is informal but you must still use correct spelling, grammar and punctuation.

If you wish to do so, you can plan your work on the blank pages your tutor will hand you.

Functional Skills English Level 2  Summative Assessment Papers, Marking Scheme,  and Tutors' Guide — ISBN: 978-1-9049955-5-5

# Fact Sheet Plan/Notes

Functional Skills English Level 2  Summative Assessment Papers, Marking Scheme, and Tutors' Guide – ISBN: 978-1-9049955-5-5

# Personal Letter Plan/Notes

---

Functional Skills English Level 2  Summative Assessment Papers, Marking Scheme, and Tutors' Guide – ISBN: 978-1-9049955-5-5

# GUIDE TO SHOPPING SAFELY USING THE INTERNET

**The Internet has made it is easier and quicker to shop from the comfort of your home. But what are the facts and hazards of Internet shopping?**

Buying on the Internet is known as "distance selling" and as such is subject to the Distance Selling Regulations and Electronic Commerce Regulations.

In the UK, Internet shopping is estimated to be worth over £21 billion and in 2007 it is believed that over 20 million people shopped online, with only two-thirds spending under £1000.

**Tips for safe shopping on the Internet**

**Before you buy**: make a note of the company's contact details (their full address and telephone number). It is not sufficient to only have their email address.

If their address is not available **DON'T BUY.**

**Paying for the goods**   Consider paying by credit card because if the cost is over £100 and you pay by credit card you **may** be protected by the Consumer Credit Act.  This says that the credit card company is **equally** liable for any defects.  So if there are any problems (faulty electrical equipment, faulty watch, an item of clothing where the zip falls out, etc.), you can claim either from the seller or the credit card company.

**Beware of buying goods from a seller based outside the UK**, even in the EU, because UK consumer law may not cover your purchase and it may be difficult to get a refund from a company based abroad.

**Print a copy of the order** and keep it safely.

**Always check bank and credit card statements** very carefully when you have used a debit or credit card to buy anything on the Internet.  If you have any doubt about an entry, ring the financial institution **immediately** and launch an investigation into the queried entry.

NEVER, NEVER, NEVER divulge your PIN number to anyone.

NO REPUTABLE COMPANY WILL ASK FOR THIS, EITHER VERBALLY, IN WRITING OR ONLINE.

Functional Skills English Level 2 Summative Assessment Papers, Marking Scheme, and Tutors' Guide – ISBN: 978-1-9049955-5-5

# CONSUMER PROTECTION (DISTANCE SELLING) REGULATIONS 2000 AND THE BUYER

A "Distance" contract is one where there is no face-to-face contact between the customer (consumer) and the business.

These regulations cover goods and services bought by a consumer from a supplier. These do not cover sales between businesses, i.e. business to business.

Consumers who buy goods or services via mail order, the Internet, digital television, telephone and fax are covered by the Consumer Protection (Distance Selling) Regulations 2000.

The business from which you buy must:

- give you clear information about the goods or services offered, the delivery arrangements and payment arrangements — whether the business accepts debit or credit cards or cheques or postal orders, etc.;
- provide you with full details of the supplier (name and contact details — not just an email address, or a post office box number);
- tell you about your cancellation rights **before you complete the purchase**;
- allow you a "cooling-off" period of seven working days;
- send you confirmation of your order (by letter, fax or email). However, if you have ordered from a catalogue or an advertisement this is deemed confirmation and the business does not have to provide additional confirmation to you.

## SAFE INTERNET BANKING AND BUYING GOODS VIA THE INTERNET

Online banking is generally safe, but you must use the system correctly and safely to try to ensure you are not open to **Internet Fraud**.

### TIPS

1   If you receive an email from a financial institution (bank, building society, credit card company) asking you for your security information such a PIN number or account number **IT IS A HOAX** because financial institutions **NEVER** ask for this information.  Do not reply to the email.

2   Keep your personal information safe (not next to the computer!) and never reveal the information, or your PIN number, to anyone.

3   Protect your PC by installing anti-virus software and anti-spyware to prevent unauthorised access and viruses being downloaded onto your PC when you are online.

4   Don't buy goods over the Internet unless you are using your **own** PC.

5   If you have any doubt about whether you can safely purchase online, or have entered your **real** financial institution's website, look for the locked padlock or unbroken key on your browser window. You can check the Security Certificate is authentic by double clicking on the padlock/key.

6   Safe website addresses usually change from http:  to https: ("s" signifying "secure").

7   Always log out of your account properly and never leave your computer unattended when it is logged on to a purchase site or a banking site.

Functional Skills English Level 2  Summative Assessment Papers, Marking Scheme, and Tutors' Guide – ISBN:  978-1-9049955-5-5

# RELOGIO WATCHES

## *TIMEPIECES OF DISTINCTION*

Welcome to Relogio Watches — the UK's leading **Direct Mail Watch Retailer.**

**We have timepieces to suit every person and every occasion.**

**Our watches are made to the highest standards and are covered by a 5-year guarantee.**

## THIS MONTH'S SPECIAL OFFERS

| | |
|---|---|
| **RW51 [CLICK TO SEE PHOTOGRAPH AND FULL DESCRIPTION]** | **£150** |
| Stainless steel solid link strap. Mother-of-pearl face. Gent's sports-watch with Swiss movement. | *Buy Now* |
| **RW511 [CLICK TO SEE PHOTORAPH AND FULL DESCRIPTION]** | **£140** |
| Gent's sports-watch, with Swiss movement. It has black leather strap and stainless steel face. | *Buy Now* |
| **RW73 [CLICK TO SEE PHOTORAPH AND FULL DESCRIPTION]** | **£185** |
| This ladies' dress-watch with champagne mother-of-pearl dial has six diamonds delightfully complemented by gold-finish strap. | *Buy Now* |
| **RW738 [CLICK TO SEE PHOTORAPH AND FULL DESCRIPTION]** | **£180** |
| Gent's date-watch with a green satin dial and 11 diamonds. Stainless steel case and solid stainless steel, or gold, strap with butterfly fastening. | *Buy Now* |
| **RW987 [CLICK TO SEE PHOTORAPH AND FULL DESCRIPTION]** | **WAS £200** <br> **NOW £150** |
| Gold ladies' watch. Black dial with 4 diamonds. Luxury leather strap available in black or taupe. Gold finish hands. Date set, unusually, at 5 o'clock space. | *Buy Now* |
| **RW983 [CLICK TO SEE PHOTORAPH AND FULL DESCRIPTION]** | **WAS £300** <br> **NOW £177** |
| Gents' retro black diamond watch. The elegant pitch black dial is tastefully adorned with eight magnificent diamonds (0.062ct). Gold finish and 9 Arabic numerals, calendar at the 6 o'clock position. Colour co-ordinated leather strap. | *Buy Now* |
| **RW983A [CLICK TO SEE PHOTORAPH AND FULL DESCRIPTION]** | **WAS £270** <br> **NOW £150** |
| Ladies' retro black diamond watch. The elegant pitch black dial is tastefully adorned with six magnificent diamonds (0.050ct). Gold, or silver, finish and 9 Arabic numerals, calendar at the 9 o'clock position. Gold or silver colour co-ordinated metal strap with butterfly fastening. | *Buy Now* |

Purchase with absolute confidence at Relogio Watches and immediately receive our full comprehensive after sales care package that consists of a 28-day money back guarantee, our 5 year movement warranty, a complete service and battery care programme. Orders are delivered within 14 working days of being received. Contact us on 01778 838383 9.30 — 5.30 7 days a week. Registered UK office : 18 Lower Bath Street, BRISTOL, BT8 3ST

# Functional Skills English Level 2 Assessment Paper

Student's Name

Paper's Title

**TRINITY HOUSE**

Date Set

Hand-in Date

| Activity | Possible Marks | | Marks Awarded | Totals |
|---|---|---|---|---|
| 1  Reading and Writing | Q1 | 1 | | |
| | Q2 | 1 | | |
| | Q3 | 1 | | |
| | Q4 | 1 | | |
| | Q5 | 1 | | |
| | Q6 | 2 | | |
| | Q7 | 3 | | |
| | | | Activity 1 | |
| 2  Reading and Writing | Q1 | 4 | | |
| | Q2 | 1 | | |
| | Q3 | 3 | | |
| | Q4 | 1 | | |
| | Q5 | 1 | | |
| | Q6 | 3 | | |
| | | | Activity 2 | |
| 3  Researching and Writing | Q1 | 15 | | |
| | Q2 | 12 | | |
| | | | Activity 3 | |
| | | | PAPER TOTAL | |
| | | | **PERCENTAGE** | |

| Result | PASS |
|---|---|
| Circle the appropriate result | FAIL |

Assessor's Signature ........................................................................ Date ...........................

Functional Skills English Level 2  Summative Assessment Papers, Marking Scheme, and Tutors' Guide – ISBN: 978-1-9049955-5-5

# TRINITY HOUSE

## Assessor's Comments

| Activity | Comments |
|---|---|
| 1 | |
| 2 | |
| 3 | |

Functional Skills English Level 2 Summative Assessment Papers, Marking Scheme, and Tutors' Guide – ISBN: 978-1-9049955-5-5

# TRINITY HOUSE

This paper has **3** sections:

Sections 1 and 2    involve reading and writing

Section 3    involves researching and writing a fact sheet and an invitation

There are **two** documents for you to read.

Read the documents **before** you begin to answer the questions and keep referring to them when you work through the sections.

You are reminded that clear written English and correct spelling and punctuation are important, together with presenting work neatly and making sure it is suitable for the purpose and the audience.

Functional Skills English Level 2  Summative Assessment Papers, Marking Scheme, and Tutors' Guide – ISBN: 978-1-9049955-5-5

## TRINITY HOUSE

ACTIVITY 1 - Reading and Writing

You will be assessed on the following:

— reading, finding and summarising facts and ideas from different types of document;

— identifying the purpose and effectiveness of texts;

— presenting your work and ideas clearly and logically;

— using a range of sentence structures, including complex sentences;

— using spelling, grammar and punctuation accurately and correctly.

Read **Document 1**, which includes charts, then answer the following questions.

You should spend no longer than 30 minutes on questions 1 — 7.

For questions 1 — 5 choose one answer, A, B, C or D and put a ✓ (tick) in the box.

1 mark is awarded for each of the multiple-choice questions.

1    Select the option which **best** describes the main purpose of Document 1.

    A       to persuade        ☐

    B       to instruct         ☐

    C       to inform         ☐

    D       to advertise      ☐

2    Using the information in the document, select the correct statement from the following.

    A       Trinity House is a charity concerned with lighthouses    ☐

    B       Trinity House has been concerned with the safety of shipping for almost 400 years    ☐

    C       Trinity House maintains 60 lighthouses and 412 buoys in the United Kingdom    ☐

    D       Trinity House is a charity concerned with the safety of mariners and with protecting the environment    ☐

3  Looking at **Charts 1 and 2**, what would be appropriate titles for each of them?

    A       Some lighthouse statistics   ☐

    B       1.    The height of 12 lighthouses   ☐

               2.    Distance at which the light is visible

    C       Details of 12 Lighthouses   ☐

    D       1.    Details of the tallest and lowest lighthouses   ☐

               2.    The distances the lighthouse lights travel

4  Looking at **Chart 1**, select the correct statement from the following.

    A       South Stack and Lizard are 20m high   ☐

    B       Alderney is the tallest lighthouse and Whitby the shortest   ☐

    C       Portland Bill is 41m high and Whitby is 15m high   ☐

    D       Alderney is 32m high and 12m shorter than South Stack   ☐

5  Comparing **Charts 1 and 2**, select the correct statement from the following.

    A       Whitby is the shortest lighthouse and also has the shortest light range   ☐

    B       the tallest lighthouse also has the longest light range   ☐

    C       Europoint and South Stack have identical heights and light ranges   ☐

    D       of the lighthouses which have a 26 nautical mile light range, Bardsey is the tallest   ☐

Functional Skills English Level 2  Summative Assessment Papers, Marking Scheme, and Tutors' Guide – ISBN: 978-1-904995-5-5

6   The information contained in **Charts 1 and 2** could have been displayed in another format.  Suggest what this could have been **and** say why you think the writer has chosen to use charts and whether, in your opinion, they are an effective communication method for the information.   **2 marks**

_____

_____

_____

_____

7   It is suggested that Trinity House helps to take care of the environment.  Identify **three** ways in which it does this.  **3 marks**

_____

_____

_____

_____

## TRINITY HOUSE

ACTIVITY 2 — Reading and Writing

You will be assessed on the following:

— reading, finding and summarising facts and ideas from different types of document;

— identifying the purpose and effectiveness of texts;

— presenting your work and ideas clearly and logically;

— using a range of sentence structures, including complex sentences;

— using spelling, grammar and punctuation accurately and correctly.

Read **Document 2** then answer the following questions.

You should spend no longer than 25 minutes on questions 1 — 6.

1    According to the text, what were the disadvantages of the privately-owned lighthouses? **4 marks**

_____

_____

_____

_____

_____

2    What occurred in the year 1836? **1 mark**

_____

_____

_____

_____

Functional Skills English Level 2 Summative Assessment Papers, Marking Scheme, and Tutors' Guide – ISBN: 978-1-9049955-5-5

3   What were the advantages of wood- and coal-fired lights being replaced with oil and electric lamps?  **3 marks**

_____

_____

_____

4   Which lighthouse has a pattern of light with 4 white flashes every 10 seconds?  **1 mark**

_____

5   Why do some lighthouses not have fog horns?  **1 mark**

_____

_____

6   Lighthouses are supposed to help mariners.  Each lighthouse has different patterns of light and sound.  How does this help mariners in the dark or in foggy conditions?  **3 marks**

_____

_____

_____

_____

# TRINITY HOUSE

ACTIVITY 3 — Researching and Writing

## Writing a Fact Sheet/Brochure and an Invitation

You will be assessed on the following:

— locating relevant information from research;

— summarising the research documents and the information/ideas they contain;

— adapting research information to prepare documents;

— producing work which is suitable for the situation, purpose and audience;

— presenting your work clearly, including appropriate illustration(s);

— using a range of sentence structures, including complex sentences;

— using a range of writing styles for different purposes;

— using spelling, grammar and punctuation accurately and correctly.

**There are no suggested timings for this activity.**

## Scenario

You work for Trinity House and have been asked to find some information on Strumble Head Lighthouse because it was 100 years old on 20th January 2008 and there is to be a belated birthday party on the 24th of next month.

## 1    Research and Fact Sheet/Brochure   15 marks

The Fact Sheet/Booklet will be handed to guests at the birthday celebration.  It has been started **(Document 3)** but you have been asked to carry out research and complete the document, which will be given out as a souvenir of the event.

You should consider that the audience will be interested in details of its location and history and that you must provide facts.

The picture which has been included in **Document 3** is a picture of a lighthouse, and you should consider including a picture of Strumble Head Lighthouse instead.

Your Fact Sheet/Brochure should contain at least 500 words and you are advised to make use of headings and sub-headings and other methods of enhancing the display.

Keep copies of your research documents to hand in with your work.

If you wish to do so, you can plan your work on the blank pages your tutor will hand you.

Functional Skills English Level 2 Summative Assessment Papers, Marking Scheme, and Tutors' Guide – ISBN: 978-1-9049955-5-5

# Research Notes

---

Functional Skills English Level 2 Summative Assessment Papers, Marking Scheme, and Tutors' Guide – ISBN: 978-1-9049955-5-5

# Fact Sheet Plan/Notes

Functional Skills English Level 2  Summative Assessment Papers, Marking Scheme,  and Tutors' Guide — ISBN:  978-1-9049955-5-5

## 2    Invitation to the party   12 marks

To mark the occasion, around 30 guests (some of the former keepers of the lighthouse, members of Trinity House and members of the local community) will be invited to attend a "Service of Dedication and Readings from the Lighthouse log of Events" at 2pm in the lighthouse, the event to be followed by afternoon tea. There will be a cake especially designed and decorated for the occasion.  The event will end at 5pm.

Your task is to design the invitation which will be sent to each invited guest.  (It has been started **(Document 4)** but you have to complete it.  You may wish to amend what has already been written.)

Remember you will need to include the date and time of the occasion.  Also to be included will be details of the event, and a line for the individual name(s) to be included in handwriting once the invitations have been printed.

You must add the initials  **RSVP**  (this is always added to invitations and it is the request from the sender that the recipient should reply to say whether or not they will be attending the event).  Next to RSVP add "by 11th (next month)" then include the name Peter Hopper, his title Former Lighthouse Keeper, and make up an address.

**Remember the purpose of the invitation** is to encourage people to attend and to fully describe the event.


If you wish to do so, you can plan your work on the blank pages your tutor will hand you.

# Invitation Plan

Functional Skills English Level 2 Summative Assessment Papers, Marking Scheme, and Tutors' Guide – ISBN: 978-1-9049955-5-5

**Document 1**

TRINITY HOUSE

**Trinity House** was established in 1514 by a Charter granted by King Henry VIII.

Today, more than 400 years later, the safety of shipping and the well-being of seafarers is its concern.

The charitable organisation has three functions:

1.    It is the General Lighthouse Authority for England, Wales, the Channel Islands and Gibraltar and is responsible for a range of navigational aids ranging from lighthouses to radar beacons.

2.    It is dedicated to the safety, welfare and training of mariners.

3.    It provides expert navigators for ships crossing Northern European waters.

Its area covers the sea from Berwick upon Tweed on the North East coast, to the Solway Firth on the North West coast, and Gibraltar off the Spanish mainland.

**Not just lighthouses**

Trinity House has a selection of almost 600 visual, audible, electronic, fixed and floating <u>aids to sea navigation</u>. Included in this list are lighthouses, light vessels, beacons and buoys to modern global positioning aids, known as DGPS.

In total there are:

69 Lighthouses

10 Light Vessels / Light Floats

412 Buoys

19 Beacons

48 Radar Beacons

7 DGPS Reference Stations

On the following page are some statistics on 12 of the 69 lighthouses.

Functional Skills English Level 2 Summative Assessment Papers, Marking Scheme, and Tutors' Guide – ISBN: 978-1-9049955-5-5

**Chart 1**

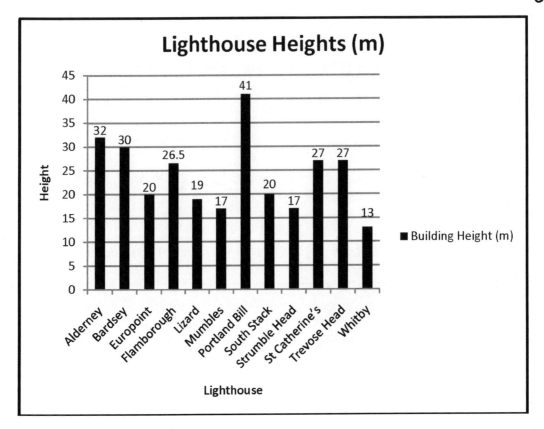

**Chart 2**

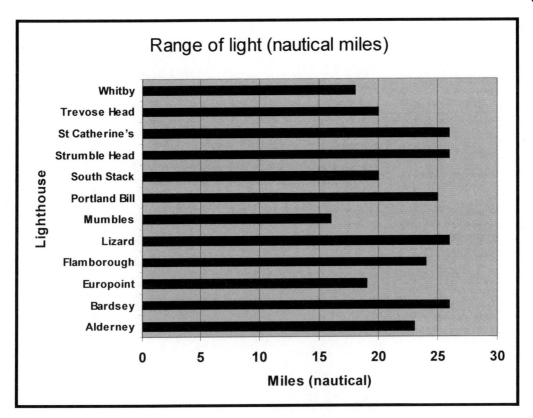

Functional Skills English Level 2 Summative Assessment Papers, Marking Scheme, and Tutors' Guide – ISBN: 978-1-9049955-5-5

## CARING FOR THE ENVIRONMENT

Whilst the Charity's main objectives are to ensure safety at sea, prevent human injury or loss of life, it is also aware that it must not damage the environment if at all possible.

This responsibility includes:

- reducing the risk of pollution caused by shipping accidents;

- using renewable energy to power the navigational aids;

- using solar, wind and wave energy;

- any helicopter flight to a lighthouse is planned in order to minimise disruption to nesting birds;

- water used to clean buoys returned to a Trinity House depot is filtered so as not to contaminate the local environment.

As a result of using renewable energy, Trinity House has almost eliminated carbon emissions. This saves up to 15 tonnes per year from every offshore lighthouse or light vessel.

Functional Skills English Level 2 Summative Assessment Papers, Marking Scheme, and Tutors' Guide – ISBN: 978-1-9049955-5-5

## HOW LIGHTHOUSES DEVELOPED

Early lighthouses must have been a little confusing to mariners. They were fuelled by wood or coal and were dependent upon people (lighthouse keepers) keeping the fire(s) burning. No fire, no light. No light, no signal. No signal, no assistance to passing sailors.

The first lighthouse was at Lowestoft in 1609. This was one of a series of lights provided to guide vessels through the maze of sandbanks in the area.

Over the following two hundred years, many lighthouses were built, some were privately owned and financed by an annual fee. The owners of private lighthouses were allowed to charge a fee of the passing ships once those ships arrived in port.

The reliability of the privately-owned lighthouses was uncertain. Unlike the Trinity House lighthouses, some gave signals differently to other lighthouses and there was no regulation related to brightness or the position of the light. Most did not effectively mark out the real hazards the mariners faced.

Legislation in 1836 established the compulsory purchase of all the private lighthouses in England, Wales and the Channel Islands and all were put under the management of Trinity House.

## Who pays for the lighthouses?

Lighthouses, and the other navigational aids round the coast, are paid for by `dues'. These are charges collected from every ship that uses a British or Irish port.

For England, Wales and the Channel Islands, this money goes to Trinity House. For Scotland and the Isle of Man it goes to the Commissioners of Northern Lighthouses, and for Ireland the money goes to the Commissioners for Irish Lights.

## The distinctive signals of each lighthouse's light

When wood- and coal-fired lights were replaced with oil and electric lamps, the lamps gave far stronger beams, which were concentrated by powerful lenses and could be seen over greater distances. There was also another big advantage, the lights could be made to flash or rotate.

This led to individual lighthouses having distinctive patterns, so mariners could identify them from how often they flashed in a given time.

The table describes the distinctive signals emitted by the 12 lighthouses featured in the graphs.

Lighthouses are not much use to a mariner in fog, so many have audible signals which are switched on when visibility is poor. Even the fog horns sound differently for each lighthouse and this information is shown in the table on the next page.

Functional Skills English Level 2 Summative Assessment Papers, Marking Scheme, and Tutors' Guide – ISBN: 978-1-9049955-5-5

| Lighthouse | Pattern of the light | Pattern of the fog horn* |
|---|---|---|
| Alderney | 4 white flashes every 15 seconds | 1 blast of 3 seconds duration every 30 seconds |
| Bardsey | White flash 5 times every 15 seconds | Sounding twice every 45 seconds |
| Europoint | 2 white and red flashes every 15 seconds | No fog horn attached to this lighthouse |
| Flamborough | 4 white flashes every 10 seconds | 2 blasts every 90 seconds |
| Lizard | One white flash every 3 seconds | 1 blast every 30 seconds |
| Mumbles | 4 white flashes every 20 seconds | 3 blasts every 60 seconds |
| Portland Bill | White group flashing 4 times every 20 seconds | 3.5 second blast every 30 seconds |
| South Stack | White flash every 10 seconds | 1 second blast every 30 seconds |
| Strumble Head | 4 white flashes every 15 seconds | No fog horn attached to this lighthouse |
| St Catherine's | One white flash every 5 seconds | No fog horn attached to this lighthouse |
| Trevose Head | 1 white flash every 7.5 seconds | 2 blasts every 30 seconds |
| Whitby | White and red phase every 5 seconds | No fog horn attached to this lighthouse |

* Those lighthouses which do not have a fog horn are those which are most generally not located in the sea but on the land, usually a cliff close to the sea.

Functional Skills English Level 2 Summative Assessment Papers, Marking Scheme, and Tutors' Guide – ISBN: 978-1-9049955-5-5

**Document 3**

**Strumble Head Lighthouse** stands on St. Michael's Island, an islet to the west of Fishguard in Pembrokeshire, Wales.

The lighthouse was built in 1908.

Functional Skills English Level 2 Summative Assessment Papers, Marking Scheme, and Tutors' Guide – ISBN: 978-1-9049955-5-5

# HAPPY BIRTHDAY STRUMBLE HEAD

**Strumble Head lighthouse was 100 years of age on 20th January 2008**

## YOU ARE INVITED TO

## STRUMBLE HEAD'S BIRTHDAY PARTY

Functional Skills English Level 2  Summative Assessment Papers, Marking Scheme, and Tutors' Guide – ISBN:  978-1-9049955-5-5

## Functional Skills English Level 2 Assessment Paper

Student's Name

Paper's Title

**CLIMATE CHANGE**

Date Set

Hand-in Date

| Activity | Possible Marks | | Marks Awarded | Totals |
|---|---|---|---|---|
| 1  Reading and Writing | Q1 | 2 | | |
| | Q2 | 2 | | |
| | Q3 | 2 | | |
| | Q4 | 1 | | |
| | Q5 | 1 | | |
| | Q6 | 1 | | |
| | Activity 1 | | | |
| 2  Reading and Writing | Q1 | 2 | | |
| | Q2 | 1 | | |
| | Q3 | 1 | | |
| | Q4 | 1 | | |
| | Q5 | 1 | | |
| | Q6 | 3 | | |
| | Activity 2 | | | |
| 3  Researching and Writing | Q1 | 16 | | |
| | Activity 3 | | | |
| 4  Researching, Writing and Making a Presentation | Q1 | 16 | | |
| | Activity 4 | | | |
| | PAPER TOTAL | | | |
| | **PERCENTAGE** | | | |

| Result | | PASS |
|---|---|---|
| Circle the appropriate result | | FAIL |

Assessor's Signature ................................................................... Date ...........................

Functional Skills English Level 2 Summative Assessment Papers, Marking Scheme, and Tutors' Guide – ISBN: 978-1-9049955-5-5

Functional Skills English Level 2  Summative Assessment Papers, Marking Scheme, and Tutors' Guide – ISBN: 978-1-9049955-5-5

| Activity | Comments |
|---|---|
| 1 | |
| 2 | |
| 3 | |
| 4 | See also my comments on the Speaking and Listening Observation Sheet |

# CLIMATE CHANGE

This paper has **4** sections:

Sections 1 and 2    involve reading and writing

Section 3             involves researching and writing two illustrated articles

Section 4             involves researching and making a presentation

There are **three** documents for you to read.

Read the documents **before** you begin to answer the questions and keep referring to them when you work through the sections.

You are reminded that clear written and spoken English and correct spelling and punctuation are important, together with presenting work neatly and making sure it is suitable for the purpose and the audience.

Functional Skills English Level 2  Summative Assessment Papers, Marking Scheme, and Tutors' Guide – ISBN: 978-1-9049955-5-5

## CLIMATE CHANGE

ACTIVITY 1 — Reading and Writing

You will be assessed on the following:

— reading, finding and summarising information and ideas from text;

— presenting your work and ideas clearly and logically;

— using a range of sentence structures, including complex sentences;

— using spelling, grammar and punctuation accurately and correctly.

Read **Document 1** then answer the following questions.

You should spend no longer than 20 minutes on questions 1 — 6.

1 Explain what the term "climate" means.  **2 marks**

_____

_____

_____

_____

_____

2 What is occurring in the Alps as a result of temperature rises?  **2 marks**

_____

_____

_____

_____

3    Why does the article suggest warmth from the earth's surface does not escape into space, and what happens as a result?   **2 marks**

_____

_____

_____

_____

4    Which gas is released from rotting household rubbish? **1 mark**

_____

_____

5    What is the collective name for natural gas, coal and oil?   **1 mark**

_____

6    Some countries are heavily involved in felling trees.  Which gas are these countries responsible for emitting into the atmosphere? **1 mark**

_____

Functional Skills English Level 2  Summative Assessment Papers, Marking Scheme, and Tutors' Guide – ISBN:  978-1-9049955-5-5

## CLIMATE CHANGE

ACTIVITY 2 — Reading and Writing

In this section you are expected to **write** sentences reflecting your opinion and give reasons for those opinions.

You will be assessed on the following:

— reading, finding and summarising information and ideas from text;

— identifying the purpose and effectiveness of texts;

— presenting your work and ideas clearly and logically;

— using a range of sentence structures, including complex sentences;

— using spelling, grammar and punctuation accurately and correctly.

Read **Document 2** then answer the following questions.

You should spend no longer than 20 minutes on questions 1 — 6.

1    The first paragraph includes the phrase "this unwelcome status". Explain what this phrase means.   **2 marks**

_____

_____

_____

_____

For questions 2 — 5 choose one answer, A, B, C or D and put a ✓ (tick) in the box.

1 mark is awarded for each correct answer.

2    How many countries are expected to meet the targets stated in the Kyoto Treaty?

| | | |
|---|---|---|
| A | 15 | ☐ |
| B | 2 | ☐ |
| C | 0 | ☐ |
| D | 12 | ☐ |

3    Under the ECCP programme, what will happen to members of the airline industry if they fail to take responsibility for polluting the atmosphere?

    A     they will be charged            ☐

    B     they will be prevented from flying    ☐

    C     they will not be allowed to operate    ☐

    D     they will have to build lighter planes    ☐

4    If the iron and steel, or the paper and card, industries do not meet their restricted carbon emissions targets, what will happen?

    A     they will be forced to stop manufacturing    ☐

    B     they will receive penalties    ☐

    C     they will have to report their emission output    ☐

    D     they will be excluded from the scheme    ☐

5    How are "wind farms" described in the article?

    A     as green alternatives    ☐

    B     as "green" energy    ☐

    C     as renewable energy    ☐

    D     as fossil fuels    ☐

6    Consider the title of the document and say whether you think the content effectively covers this? Give reasons for what you say.  **3 marks**

_____

_____

_____

_____

_____

_____

_____

Functional Skills English Level 2 Summative Assessment Papers, Marking Scheme, and Tutors' Guide – ISBN: 978-1-9049955-5-5

# CLIMATE CHANGE

ACTIVITY 3 — Researching and Writing

## Writing two illustrated articles

You will be assessed on the following:

— locating relevant information from research;

— summarising the research documents and the information and ideas they contain;

— adapting research information to prepare documents;

— presenting your written work clearly and logically;

— presenting information and ideas clearly and persuasively;

— using a style of writing suited to the situation and the audience;

— using a range of sentence structures, including complex sentences;

— using spelling, grammar and punctuation accurately and correctly.

**There are no suggested timings for this activity.**

## Scenario

You work for Shorfield-on-Sea District Council in the Environment Department.  The Council is holding a two-day exhibition in its offices aimed at informing local residents and businesses how they can help reduce climate change by living, working and travelling in an energy-saving way.  It plans to put this information into a booklet which will be available at the event.

**Document 3** is one of the articles that will appear in the booklet.  You must now produce **two** similar articles suitable for the intended readers.

The **two** articles you will write, and illustrate appropriately, are to be:

1    **Either** — How to travel in a greener form (assume you are aiming this at car drivers and/or aeroplane travellers [energy saving holidays]).

     **Or** — Energy saving in the garden at home.

2    Energy saving in the office environment.

Functional Skills English Level 2  Summative Assessment Papers, Marking Scheme, and Tutors' Guide – ISBN:  978-1-9049955-5-5

# 1  Researching and Writing the Articles          16 marks

A useful research starting point might be to visit  www.energysavingsecrets.co.uk

The aim of your articles, similar to **Document 3**, is to inform the reader about the topic and persuade a course of action.

Document 3 is informative and persuasive (because it keeps returning to the 'save money' theme and giving examples of how money can be saved).  It has occasional moments of humour because it is aiming to get the reader to change their ways and uses humour to reinforce some points.

Each article you write should contain no fewer than 400 words.  You can illustrate one, or both, articles with appropriate images designed to enhance the reader's understanding or maintain their interest.

Keep copies of your research documents to hand in with your work.

If you wish to do so, you can plan your work on the blank pages your tutor will hand you.

Functional Skills English Level 2  Summative Assessment Papers, Marking Scheme, and Tutors' Guide – ISBN: 978-1-9049955-5-5

# Research Notes and Article Plan

Functional Skills English Level 2  Summative Assessment Papers, Marking Scheme,  and Tutors' Guide – ISBN:  978-1-9049955-5-5

## CLIMATE CHANGE

ACTIVITY 4 — Researching and Making a Presentation

## Making a Presentation

You will be assessed on the following:

— locating relevant information from research;

— summarising the research documents and the information and ideas they contain;

— adapting researched information to prepare documents;

— presenting information and ideas clearly and persuasively to the audience.

**There are no suggested timings for this activity.**

## Scenario

As part of the Council's two-day exhibition you have to make a presentation, the title of which is 'An Energy-Efficient School Run'. The aim of this presentation is to give facts about how individual families using individual cars not only causes congestion but emits greenhouse gases into the atmosphere and helps to pollute the immediate environment. You also wish to offer alternative suggestions for coping with this twice-daily (sometimes four-times daily) routine.

## 1    Research and Presentation   16 Marks

Carry out some research into the topic and put together a presentation which must last no fewer than four minutes and no longer than six minutes.

The people likely to make up your audience will be parents who are interested in the topic, or who are against the topic on the grounds of the safety of their children. Be aware that you might have to 'win over' your audience.

There is no need to produce any handouts or other documents to accompany this presentation. Be prepared for questions from your audience.

Keep copies of your research documents to hand in with your work.

If you wish to do so, you can plan your work on the blank pages your tutor will hand you.

Functional Skills English Level 2 Summative Assessment Papers, Marking Scheme, and Tutors' Guide — ISBN: 978-1-9049955-5-5

# Research Notes/Presentation Plan

Functional Skills English Level 2  Summative Assessment Papers, Marking Scheme, and Tutors' Guide – ISBN:  978-1-9049955-5-5

## WHAT IS CLIMATE CHANGE?

We've all heard the term 'climate change', but what is it?

Climate means the **average weather** experienced over a long period. Climate includes temperatue, wind and rainfall patterns and trends. Scientists know that the earth's temperature has increased by 0.74°C since 1908 and that 0.4°C of this has occurred since the 1970s.

As temperatures rise on planet earth, this results in:

— changes to weather patterns;

— rising sea levels;

— extremes of weather.

In turn, these changes have produced other changes, such as:

— glaciers are melting;

— the corals of the Great Barrier Reef in Australia are dying;

— skiing in the Alps is now only possible for a reduced number of days as the snow is either not falling, as temperatures rise, or melting more quickly.

## WHY IS CLIMATE CHANGE HAPPENING?

The main influence of human beings in contributing towards climate change is our emission of greenhouse gases — carbon dioxide, ($CO_2$), methane and nitrous oxide.

The energy from the sun warms the earth's surface. The earth sends some of this energy back into the atmosphere. Atmosphere is the air which surrounds the earth and extends as far as 1,6000 kilometres above its surface.

The greenhouse gases, already in the atmosphere and effectively forming a blanket, stop some of the heat escaping into space, beyond the atmosphere, trapping it. This trapped heat is known as the 'greenhouse effect' and effectively warms up the planet.

## HOW DO WE CAUSE GREENHOUSE GASES?

We already know that greenhouse gases are made up of such things as carbon dioxide, methane and nitrous oxide, to name but a few. But how do these occur?

**Carbon Dioxide** is released into the atmosphere when solid waste, fossil fuels (oil, natural gas, and coal), wood and wood products are burned. Carbon dioxide is also released into the atmosphere when trees are felled during land clearing operations.

**Methane** is emitted during the production and transport of coal, natural gas, gas and oil. The Council rubbish tips — landfill sites — also result in methane emissions.

**Nitrous oxide** is emitted during agricultural and industrial activities as well as during burning of solid waste and fossil fuels.

Functional Skills English Level 2 Summative Assessment Papers, Marking Scheme, and Tutors' Guide – ISBN: 978-1-9049955-5-5

**Document 2**

<u>HOW IS EUROPE TACKLING CLIMATE CHANGE?</u>

Europe is one of the biggest $CO_2$ emitters, but the good news is that Europe is trying to change this unwelcome status by pledging a commitment to a number of courses of action. These are aimed at the continent, and every country within it, becoming "greener".

These courses of action are contained in three main treaties.

## 1 The Kyoto Treaty

This Treaty is the main part of Europe's commitment to tackling climate change. The Treaty allocates mandatory targets for the reduction of greenhouse gases to all nations who have signed up to it. In May 2002 there were 15 member-states and they all signed up to the Treaty's targets.

The target is that by the year 2012 Europe will reduce $CO_2$ emissions by 12.5 per cent from the levels that were recorded in the year 1990.

It is likely that many of the EU countries will fail to meet these targets. However, it is thought though that Britain and Sweden are expected to meet the targets.

## 2 The European Climate Change Programme (ECCP)

This was set up to devise a framework which could be followed by European countries so they were able to meet the agreements made in the Kyoto Treaty.

This Programme sets targets for the transport and energy industries, and includes such things as producing lighter vehicles; making the aviation companies responsible for the pollution resulting from air travel (and charging them if they fail to reduce their contribution); working towards relying less on fossil fuels and more on renewable energy (wind farms for instance).

## 3 The European Union Greenhouse Gas Emission Trading Scheme

This is the largest 'green scheme' in the world. The companies involved represent the energy sector — iron- and steel-making companies, and paper- and card-making businesses. Restrictions on carbon emissions apply to these industries, along with penalties if the restrictions are broken. Such business have to apply for a permit to operate and must regularly report on their emission outputs.

Other industries might be included in this scheme in the future.

## SAVING ENERGY IN THE HOME

## WHAT WE CAN ALL DO TO HELP OUR PLANET

A recent survey found that in the European countries of Germany, UK, Spain and France, the Germans were the best energy savers whilst we in Britain were the worst for energy wasting.

Clearly in the UK we need to be more aware of what we are doing and this document is related to energy-saving (and money saving) tips in the home.

There are a number of things we can all do to help save energy in our homes and, at the same time, learn to change the bad, energy-sapping habits we have perhaps got into without thinking.

**Bad habits that sap energy (and cost us more)**

1    Leaving applicances on standby. Think about it. From the television to the music centre, this is the worst energy-sapping practice in the home.  It costs UK householders up to £37 a year each.  Not leaving electrical items switched on at the mains could save enough electricity to power 1.2 million homes every year. Quite some saving.

2    Leaving chargers plugged in.  Sixty-five per cent of UK consumers do this at least once a week.  Only the Italians confess to being worse than us in the UK. Next time you charge an MP3 player, or your mobile phone, once it is done, remove the charger from the mains.  Forgotten chargers account for 250,000 tonnes of $CO_2$ every year — that's enough electricity to power 100,000 homes.

**HEY : TURN ME OFF!!**

**Help the planet**

Functional Skills English Level 2  Summative Assessment Papers, Marking Scheme,  and Tutors' Guide – ISBN:  978-1-9049955-5-5

3    Forgetting to switch the lights off when you leave a room.  Whilst across Europe this causes massive energy wastage, in the UK up to 63 per cent of people admit to doing this at least once a week.  The French admit to half this percentage, and the Germans to one-quarter of the UK percentage.  Lighting our homes can cost up to £1.9 billion a year, so turning off the unwanted lights would cut $CO_2$ emissions (and our household fuel bills).  It's got to be worth leaving an empty room in darkness!

## SAVING ENERGY IN THE KITCHEN

Every household has its 'labour-saving' appliances and most of these are to be found in the kitchen.  Here are some tips for energy-saving in the kitchen.

- Don't leave appliances on standby.

- Buy energy-efficient appliances — when buying new electrical products such as a washing machine, tumble drier, a refrigerator or a freezer, look for the Energy Saving Recommended logo.  This logo indicates where the item is in the 'most energy efficient' category.

- What can you save by buying a freezer with the logo?  It will run effeciently and use less electricity — in fact it'll save you enough money each year to buy 39 pints of milk!

- What can you save by buying a dishwasher with the logo?  It will run efficiently and use less electricity and water.  On average a cycle of a dishwasher costs 9p for an energy-efficient appliance, compared with up to 16p a cycle for one not energy-efficient.

- Use appliances economically (don't run a dishwasher for instance, until it is full — never run on half a load; only boil the kettle filled with enough water you need, don't fill the kettle to the brim if you only want one cup of tea!).

ALL IT TAKES IS SOME
THOUGHT:
- THINK
- REDUCE
- SAVE

# Functional Skills English Level 2 Assessment Paper

Student's Name

Paper's Title

**THE YORKSHIRE THREE PEAKS CHALLENGE WALK**

Date Set

Hand-in Date

| Activity | Possible Marks | | Marks Awarded | Totals |
|---|---|---|---|---|
| 1  Reading | Q1 | 1 | | |
| | Q2 | 1 | | |
| | Q3 | 1 | | |
| | Q4 | 1 | | |
| | Q5 | 1 | | |
| | Q6 | 1 | | |
| | Q7 | 1 | | |
| | Q8 | 1 | | |
| | Q9 | 1 | | |
| | Q10 | 1 | | |
| | Q11 | 1 | | |
| | Q12 | 1 | | |
| | Activity 1 | | | |
| 2  Reading and Writing | Q1 | 1 | | |
| | Q2 | 1 | | |
| | Q3 | 4 | | |
| | Q4 | 5 | | |
| | Q5 | 1 | | |
| | Q6 | 3 | | |
| | Activity 2 | | | |
| 3  Reading and Speaking | Q1 | 10 | | |
| | Activity 3 | | | |
| 4  Researching and Writing | Q1 | 13 | | |
| | Activity 4 | | | |
| | PAPER TOTAL | | | |
| | PERCENTAGE | | | |

| Result | | PASS |
|---|---|---|
| Circle the appropriate result | | FAIL |

Assessor's Signature ................................................................. Date ...........................

Functional Skills English Level 2  Summative Assessment Papers, Marking Scheme, and Tutors' Guide – ISBN: 978-1-9049955-5-5

# THE YORKSHIRE THREE PEAKS CHALLENGE WALK

## Assessor's Comments

| Activity | Comments |
|---|---|
| 1 | |
| 2 | |
| 3 | See also my comments on the Speaking and Listening Observation Sheet |
| 4 | |

Functional Skills English Level 2  Summative Assessment Papers, Marking Scheme, and Tutors' Guide – ISBN: 978-1-9049955-5-5

# THE YORKSHIRE THREE PEAKS CHALLENGE WALK

This paper has **4** sections:

| Section 1 | involves reading |
|---|---|
| Section 2 | involves reading and writing |
| Section 3 | involves reading and taking part in a telephone call |
| Section 4 | involves researching and writing a business letter |

There are **two** documents for you to read.

Read both documents **before** you begin to answer the questions and keep referring to them when you work through the sections.

You are reminded that clear written and spoken English and correct spelling and punctuation are important, together with presenting work neatly and making sure it is suitable for the purpose and the audience.

Functional Skills English Level 2 Summative Assessment Papers, Marking Scheme, and Tutors' Guide – ISBN: 978-1-9049955-5-5

# THE YORKSHIRE THREE PEAKS CHALLENGE WALK

ACTIVITY 1 — Reading

You will be assessed on the following:

— reading, finding and summarising information and ideas from text;

— identifying the purpose of text.

**Document 1** is an advertisement which has been placed in the weekly specialist magazine *Walkers' World*. Read the document then answer the following questions.

You should spend no longer than 25 minutes on questions 1 — 12.

For each question choose one answer, A, B, C or D and put a ✓ (tick) in the box.

1 mark is awarded for each correct answer.

1      What is the length of The Yorkshire Three Peaks Challenge Walk?

     A      690 miles      ☐

     B      720 miles      ☐

     C      25 miles      ☐

     D      5,200 feet      ☐

2      Where does the walk begin?

     A      17 High Road, Whernside      ☐

     B      Pen-y-ghent      ☐

     C      Ingleborough      ☐

     D      Horton-in-Ribblesdale      ☐

3      If a walker was <u>not</u> adopting a leisurely approach to the challenge, in how long would she/he aim to complete the walk?

     A      12 days      ☐

     B      12 hours      ☐

     C      under 12 hours      ☐

     D      24 hours      ☐

4   How is the region of the walk described?

   A   rainy   ☐

   B   mountainous   ☐

   C   sunny   ☐

   D   hard ground   ☐

5   Apart from being physically fit, what do walkers need to have?

   A   a map   ☐

   B   first aid experience   ☐

   C   mountain equipment   ☐

   D   a first aid kit   ☐

6   According to the text, what experience does a party leader need?

   A   the ability to detect signs of exposure   ☐

   B   the ability to detect signs of hypothermia   ☐

   C   the ability to detect signs of hypothermia and exposure   ☐

   D   the ability to map read   ☐

7   According to the text, what can cause hard ground to become boggy?

   A   mist   ☐

   B   rain   ☐

   C   mist and heavy rain   ☐

   D   heavy rain   ☐

8   What is the purpose of contacting Mike?

   A   to check the weather conditions   ☐

   B   to arrange a guided climb   ☐

   C   to get permission to climb   ☐

   D   to find out more information   ☐

Functional Skills English Level 2 Summative Assessment Papers, Marking Scheme, and Tutors' Guide – ISBN: 978-1-9049955-5-5

9    What is the purpose of the information displayed in the box?

    A    to promote tourism ☐

    B    to give detailed information on accommodation in the area ☐

    C    to make sure the reader books accommodation ☐

    D    to advertise nearby accommodation ☐

10    What **best** describes the tone of the main text?

    A    persuasive ☐

    B    informative ☐

    C    fictional ☐

    D    amusing ☐

11    For which organisation do you think the document was written?

    A    Mike ☐

    B    the owner of the Golden Lion ☐

    C    all the guest house owners ☐

    D    Yorkshire Three Peak Challenge Club ☐

12    Why do you think the image has been included in the advertisement?

    A    to encourage people doing the walk to take photographs ☐

    B    to use some of the page space ☐

    C    because it draws the reader's attention to the topic ☐

    D    because is shows what the area is like on a sunny day ☐

## THE YORKSHIRE THREE PEAKS CHALLENGE WALK

ACTIVITY 2 — Reading and Writing

You will be assessed on the following:

— reading, finding and summarising information and ideas from text;

— identifying the purpose of text;

— presenting your work and ideas clearly and logically;

— using a range of sentence structures, including complex sentences;

— using spelling, grammar and punctuation accurately and correctly.

**Document 2** is another advertisement placed in the magazine *Walkers' World*. Read the document then answer the following questions.

You should spend no longer than 15 minutes on questions 1 — 6.

For questions 1 and 2, choose one answer from options A, B, C or D and put a ✓ (tick) in the box.

1 mark is awarded for each correct question.

1    Referring to the document, select the correct statement from those below.

    A    two hotels have an indoor swimming pool and one has an ☐
outdoor pool

    B    the Golden Lion has the fewest number of bedrooms ☐
and the White Swan has the most

    C    Helwith Park has 13 double bedrooms and is set in 30 ☐
acres

    D    Helwith Park has 20 double bedrooms and Colin ☐
Chatham thinks the hotel is perfect for weddings

2    Which hotel has only recently been reopened?

    A    Golden Lion ☐

    B    Helwith Park ☐

    C    Moss Grove Inn ☐

    D    White Swan ☐

Functional Skills English Level 2  Summative Assessment Papers, Marking Scheme,  and Tutors' Guide – ISBN: 978-1-9049955-5-5

3    Which hotel, in your opinion, gives the most information about the surrounding area?  Give reasons for your choice.  **4 marks**

_____

_____

_____

_____

_____

_____

4    Some hotels, more than others, seem to have recognised they are situated in the area of the Three Peaks Challenge Walk.  Which hotels do you think have achieved this?  Give reasons for the choices you make.   **5 marks**

_____

_____

_____

_____

_____

_____

5    What has happened to the former stable block of Moss Grove Inn?   **1 mark**

_____

_____

_____

Functional Skills English Level 2  Summative Assessment Papers, Marking Scheme, and Tutors' Guide – ISBN:  978-1-9049955-5-5

6      If you were directing someone to Helwith Park, where would you say the hotel
       was situated?  **3 marks**

_____

_____

_____

_____

Functional Skills English Level 2  Summative Assessment Papers, Marking Scheme, and Tutors' Guide – ISBN: 978-1-9049955-5-5

# THE YORKSHIRE THREE PEAKS CHALLENGE WALK

ACTIVITY 3 — Reading and Speaking

In this activity you are expected to read **Document 2** then **make a telephone call** to book accommodation.

You will be assessed on the following:

— reading and summarising information and ideas;

— detecting points of view and meaning and bias in text;

— speaking clearly so that others understand your contribution;

— speaking in a way which suits the situation and purpose;

— making contributions to the discussion and closing the discussion.

**There are no suggested timings for this activity.**

## Scenario

Some members of your family have decided to do the Yorkshire Three Peaks Challenge Walk, and their partners have decided to accompany them and take advantage of a few days' short break to explore the surrounding area. You will now select accommodation and telephone to make the booking.

## 1    Telephone Call    10 marks

Study **Document 2** and decide which accommodation will be the most suitable for your family's stay. Take into account the following:

1    your father and his brother, your uncle, will be doing the challenge walk on the second Saturday and Sunday of next month;

2    their partners will be accompanying them for the short break which will last from Friday to Tuesday (they will be going home on the Tuesday);

3    you will need to book two double rooms for their stay;

4    the ladies will have use of your father's car so will be able to visit not just the immediate vicinity of the accommodation, but tourist sites further afield.

Your tutor will take the part of the receptionist/proprietor/manager of the hotel you select.

Telephone the hotel to enquire if accommodation is available for the dates and days. You can expect to have to give the name and address of the guests (as your father and

Functional Skills English Level 2 Summative Assessment Papers, Marking Scheme, and Tutors' Guide – ISBN: 978-1-9049955-5-5

uncle are brothers they will have the **same** surname, remember).

Tell the person to whom you speak **why** you have chosen their hotel.

Ask for room and breakfast rates.

The guests' estimated time of arrival will be around 2pm on the Friday and they will be leaving after breakfast on the Tuesday.

Explain that the two men are doing the Yorkshire Three Peak Challenge Walk but the ladies are not, so they plan to explore the area. Ask the person to whom you are speaking if they can send details about places of interest.

Expect to be asked for your name and address so the person to whom you are speaking can forward the information you request.

If you wish to do so, you can plan your telephone call and/or make rough notes on the blank pages your tutor will hand you.

Functional Skills English Level 2 Summative Assessment Papers, Marking Scheme, and Tutors' Guide – ISBN: 978-1-9049955-5-5

# Telephone Call Plan

# THE YORKSHIRE THREE PEAKS CHALLENGE WALK

ACTIVITY 4 — Researching and Writing

## Writing a business letter

You will be assessed on the following:

— locating relevant information from research;

— summarising the research documents and the information and ideas they contain;

— adapting researched information to prepare documents;

— presenting information and ideas clearly and persuasively;

— using spelling, grammar and punctuation accurately and correctly;

— making contributions which suit the audience, the purpose and the situation.

**There are no suggested timings for this activity.**

## Scenario

Following the booking and information request, you are now to assume the role of the hotel proprietor/owner and do some research into tourist attractions in the area so you can write to the person you spoke to on the telephone, firstly in order to confirm their booking, and to give details of attractions which might be interest.

## Research

Locate the area involved in this assessment activity on a map. It is in the Wensleydale area of North Yorkshire.

Conduct some research — you might find it appropriate to begin by visiting www.wensleydale.net. Some areas to consider researching are Leyburn, the Wensleydale Railway, Kirby Lonsdale and Settle.

Try to find information on forthcoming attractions (remembering the guests will be staying early **next** month).

The **aim** of your research is to be able to include details of three or four places/ attractions/events in the letter you write.

Keep copies of your research documents to hand in with your work.

If you wish to do so, you can plan your work on the blank pages your tutor will hand you.

Functional Skills English Level 2 Summative Assessment Papers, Marking Scheme, and Tutors' Guide – ISBN: 978-1-9049955-5-5

# Research Notes

# 1    Business Letter    13 Marks

Ask your tutor for a letter heading which represents the appropriate Inn/Hotel and write your letter to the guest whose name and address you used in Activity 3.

The aim of the letter is to:

—    confirm the booking and the costs and dates involved;

—    provide details from your research.

The tone should be welcoming.

The manager/proprietor will sign the letter.

Your finished letter must contain no fewer than 500 words.

If you wish to do so, you can plan your work on the blank pages your tutor will hand you.

Functional Skills English Level 2  Summative Assessment Papers, Marking Scheme, and Tutors' Guide – ISBN: 978-1-9049955-5-5

# Business Letter Plan

Functional Skills English Level 2  Summative Assessment Papers, Marking Scheme,  and Tutors' Guide – ISBN:  978-1-9049955-5-5

GOLDEN LION

15 HIGH STREET

SKERWITH

WENSLEYDALE

SY2 3PP

01665 334378

Functional Skills English Level 2  Summative Assessment Papers, Marking Scheme, and Tutors' Guide – ISBN: 978-1-9049955-5-5

Helwith Park

Helwith Park Estate

Helwith Bridge

JJ6 2BY

01553 889354

www.helwith.parkestate.co.uk

Functional Skills English Level 2 Summative Assessment Papers, Marking Scheme, and Tutors' Guide – ISBN: 978-1-9049955-5-5

# MOSS GROVE INN

LOWER WYND

HIGH  BIRKWITH

NORTH YORKSHIRE

NY46 2PW

**0449  774642**

Functional Skills English Level 2  Summative Assessment Papers, Marking Scheme,  and Tutors' Guide – ISBN:  978-1-9049955-5-5

# WHITE SWAN

## SETHCOTE STREET, WHERNSIDE, NORTH YORKSHIRE  SY37 4GH

**01549 222901**

**www.whiteswan.sethcote.co.uk**

Functional Skills English Level 2  Summative Assessment Papers, Marking Scheme,  and Tutors' Guide – ISBN:  978-1-9049955-5-5

# The Yorkshire Three Peaks Challenge Walk

This is a challenging, established walk with a 25 mile circuit, beginning and ending in Horton-in-Ribblesdale.

The "Three Peaks" are the three <u>highest</u> peaks in Yorkshire :

1. Pen-y-ghent    690m (approx)

2. Whernside     730m (approx)

3. Ingleborough  720m (approx)

The aim of many walkers is to complete the circuit and climbs in fewer than 12 hours, but a more leisurely pace is quite common!!

<u>Walk Level</u>  The level of the walk is <u>demanding</u> with a total climb of approximately 5,200 metres.

Good navigating skills are essential, especially as in some sections the walker will likely encounter poor visibility.  Accordingly walkers should have a good standard of fitness and stamina and have mountain equipment.  Outdoor experience is essential before undertaking this Three Peaks Challenge.

<u>Party leaders</u> are advised to have a knowledge of first aid  and what to do in an emergency and enough experience to be able to detect the signs of exposure in any party members, together with the symptoms of hypothermia.

<u>Weather</u>

It is a mountainous region and the weather can change frequently and quickly.  Sunshine can turn into swirling mist with little warning and heavy rain can make hard ground suddenly become boggy.

TO ARRANGE A GUIDED CLIMB CONTACT

YORKSHIRE THREE PEAK CHALLENGE CLUB, 17 HIGH ROAD, WHERNSIDE, NY23 7JM
01549 227461

www.ytpcc.org.uk or email mike@ytpcc.co.uk

**Staying in the area for a few days ?**

The following Inns and Guest Houses are nearby.

Golden Lion, Skerwith

01665 334378

Dale Lodge, Helwith Bridge

01553 889354

Moss Grove Inn, High Birkwith

01439 774642

White Swan, Whernside

01549 222901

**Accommodation details available on request**

Functional Skills English Level 2  Summative Assessment Papers, Marking Scheme, and Tutors' Guide – ISBN:  978-1-9049955-5-5

# ACCOMMODATION IN THE WENSLEYDALE AREA

| | |
|---|---|
| **Golden Lion, Skerwith**<br><br>01665 334378 | 15 High Street, Skerwith<br><br>Proprietor : Mary Swales<br><br>This charming 18th Century inn is situated in the village of Skerwith. It's an ideal base for those doing the Three Peaks Challenge Walk and a warm welcome is extended by the proprietor and her staff. Situated in Wensleydale the Golden Lion is perfectly placed for exploring the picturesque surrounding area. There are eight double bedrooms and three single bedrooms, each with en suite facilities. Brochure available on request. |
| Helwith Park, Helwith Bridge<br><br>Manager : Colin Chatham<br><br>This Victorian former manor house has reopened after six months of extensive renovation. The hotel is set in the 30 acres of the Helwith Park Estate, one mile to the east and two miles to the south of the village of Helwith Bridge. It comprises 33 bedrooms, of which 13 are single, the remainder are double. All have en suite facilities, mini-bar and tea/coffee making facilities. The hotel has a heated, indoor swimming pool and a small health spa. The perfect venue for weddings. Prices available on request. | **Helwith Park Estate, Helwith Bridge**<br><br>01553 889354 |
| **Moss Grove Inn, High Birkwith**<br><br>01449 774642 | Lower Wynd, High Birkwith<br><br>Proprietors : Terry and Fiona Ford<br><br>The village of High Birkwith is situated on the edge of the Yorkshire Dales National Park. Leyburn is situated to the North East and Kirby Lonsdale to the East. Ideally situated in an area where there are lots of tourist attractions and a perfectly situated base for the Yorkshire Three Peaks Challenge Walk. The Inn was formerly a 17th Century coaching inn and retains many of its original features including a courtyard with stable block (today the stable block has been turned into a heated indoor swimming pool and jacuzzi area). The Inn has ten double and four single bedrooms, each furnished to the highest standard. Accommodation and meal costs available on request. |
| Sethcote Street, Whernside<br><br>Proprietors : Neil Camberley and Todd Scott<br><br>The White Swan is an attractive whitewashed building in the heart of the village of Whernside. Outside the village is the peak of Whernside which is part of the Yorkshire Three Peaks Challenge Walk. There are seven double bedrooms and three single bedrooms, each furnished and decorated individually and with care. Ideally situated for those taking part in, or just supporting those taking part in, the Yorkshire Three Peaks Challenge. A homely atmosphere, good food, quiet surroundings and fantastic views from the conservatory dining room at the rear. Call for prices and brochures. | **White Swan, Whernside**<br><br>01549 222901 |

Functional Skills English Level 2 Summative Assessment Papers, Marking Scheme, and Tutors' Guide – ISBN: 978-1-9049955-5-5

## Functional Skills English Level 2 Assessment Paper

Student's Name

Paper's Title

**SWIM BETTER — FEEL FITTER**

Date Set

Hand-in Date

| Activity | Possible Marks | | Marks Awarded | Totals |
|---|---|---|---|---|
| 1  Reading and Writing | Q1 | 1 | | |
| | Q2 | 1 | | |
| | Q3 | 1 | | |
| | Q4 | 1 | | |
| | Q5 | 1 | | |
| | Q6 | 4 | | |
| | Q7 | 1 | | |
| | | | Activity 1 | |
| 2  Reading and Writing | Q1 | 1 | | |
| | Q2 | 3 | | |
| | Q3 | 2 | | |
| | Q4 | 4 | | |
| | | | Activity 2 | |
| 3   Researching and Writing | Q1 | 30 | | |
| | | | Activity 3 | |
| | | | PAPER TOTAL | |
| | | | **PERCENTAGE** | |

| **Result** | PASS |
|---|---|
| Circle the appropriate result | FAIL |

Assessor's Signature ................................................................................ Date ...............................

152

Functional Skills English Level 2  Summative Assessment Papers, Marking Scheme, and Tutors' Guide – ISBN: 978-1-9049955-5-5

# SWIM BETTER — FEEL FITTER

## Assessor's Comments

| Activity | Comments |
|---|---|
| 1 | |
| 2 | |
| 3 | |

Functional Skills English Level 2  Summative Assessment Papers, Marking Scheme, and Tutors' Guide – ISBN: 978-1-9049955-5-5

# SWIM BETTER — FEEL FITTER

This paper has **three** sections:

Sections 1 and 2    involve reading and writing

Section 3              involves researching and writing a report

There are **three** documents for you to read.

Read the documents **before** you begin to answer the questions and keep referring to them when you work through the sections.

You are reminded that clear written English and correct spelling and punctuation are important, together with presenting work neatly and making sure it is suitable for the purpose and the audience.

Functional Skills English Level 2 Summative Assessment Papers, Marking Scheme, and Tutors' Guide – ISBN: 978-1-9049955-5-5

# SWIM BETTER — FEEL FITTER

ACTIVITY 1 — Reading and Writing

You will be assessed on the following:

— reading, finding and summarising information and ideas from text;

— presenting your work and ideas clearly and logically;

— using a range of sentence structures, including complex sentences;

— using spelling, grammar and punctuation accurately and correctly.

**Document 1** is an extract from a Health Club's monthly swimming newsletter. Read the document then answer the following questions.

You should spend no longer than 20 minutes on questions 1 — 7.

For questions 1 — 5 choose one answer, A, B, C or D and put a ✓ (tick) in the box.

1 mark is awarded for each correct answer.

1    According to the Newsletter, what is important about exercise?

    A     a varied routine is essential when exercising    ☐

    B     it has limited health benefits    ☐

    C     it helps reduce weight and boost energy levels    ☐

    D     it helps manage weight, keep a heart healthy and    ☐
            encourage better levels of energy

2    Apart from making fitness training more interesting, what benefit does swimming offer?

    A     it helps build stamina    ☐

    B     different muscles will be used to those used in the gym    ☐

    C     it is less boring than training n the gym    ☐

    D     swimmers lose weight more quickly    ☐

3    What will it take for a swimmer to burn 360 calories?

    A     an hour's swimming    ☐

    B     an hour's leisurely swimming    ☐

    C     half an hour of swimming different strokes    ☐

    D     half an hour of vigorous swimming    ☐

Functional Skills English Level 2  Summative Assessment Papers, Marking Scheme, and Tutors' Guide – ISBN:  978-1-9049955-5-5

4    For which stroke(s) is the swimmer advised to use the fast lane of the pool?

   A    breaststroke and butterfly    ☐

   B    breaststroke and crawl    ☐

   C    butterfly    ☐

   D    crawl and butterfly    ☐

5    What does the poolside board explain?

   A    the pool etiquette    ☐

   B    the directions to swim in each lane    ☐

   C    the speed at which to swim in each lane    ☐

   D    the time the lanes are open    ☐

6    List the health benefits of the front crawl.  **4 marks**

_____

_____

_____

_____

_____

7    Describe what someone interested in pool aerobics should do.  **1 mark**

_____

_____

_____

_____

156

Functional Skills English Level 2  Summative Assessment Papers, Marking Scheme, and Tutors' Guide – ISBN:  978-1-9049955-5-5

## SWIM BETTER — FEEL FITTER

ACTIVITY 2 — Reading and Writing

You will be assessed on the following:

— reading, finding and summarising information and ideas from text;

— presenting your work and ideas clearly and logically;

— using a range of sentence structures, including complex sentences;

— using spelling, grammar and punctuation accurately and correctly.

Read **Document 2** then answer the following questions.

You should spend no longer than 20 minutes on questions 1 — 4.

For question 1 choose one answer, A, B, C or D and put a ✓ (tick) in the box.

1 mark is awarded for the correct answer.

1    How much money will be invested to encourage walking?

    A    more than £75 million    ☐

    B    more than £7 million    ☐

    C    £7 million    ☐

    D    £130 million    ☐

2    Explain how some local authorities in Wales are offering increased swimming provision.    **3 marks**

_____

_____

_____

_____

_____

Functional Skills English Level 2  Summative Assessment Papers, Marking Scheme, and Tutors' Guide – ISBN:  978-1-9049955-5-5

3    As **First Steps to Fitness** is a health club with fee-paying members, in which of the Government initiatives will it probably be asked to take part? Explain your answer.  **2 marks**

_____

_____

_____

_____

_____

4    Explain why the Government is specifically targeting people as young as 16 in the Fit for the Future scheme.  **4 marks**

_____

_____

_____

_____

_____

158

Functional Skills English Level 2  Summative Assessment Papers, Marking Scheme, and Tutors' Guide – ISBN:  978-1-9049955-5-5

# SWIM BETTER — FEEL FITTER

ACTIVITY 3 — Researching and Writing

## Writing a Report

You will be assessed on the following:

— locating relevant information from research;

— summarising the research documents and the information and ideas they contain;

— reading and summarising information shown in graphs;

— adapting researched information to prepare documents;

— presenting written work clearly and logically;

— presenting information and ideas clearly and persuasively;

— using a style of writing suited to the situation and the audience;

— using a range of sentence structures, including complex sentences;

— using spelling, grammar and punctuation accurately and correctly.

**There are no suggested timings for this activity.**

## Scenario

You work for **First Steps to Fitness**. The branch of the organisation near your home is one of 29 in Wales. Although it is a private, members-only, fee-paying fitness centre, the management is aware of the Welsh Assembly Government's swimming initiative.

The management has realised there might be a business opportunity to work with local councils that have to consider providing free swimming and who will need to renovate and upgrade their pools. You have been asked to research the topic in order to present some information to the management so it can decide what it will do to be part of this Free Swimming initiative.

## Researching and Writing your Report     30 marks

A useful starting point, if you are going to use the Internet to search for information, would be to enter "Welsh Assembly Free Swimming" into the search engine. This will probably direct you to various councils' websites which will explain what, if anything, each plans to do if they decide to take part in the initiative.

Keep copies of your research documents to hand in with your work.

Your report will need to contain the following:

1.  A cover sheet with:

    the title "Government's Initiative Free Swimming"

    Your name

    Report for the Management of First Steps to Fitness

    Today's date

2.  Heading "Terms of Reference"

    **To advise the management of First Steps to Fitness about the Welsh Assembly's Free Swimming inititative.**

3.  **Title: "Comparing the provisions being made by some local councils in Wales"**

4.  Findings

    Look in your research for such information as:

    —   the type of activities included in the swimming sessions;

    —   the length of the sessions;

    —   what people have to do to take part;

    —   why swimming is regarded as important.

There will be other things you might wish to include but as far as possible, try to include the same information for each local council you investigate so you can write a comparison — possibly in the form of a table.  You do not need to write sentences for this information, so if you don't use a table consider bullet points or a numbered list.

Compare the plans of **four** local councils.

Functional Skills English Level 2  Summative Assessment Papers, Marking Scheme,  and Tutors' Guide — ISBN:  978-1-9049955-5-5

5.   Recommendations

In this section you will recommend to the management how you think First Steps to Fitness could get involved (how often it could offer sessions, the length of the sessions, etc.).  **Remember**, each branch of First Steps to Fitness is already open from 7am until 10pm Monday to Saturday, and 8am to 4pm on a Sunday.  Each branch has two 25m pools and a 12m pool.

The company would be helping out the local council by offering their facilities and poolside staff (life guard and/or swimming coach) for a short time each week.  Any time used in this way is likely to inconvenience the fee-paying members, so you cannot use every pool and you cannot offer sessions more than twice a week.

Look at the graphs in **Document 3** that will help you locate the times when each of the pools has the least activity.

Your report must contain a minimum of 500 words.

If you wish to do so, you can plan your work on the blank pages your tutor will hand you.

Functional Skills English Level 2  Summative Assessment Papers, Marking Scheme, and Tutors' Guide – ISBN:  978-1-9049955-5-5

# Research Notes and Report

Functional Skills English Level 2 Summative Assessment Papers, Marking Scheme, and Tutors' Guide – ISBN: 978-1-9049955-5-5

Functional Skills English Level 2  Summative Assessment Papers, Marking Scheme, and Tutors' Guide – ISBN: 978-1-9049955-5-5

**DOCUMENT 1**

## Health Club

*www.fstf.health.com*                    *01533 670082*

## MONTHLY  SWIMMING  NEWSLETTER

### HEALTH BENEFITS OF SWIMMING

Swimming is an excellent form of exercise and the health benefits are numerous.

Swimming is exercise and exercise is key to weight management, a healthy heart and greater energy levels.

Add swimming to your regular fitness regime

Swimming just once a week will add variety to your gym routine. It will work different muscles to those you exercise in the gym area and will add more interest to your fitness training.

Burning those calories

Look upon swimming as part of your workout.  Doing half an hour of vigorous swimming can burn 360 calories — that's the equivalent of running 12 kph on our running track for the same length of time.

The water is cooling and means you are not conscious of sweating as you would be during your gym workout and this allows and encourages you to work longer and harder.

Do vary your swimming strokes, if possible, as this will involve working different muscles.

### SWIMMING ETIQUETTE

At First Steps to Fitness there are "Swimming Etiquette" posters all around the pool and aqua-fitness area.  If you haven't read them — or worse still, if you haven't noticed them — here's a reminder.

**DO**

1. Choose the right lane for your speed.  We have slow, medium and fast lanes available.

   Swim breaststroke in the slow lane or the medium lane.

   Swim crawl (freestyle) in the medium or fast lane, but if there are people doing the breaststroke in the medium lane, choose the fast lane.

   Swim butterfly in the fast lane.  If you choose the slow lane, because of the amount of water displacement involved in this stroke, you will disturb the swimmers in the slow lane, and possibly empty the pool!

2. Swap lanes if you find yourself holding up another swimmer, or move to the larger, unlaned section of the pool.

3. Wear goggles so you can see where you are going.

4. Keep to your side of the lane — follow the directional arrows shown on the board at the poolside.

163

**DON'T**

1.      Walk up and down when in the pool. At First Steps to Fitness we promote the pool as a "training pool". Walking up and down lanes blocks them and takes space away from the serious swimmers we encourage. If you want to engage in water aerobics, go into the smaller, children's pool or better still, join one of our many water aerobics classes.

2.      Wear inappropriate swimwear.

3.      Jump in or dive in. At First Steps to Fitness this is strictly forbidden.

4.      Swim in the lanes chatting to your friend. The lanes are for continuous swimming.

> **REMEMBER:**
> **YOU MUST**
> **WEAR A**
> **SWIMMING HAT**
>
>
>
> **NO HAT — NO SWIMMING**

### SWIMMING TIPS

### Improving your Crawl

**Benefits of the stroke**

The front crawl strengthens the back, tones the arms and legs, increases the mobility of the shoulders and hips, as well as improves cardiovascular fitness.

**Alignment**

The body roll is vital in the front crawl.

Hips and shoulders should rotate. Keep your head still.

**Kicking**

The kick in this stroke is known as the "flutter kick". Keep your ankles and feet floppy, the kick should come from your upper leg and thighs.

**Arm action**

Slip your hand into the water  with the elbow and forearm high.  As your elbow follows your hand into the water, extend the hand and forearm forward (as if you were going to shake someone's hand).

**Breathing**

As your body rotates to the side (see *Alignment* above) turn your head only slightly to get a comfortable breath (see the photo above). Always exhale fully with your face in the water before breathing.

> **WEEKLY WATER AEROBICS CLASSES**
>
> Classes are now held three times weekly. Check the timetable at Reception.
>
> Book your place with the instructors Karen, Tim or Stephanie.
>
>

Functional Skills English Level 2 Summative Assessment Papers, Marking Scheme, and Tutors' Guide – ISBN: 978-1-9049955-5-5

# THE GOVERNMENT'S INITIATIVES TO GET UK CITIZENS FITTER BY 2012

## Swimming

In 2008, the Government announced an initiative offering free swimming for everyone, but in July 2010 the new coalition Government in England announced it was unable to continue to fund the project. The Welsh Assembly Government is funding free swimming in Welsh local authority pools for children and young people aged up to 16 during all school holidays and weekends. Anyone aged 60 and over can swim for free outside school holidays.

Some local authorities have extended the scheme to provide 60+ free swimming all year round.

The Welsh Assembly Government has invested over £3.5m per year in the Free Swimming initiative, via Sport Wales.

## Walking

Seven million pounds worth of programmes have been introduced to encourage people to walk more each day. This includes a "Schools Walking Challenge" which aims to encourage more children to walk to, and outside of, school.

## Changing children's diet

More than £75 million has been targeted to support parents in changing children's diet and increasing levels of physical activity.

## 16–22 year old scheme

Working with the fitness industry to offer a "Fit for the Future" incentive for those in the 16–22 age group will, the Government believes, help deal with the problem of those who have left school and not continued a fitness regime after their school's weekly physical exercise classes ended. A commitment of more than £1 million will help offer subsidised gym and fitness club membership.

Functional Skills English Level 2 Summative Assessment Papers, Marking Scheme, and Tutors' Guide – ISBN: 978-1-9049955-5-5

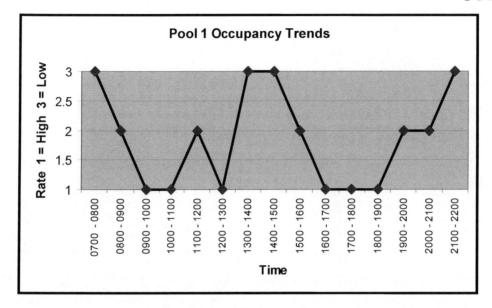

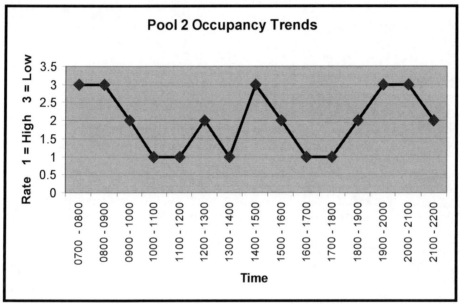

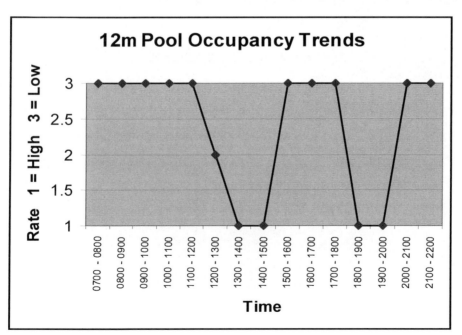

Functional Skills English Level 2  Summative Assessment Papers, Marking Scheme,  and Tutors' Guide – ISBN:  978-1-9049555-5-5

# Functional Skills English Level 2 Assessment Paper

Student's Name

Paper's Title

**THINK ABOUT RECYCLING**

Date Set

Hand-in Date

| Activity | Possible Marks | | Marks Awarded | Totals |
|---|---|---|---|---|
| 1   Reading and Writing | Q1 | 1 | | |
| | Q2 | 1 | | |
| | Q3 | 1 | | |
| | Q4 | 1 | | |
| | Q5 | 1 | | |
| | Q6 | 2 | | |
| | Q7 | 4 | | |
| | Q8 | 4 | | |
| | | | Activity 1 | |
| 2   Reading and Writing | Q1 | 4 | | |
| | Q2 | 3 | | |
| | Q3 | 4 | | |
| | Q4 | 8 | | |
| | | | Activity 2 | |
| 3   Reading | Q1 | 1 | | |
| | Q2 | 1 | | |
| | Q3 | 1 | | |
| | Q4 | 1 | | |
| | Q5 | 1 | | |
| | | | Activity 3 | |
| 4   Researching and Writing | Q1 | 11 | | |
| | | | Activity 4 | |
| | | | PAPER TOTAL | |
| | | | **PERCENTAGE** | |

| Result | | PASS |
|---|---|---|
| Circle the appropriate result | | FAIL |

Assessor's Signature ................................................................. Date ............................

Functional Skills English Level 2  Summative Assessment Papers, Marking Scheme,  and Tutors' Guide – ISBN:  978-1-9049955-5-5

# THINK ABOUT RECYCLING

## Assessor's Comments

| Activity | Comments |
|----------|----------|
| 1        |          |
| 2        |          |
| 3        |          |
| 4        |          |

Functional Skills English Level 2 Summative Assessment Papers, Marking Scheme, and Tutors' Guide – ISBN: 978-1-9049955-5-5

# THINK ABOUT RECYCLING

This paper has **4** sections:

Sections 1 and 2    involve reading and writing

Section 3           involves reading

Section 4           involves researching and writing a publicity leaflet

There are **three** documents for you to read.

Read the documents **before** you begin to answer the questions and keep referring to them when you work through the sections.

You are reminded that clear written English and correct spelling and punctuation are important, together with presenting work neatly and making sure it is suitable for the purpose and the audience.

Functional Skills English Level 2  Summative Assessment Papers, Marking Scheme, and Tutors' Guide – ISBN: 978-1-9049955-5-5

## THINK ABOUT RECYCLING

ACTIVITY 1 — Reading and Writing

You will be assessed on the following:

— reading, finding and summarising information and ideas from text;

— presenting your work and ideas clearly and logically;

— identifying the purpose of the text;

— using a range of sentence structures, including complex sentences;

— using spelling, grammar and punctuation accurately and correctly.

**Document 1** is an extract from an article about how goods are over-packaged. Read the document then answer the following questions.

You should spend no longer than 15 minutes on questions 1 — 5.

You should spend no longer than 20 minutes on questions 6 — 8.

For questions 1 — 5 choose one answer, A, B, C or D and put a ✓ (tick) in the box.

1 mark is awarded for each correct answer.

1    What does the figure of seventy per cent represent?

    A    packaging surrounding goods which householders buy    ☐

    B    the volume of packaging householders throw away    ☐

    C    the number of industries using too much packaging    ☐

    D    the figure by which packaging must be reduced    ☐

2    In 2009, how much waste packaging was recovered or recycled?

    A    59%    ☐

    B    10.5 million tonnes    ☐

    C    59% of 10.5 million tonnes    ☐

    D    59 million tonnes    ☐

Functional Skills English Level 2 Summative Assessment Papers, Marking Scheme, and Tutors' Guide – ISBN: 978-1-9049955-5-5

3   For what **approximate** percentage of landfill waste is the business sector responsible?

   A   59%   ☐

   B   90%   ☐

   C   20%   ☐

   D   47%   ☐

4   What has risen by twenty per cent in the last ten years?

   A   landfill by the business sector   ☐

   B   recycling of packaging   ☐

   C   domestic waste recycling   ☐

   D   the cost of producing packaging   ☐

5   What are householders being asked to do to try to reduce the volume of packaging used by manufacturers?

   A   contact companies to ask them to produce more environmentally-friendly packaging materials   ☐

   B   write to companies to ask them to only use environmentally-friendly packaging   ☐

   C   write to companies to ask them to reduce packaging   ☐

   D   contact companies and ask them to reduce packaging and use materials which are less damaging to the environment   ☐

6   Describe what you think are the main purposes of this article?   **2 marks**
(1)

_____

_____

_____

_____

_____

171

(2)

_____

_____

_____

_____

7    The document suggests one of the things householders could do to "get the message to the business sector" is to buy food at local markets and farmers' markets **and** write to manufacturers and retailers.  Why do you think these actions might help make the point to the business sector?    **4 marks**

_____

_____

_____

_____

8    The article suggests that some packaging is essential.   Name two occasions when you think packaging is necessary?  Explain each point you make.   **4 marks**

(1)

_____

_____

_____

_____

172

Functional Skills English Level 2  Summative Assessment Papers, Marking Scheme,  and Tutors' Guide – ISBN:  978-1-9049955-5-5

(2)

_____

_____

_____

_____

_____

Functional Skills English Level 2  Summative Assessment Papers, Marking Scheme,  and Tutors' Guide – ISBN:  978-1-9049955-5-5

# THINK ABOUT RECYCLING

ACTIVITY 2 — Reading and Writing

You will be assessed on the following:

— reading, finding and summarising information and ideas from text;

— identifying the purpose and effectiveness of texts;

— presenting your work and ideas clearly and logically;

— using a range of sentence structures, including complex sentences;

— using spelling, grammar and punctuation accurately and correctly.

Document 2 is an article put together by a company — Riverside Products (UK) Ltd. This company has shops all over England, and it is recognised as one which cares about the environment and which tries to work in a way which is friendly to the environment.

Read the document then answer the following questions.

You should spend no longer than 25 minutes on questions 1 — 4.

1    The article gives advice about what the householder can do to help the environment by recycling. What is **another** purpose of the article?  Explain your answer.  **4 marks**

_____

_____

_____

_____

_____

_____

_____

Functional Skills English Level 2 Summative Assessment Papers, Marking Scheme, and Tutors' Guide – ISBN: 978-1-9049955-5-5

2    Which produce is available in different sizes and colours and how much would
     the customer pay for each size if the product was discounted?  Explain in your
     answer what the customer would have to do in order to claim the discount?
     **3 marks**

_____

_____

_____

_____

_____

_____

_____

_____

_____

_____

_____

3    What is the purpose of the Packaging and Packaging Waste Regulation?  **4 marks**

_____

_____

_____

4    If you received Document 2 through your letter box, would you be encouraged to shop at Riverside and recycle more?  Explain the answers you give.  **8 marks**

_____

_____

_____

_____

_____

_____

_____

_____

_____

_____

Functional Skills English Level 2  Summative Assessment Papers, Marking Scheme, and Tutors' Guide – ISBN: 978-1-9049955-5-5

# THINK ABOUT RECYCLING

ACTIVITY 3 — Reading

You will be assessed on the following:

— reading, finding and summarising information and ideas from different types of document;

— identifying the purpose of text.

**Document 3**, which includes a chart, is an article put together by Selby District Council and Selby Market Traders' Association. Read the document then answer the following questions.

You should spend no longer than 15 minutes on questions 1 — 5.

For questions 1 — 5 choose one answer, A, B, C or D and put a ✓ (tick) in the box.

1 mark is awarded for each correct answer.

1 Apart from littering the countryside, what is the **main** concern expressed in the article about the effect of plastic bags on soil and water?

    A       they only last 20 minutes    ☐

    B       the average person has up to 20 bags at home    ☐

    C       they contain toxic material which poisons the soil, waterways and sea animals and fish    ☐

    D       ninety per cent of the bags thrown away are in the world's oceans    ☐

2 During which month(s) is the Council giving away cotton bags?

    A       April    ☐

    B       April and May    ☐

    C       June and December    ☐

    D       November and December    ☐

3    **According to the chart**, which category showed the **highest** response?

A    people who had over 20 plastic bags at home ☐

B    the number of people who took bags each week from retailers ☐

C    people annoyed with plastic bags becoming litter ☐

D    the number of people who did not reuse their plastic bags ☐


4    To what does the figure "15,000" plastic bags relate?

A    half the people surveyed each admitting to accepting 10 plastic bags from retailers each week ☐

B    the number of people in the area who have up to 80 plastic bags at home ☐

C    the number floating in the sea as litter ☐

D    half the people surveyed admitting to accepting 10 plastic bags from retailers each week **and** shoppers with at least 20 plastic bags at home ☐


5    On how many days, and at what times, does Selby market trade?

A    Wednesdays and Saturdays from 8.30am to 5.30pm ☐

B    Saturdays from 0830 to 1700 hours ☐

C    Wednesdays from 0830 — 1700 hours and Saturdays from 0800 to 1700 hours ☐

D    Wednesdays and Saturdays from 8.30am to 5pm ☐

178

Functional Skills English Level 2 Summative Assessment Papers, Marking Scheme, and Tutors' Guide – ISBN: 978-1-9049955-5-5

# THINK ABOUT RECYCLING

ACTIVITY 4 — Researching and Writing

## Writing a Promotional Leaflet

You will be assessed on the following:

— locating relevant information from research;

— summarising research documents and the information and ideas they contain;

— adapting researched information to prepare documents;

— producing work which is suitable for the audience;

— presenting your work clearly, including appropriate illustration(s);

— using a range of sentence structures, including complex sentences;

— using a range of writing styles and sentence structures for different purposes;

— using spelling, grammar and punctuation accurately and correctly.

**There are no suggested timings for this activity.**

## Scenario

As **Document 3** suggests, Selby District Council and Selby Market Traders' Association have got together to promote a "Green Bag" campaign. The purpose of this campaign is to educate shoppers about the dangers which plastic bags pose to the environment **and** to living creatures, and then to persuade shoppers to use recyclable shopping bags. Shoppers will then be offered facts about the range of reusable, recyclable bags available.

You have to conduct some research and write a leaflet that promotes the bags the Council and the Market Traders are going to make available to shoppers.

## Researching the topic

Carry out some research into the dangers of plastic bags and the reusable alternatives. You might want to visit the website www.plasticbag.org.uk so you can find out about the alternatives to plastic bags. Be careful to distinguish between opinion, facts and bias.

Keep copies of your research documents to hand in with your work.

If you wish to do so, you can plan your work on the blank pages your tutor will hand you.

Functional Skills English Level 2  Summative Assessment Papers, Marking Scheme, and Tutors' Guide – ISBN:  978-1-9049955-5-5

# Research Notes

Functional Skills English Level 2 Summative Assessment Papers, Marking Scheme, and Tutors' Guide – ISBN: 978-1-9049955-5-5

# 1 Writing the Promotional Leaflet   11 Marks

As you discovered by reading **Document 3**, the market traders are encouraging shoppers to "ditch the plastic" and enjoy the free, reusable cloth bags.

You assume people have read the "Get a Green Bag" information sheet and you now want to put together a promotional leaflet which can be given out to shoppers who visit Selby market.

The purpose of the leaflet will be to explain about the bags being offered, and use the information from your research to give information about the different types of reusable bag.  The leaflet also aims to educate and encourage.

Information from Document 3 to be included in the leaflet should remind the reader:

- what is being given away, by whom, where and when;

- that the bags that will cost 30 pence;

- about the special Christmas bags.

Add to this information from your research, and any other facts you consider relevant.

If you illustrate the leaflet, make sure the illustration is relevant to the topic.

Include your research documents with the leaflet when you hand it to your tutor.

If you wish to do so, you can plan your work on the blank pages your tutor will hand you.

# Leaflet Plan

Functional Skills English Level 2  Summative Assessment Papers, Marking Scheme,  and Tutors' Guide – ISBN:  978-1-9049955-5-5

Functional Skills English Level 2  Summative Assessment Papers, Marking Scheme, and Tutors' Guide – ISBN:  978-1-9049955-5-5

## TACKLE THE COMPANIES THAT OVER-PACKAGE THE GOODS WE BUY

In the United Kingdom, the average family spends £470 a year on the packaging surrounding goods bought from supermarkets and other retailers.  Much of this sum of money could be saved if manufacturers reduced the volume of packaging.

In 2009, the UK disposed of an estimated 10.5 million tonnes of packaging waste, of which around 59 per cent was recovered and recycled.

The largest amount of packaging going into landfill, is from products bought in **supermarkets**.  Such packaging accounts for up to 70per cent  of household waste each year.

Whilst the Government's efforts to get householders to recycle seems to be working,  the message has yet to get through to retailers and supermarkets.  Over 90 per cent of landfill waste comes from the business sector.

Recycling figures for domestic waste have risen by 20 per cent over the last ten years, but excess packaging is still a major problem.  Householders question why, when manufacturers and retailers use so much packaging, it should be **their** responsibility to dispose of it.

**Every householder** should take responsibility to try to get a reduction in packaging by contacting companies directly and asking them to reduce their amount of **excess** packaging **and** change to using more environmentally-friendly packaging materials.

Remember, **over 90 per cent**, of general landfill waste comes from the business sector yet the public is the only sector being encouraged to act responsibly and recycle our waste.

### How can we get the message to the business sector?

We can:

- choose to buy larger quantities of goods;
- buy goods that use less packaging;
- buy food at local markets and farmers' markets*;
- if you do buy packaged goods (and sometimes it cannot be avoided) think about writing to the manufacturer or retailer to ask them to consider environmentally-friendly materials that will rot if sent to landfill, or are recyclable.

### Does packaging play a useful role?

Undoubtedly some packaging is essential because it protects and preserves the product it contains.  This is especially true in the case of **some** goods and foods.

However, stop and think about whether three bananas **need** to be presented on a polystyrene tray and wrapped.

It's usually only supermarkets which use this method of displaying when selling fruit and vegetables and it is not always necessary.

* Here you buy fruit and vegetables loose, not packaged.  You can further reduce the need for the stallholders to put the goods in paper bags by taking your own recyclable bags and using them again and again.  Butchers and fishmongers wrap meat and fish in greaseproof paper or newspaper, both of which can be recycled.

# RECYCLING ADVICE FROM
# RIVERSIDE PRODUCTS (UK) LTD

## REDUCE  THINK  REDUCE  THINK  REDUCE  THINK

There is a European Regulation related to Packaging and Packaging Waste which aims to reduce the impact of packaging and packaging waste on the environment.  The Regulation introduces recovery and recycling targets for packaging waste and encourages reuse of packaging materials.  However, until these targets are met by manufacturers, and encouraged by retailers, every householder has to accept they belong to the group which is mainly responsible for recycling.

We at **"Riverside Products (UK) Ltd"**® have already reduced the packaging we use for our products and are continuing to talk to our manufacturers about reducing unnecessary packaging even further. Until other companies adopt our environmentally-responsible attitude, it is the householder who will carry the main responsibility of recycling, and so we offer some advice on recycling and caring for the environment.

**Buy products which can be reused or recycled**  such as **glass** jars and bottles, rechargeable batteries and cans.

**Say "No" to plastic bags and carriers**  because over 100,000 tonnes of plastic bags are dumped in landfill every year.  Stop and think, then say **NO** when you are offered a plastic carrier or bag.

**Buy a selection of reusable, recyclable bags** and take them with you when you go shopping, whether to a supermarket, a clothes shop, a butchers, a newsagents, or,  in fact, **anywhere and everywhere**.

**Clothes and shoes**   can be recycled and most recycling stations have containers for clothes and pairs of shoes.   You could take them to a charity shop if you really don't have anywhere nearby which recycles.

**Don't go out of your way to get to a recycling station**   you are adding to your "carbon footprint" by driving unnecessary miles and polluting the atmosphere (as well as costing yourself money by using more petrol!).

**Reuse envelopes and jiffy bags**  by sticking a label over the address and reusing. *Buy the "Super-role" adhesive labels from our stores.*  Take a copy of this advice sheet and you can purchase a roll of 240 labels for just £12.99 — that's a saving of £3 off the retail price.

**Crush your cans** and make more room in your recycling bag or box.  Buy the *"Easi-crush" can crusher* from our stores. Take a copy of this advice sheet and you can purchase it for £9.99 — that's a saving of £4 off the retail price.

Functional Skills English Level 2  Summative Assessment Papers, Marking Scheme,  and Tutors' Guide – ISBN: 978-1-9049955-5-5

Functional Skills English Level 2  Summative Assessment Papers, Marking Scheme, and Tutors' Guide – ISBN: 978-1-9049955-5-5

**Compost your uncooked food scraps** in one of our range of *"Easi-compost"* bins (prices start at just £24.99), and you'll have top quality compost to nourish your garden.

Things you **can** compost:

uncooked fruit and vegetables peelings;

tea bags;

old flowers and soft-wood cuttings;

egg shells and egg boxes;

light cardboard;

grass cuttings.

Things you **should not** compost:

any cooked and discarded food;

meat;

fish;

glossy magazines.

Keep your kitchen tidy of vegetable and fruit scraps which are on the way to the compost bin. Invest in one of our *"Kitchen-Compost" Tidies.* Available in two sizes, £7.99 and £12.99, and in a range of colours including pale blue, light grey, dark grey, olive, sandalwood, lime green and terracotta. Each is fitted with a charcoal filter which means no odours can escape. Take this advice sheet to any of our nationwide shops and receive a reduction of £1.50 on each bin you purchase.

### Make recycling part of your everyday life.  It's easy once you begin to

### THINK, REDUCE and RECYCLE.

For further information on Reducing and Recycling contact
The Environment Manager,  Riverside Products (UK) Ltd®,

Kingfisher Business Park,  Simmerton Road East,
Darlington,  Co Durham  DL17  8PP

or call us on 01368 223 445

For a catalogue of our products and details of our nationwide stores

call us on 01773 556 191

or visit our website www.riversideproducts-kingfisher.com

*Riverside Products (UK) Ltd is a registered company*

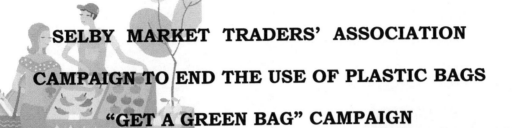

# SELBY MARKET TRADERS' ASSOCIATION

# CAMPAIGN TO END THE USE OF PLASTIC BAGS

# "GET A GREEN BAG" CAMPAIGN

> **The market is held in Abbey Square every Wednesday and Saturday from 0830 to 1700 hours**

Between 13 and 17 billion plastic bags are given free to UK shoppers every year. That's nearly 300 bags for every person in the UK.

The bags take between four hundred and one thousand years to break down. Plastic is not biodegradable, it is photodegradable, which means it breaks into smaller parts and each part is toxic so it contaminates the soil, the rivers and oceans.

When the plastic bag enters the ocean it becomes a harmful piece of litter. Many marine animals think these bags are food, swallow them and die a painful death. Nearly 90 per cent of floating litter in the world's oceans is plastic. When this toxic substance is swallowed by marine life it can enter the human food chain.

What the Selby Market Traders' Association is doing about this toxic, dangerous, unwanted product

❖ Throughout the month of April, Selby District Council is giving free, reusable, **cornstarch** bags to every person who visits the market, irrespective of whether or not they make a purchase.

❖ On every market day in May each stallholder will be placing the goods they sell in reusable **jute** bags. These bags will be given free of charge.

❖ From June onwards, the stallholders will offer for sale reusable, **unbleached cotton** shopping bags in a range of colours. These bags will cost only 30p.

❖ In November and December Selby District Council will be giving free, reusable **cotton** bags, decorated with Christmas scenes, to every person who visits the market.

How can you, the shopper, help?

You won't get plastic bags with your Selby Market purchases, but elsewhere **THINK** BEFORE YOU ACCEPT A PLASTIC CARRIER BAG.

Be aware that the average life of a supermarket plastic bag is 20 minutes before being thrown away and finding its way into a landfill site.

Carry the high-quality reusable bags we are offering. Why not buy them in a range of colours — green for fruit and vegetables, red for meat, yellow for clothes, blue for toiletries?

Functional Skills English Level 2 Summative Assessment Papers, Marking Scheme, and Tutors' Guide – ISBN: 978-1-9049955-5-5

## A survey's results

Last month Selby Market Traders' Association carried out a survey of 3,000 shoppers in an effort to establish the pattern of plastic bag usage and the attitude of shoppers to plastic bag litter.

The results are shown in this chart.

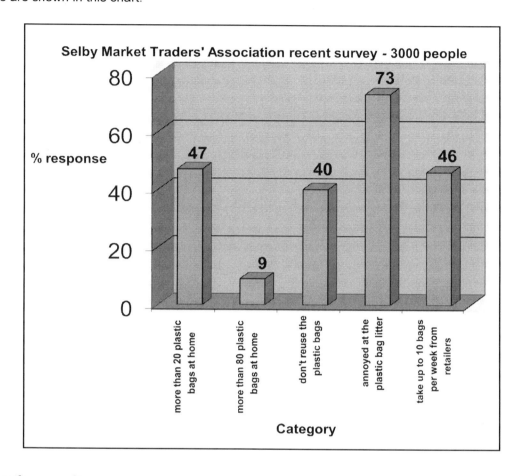

## Consider the results

Nearly 50 per cent of the 3,000 shoppers surveyed admitted to taking up to ten plastic bags a week from retailers, that's 1,500 people with a total of around 15,000 plastic bags.

Nearly 50 per cent of shoppers admitted having over 20 plastic bags at home. That's 15,000 plastic bags in this small section of the public. What's going to become of these 15,000 plastic bags? If they are at home, they are not being reused. Does that mean they will go into the household rubbish bin and end up on the landfill site, where it takes up to 1,000 years to decompose, each leaving behind a toxic footprint?

Around 10 per cent of people surveyed had more than 80 bags at home. That's 300 people with up to 80 bags each. If you do the arithmetic that adds up to another 24,000 plastic bags.

Forty per cent of people surveyed admitted they did not reuse plastic bags. If those 40 per cent also have between 20 and 80 bags at home, which will eventually find their way into the dustbin, just think how many bags are out there, ready to cause death to millions of seabirds and fish.

Please help the environment, not just for today, but for the long-term future

VISIT SELBY MARKET AND OUR "GET A GREEN BAG" CAMPAIGN

WE LOOK FORWARD TO SEEING YOU

Functional Skills English Level 2 Summative Assessment Papers, Marking Scheme, and Tutors' Guide – ISBN: 978-1-9049955-5-5

# Functional Skills English Level 2 Assessment Paper

| Student's Name | |
|---|---|

| Paper's Title | **BINGE DRINKING** | Date Set | |
|---|---|---|---|
| | | Hand-in Date | |

| Activity | Possible Marks | | Marks Awarded | Totals |
|---|---|---|---|---|
| 1   Reading and Writing | Q1 | 3 | | |
| | Q2 | 1 | | |
| | Q3 | 3 | | |
| | Q4 | 2 | | |
| | Q5 | 1 | | |
| | Q6 | 3 | | |
| | Q7 | 6 | | |
| | | | Activity 1 | |
| 2   Reading | Q1 | 1 | | |
| | Q2 | 1 | | |
| | Q3 | 1 | | |
| | Q4 | 1 | | |
| | | | Activity 2 | |
| 3   Reading and Writing | Q1 | 8 | | |
| | Q2 | 2 | | |
| | | | Activity 3 | |
| 4   Researching and Writing | Q1 | 17 | | |
| | | | Activity 4 | |
| | | | PAPER TOTAL | |
| | | | **PERCENTAGE** | |

| Result | PASS |
|---|---|
| Circle the appropriate result | FAIL |

Assessor's Signature ................................................................... Date ...........................

Functional Skills English Level 2  Summative Assessment Papers, Marking Scheme, and Tutors' Guide – ISBN: 978-1-9049955-5-5

# BINGE DRINKING

## Assessor's Comments

| Activity | Comments |
|----------|----------|
| 1        |          |
| 2        |          |
| 3        |          |
| 4        |          |

Functional Skills English Level 2  Summative Assessment Papers, Marking Scheme, and Tutors' Guide – ISBN: 978-1-9049955-5-5

## BINGE DRINKING

This paper has **4** sections:

Section 1    involve reading and writing

Section 2    involves reading

Section 3    involves reading and writing

Section 4    involves researching and writing a report

There are **three** documents for you to read.

Read the documents **before** you begin to answer the questions and keep referring to them when you work through the sections.

You are reminded that clear written English and correct spelling and punctuation are important, together with presenting work neatly and making sure it is suitable for the purpose and the audience.

Functional Skills English Level 2  Summative Assessment Papers, Marking Scheme, and Tutors' Guide – ISBN: 978-1-9049955-5-5

## BINGE DRINKING

ACTIVITY 1 — Reading and Writing

You will be assessed on the following:

— reading, finding and summarising information and ideas from text;

— presenting your work and ideas clearly and logically;

— using a range of sentence structures, including complex sentences;

— using spelling, grammar and punctuation accurately and correctly.

Read **Document 1** then answer the following questions.

You should spend no longer than 25 minutes on questions 1 — 7.


1    Name **three** terms which are used to describe **binge drinking**?    **3 marks**

_____

_____

_____

_____

_____

_____


For question 2 choose one answer, A, B, C or D and put a ✓ (tick) in the box.

2    According to the document, how many units a day can be defined as heavy
     drinking for a female ?    **1 mark**

     A     2 to 3         ☐

     B     6 to 8         ☐

     C     4 to 6         ☐

     D     3 to 4         ☐

3      In your own words, explain why the document says the recommended daily unit intake is less for a woman than it is for a man. **3 marks**

      _____

      _____

      _____

      _____

4      Name two psychological effects which result from too much alcohol. **2 marks**

      _____

      _____

5      One health effect of binge drinking can be a rise in blood pressure. What does the document say is the danger associated with high blood pressure? **1 mark**

      _____

      _____

6      Explain, in your own words, what the article suggests are the ways in which someone who has been involved in a heavy drinking session might show lack of judgement. **3 marks**

      _____

      _____

      _____

      _____

192

Functional Skills English Level 2 Summative Assessment Papers, Marking Scheme, and Tutors' Guide – ISBN: 978-1-9049955-5-5

7    In your own words, describe what the article says about the link between crime and binge drinking.   Give reasons for the points you include, i.e. say why the binge drinker might be involved in what you describe.   **6 marks**

_____

_____

_____

_____

_____

_____

_____

_____

# BINGE DRINKING

ACTIVITY 2 — Reading

You will be assessed on the following:

— reading, finding and summarising information and ideas from different types of document.

**Document 2** shows a bar chart, and text, related to units of alcohol and the recommended maximum daily intake. Study the document then answer the following questions.

You should spend no longer than 15 minutes on questions 1 — 4.

For each question choose one answer, A, B, C or D and put a ✓ (tick) in the box.

1 mark is awarded for each correct answer.

1     Which **category(ies)** of alcohol represents the **least** number of alcohol units?

     A     a pint of standard strength lager and a 125ml glass of    ☐
wine

     B     125ml of spirits    ☐

     C     275ml of alcopop and 25ml of spirits    ☐

     D     25ml of spirits    ☐

2     Which **category(ies)** of alcohol represent the **most** number of alcohol units?

     A     one measure of spirits and a 175ml glass of wine    ☐

     B     a 25ml measure of spirits and 275ml of alcopops    ☐

     C     a pint of strong lager or cider    ☐

     D     a pint of standard strength lager    ☐

3     Which **category(ies)** of alcohol represent the **highest** volume of alcohol?

     A     a pint of strong cider    ☐

     B     a pint of strong cider and a standard glass of wine    ☐

     C     wine in both standard and small glasses    ☐

     D     spirits    ☐

Functional Skills English Level 2 Summative Assessment Papers, Marking Scheme, and Tutors' Guide – ISBN: 978-1-9049955-5-5

4    Considering the **maximum** recommended daily unit intake for males, which of the following combinations of drinks could a man consume and stay **within** the recommended units?

A    a pint of strong cider and a 275ml bottle of alcopop    ☐

B    half a pint of strong lager, a small glass of wine and a measure of spirits    ☐

C    an alcopop, a measure of spirits and a standard glass of wine    ☐

D    two pints of standard strength lager and a small glass of wine    ☐

# BINGE DRINKING

ACTIVITY 3 — Reading and Writing

You will be assessed on the following:

— reading, finding and summarising information and ideas from text;

— presenting your work and ideas clearly and logically;

— identifying the purpose and effectiveness of texts;

— using a range of sentence structures, including complex sentences;

— using spelling, grammar and punctuation accurately and correctly.

Read **Document 3** then answer the following questions.

You should spend no longer than 20 minutes on questions 1 and 2.

1    Summarise, in your own words, what the survey revealed about **Year 11** students.
     **8 marks**

    _____

    _____

    _____

    _____

    _____

2    What do you think is the **tone** of Document 3?   Give reasons for your answer.
     **2 marks**

    _____

    _____

    _____

196

Functional Skills English Level 2 Summative Assessment Papers, Marking Scheme, and Tutors' Guide – ISBN: 978-1-9049955-5-5

Functional Skills English Level 2 Summative Assessment Papers, Marking Scheme, and Tutors' Guide – ISBN: 978-1-9049955-5-5

# BINGE DRINKING

ACTIVITY 4 — Researching and Writing

## Writing a Report

You will be assessed on the following:

— locating relevant information from research;

— summarising research documents and the information/ideas they contain;

— adapting researched information to prepare documents;

— producing work which is suitable for the audience;

— presenting complex subjects clearly;

— using a range of sentence structures, including complex sentences;

— using a range of writing styles and sentence structures for different purposes;

— using spelling, grammar and punctuation accurately and correctly.

**There are no suggested timings for this activity.**

## Scenario

There is more to this topic than you have read about in these documents. Your task is to carry out some research and write a short report on your findings.

### Researching the topic and Writing your Report    **17 marks**

You are to write a report and must firstly carry out research into one of the following topics:

1    the consequences of drinking (binge drinking), or

2    the dangers of alcohol for young people.

If you are going to use Internet-based research you might want to visit these sites initially.

www.drinksafely.info/home/bingedrinking; www.talkaboutalcohol.com; www.apas.org.uk; and www.patient.co.uk/health/alcohol-and-liver-disease.htm.

You will probably find other sites and other paper-based information related to your chosen topic.

Keep copies of your research documents to hand in with your work.

Your report will need to contain the following:

1.      A cover sheet which includes:

an appropriate title;

your name;

today's date.

2.      Heading

**A summary of my findings on (topic)**

3.      Findings

List these in a logical order and make use of paragraph headings to help the reader pick out and understand what you write.

4.      Summary

Provide a brief statement which draws a conclusion from your findings.

Your Report must contain a minimum of 500 words.

If you wish to do so, you can plan your work on the blank pages your tutor will hand you.

Functional Skills English Level 2  Summative Assessment Papers, Marking Scheme, and Tutors' Guide – ISBN: 978-1-9049955-5-5

# Research Notes and Report Plan

**DOCUMENT 1**

## WHAT IS BINGE DRINKING?

Binge drinking can be defined as **heavy drinking**. It is not the same as being an alcoholic, rather it is alcohol abuse, or problem drinking. This happens when a person is drinking enough to cause themselves physical or psychological harm.

How much alcohol is classed as **heavy drinking**? The Office of National Statistics defines heavy drinking as either six to eight units* of alcohol per day for men, and four to six units for females.

## UNIT GUIDELINES

Females are recommended not to exceed two or three units of alcohol a day. Males are recommended not to exceed three or four units of alcohol a day.

The recommended number of units for females is lower than the recommended number of units for males because of a woman's body composition — a woman has less water in her body than a man so if a man and woman weigh the same, and are of a similar size, the woman will get drunk more quickly.

## WHAT HEALTH PROBLEMS CAN RESULT FROM CONTINUED BINGE DRINKING?

### Short-term effects

Whilst a small amount of alcohol can have the effect of relaxing the drinker, alcohol is a depressant of the central nervous system. Therefore, increasing amounts of alcohol suppress the parts of the brain which control judgement. This, in turn, leads to a loss of inhibitions and poor judgement — this is a psychological effect of drinking alcohol. Physical effects can include dizziness, blurred vision, slurred speech and loss of balance. Drinking a large amount in one time (binge drinking) can result in unconsciousness, coma and even death. Vomiting whilst unconscious can lead to death by suffocation.

Alcohol, in any measure, contributes to a large proportion of fatal road accidents, assaults and incidents of domestic violence.

* refer to Document 2

### Long-term effects

Alcohol is a drug, and is dangerous if misused and abused. Drinking too much, too often (binge drinking) will increase the risk of physical damage to the body, and increase the risk of getting some diseases, and making some diseases worse.

Binge drinking is associated with the following:
- hepatitis and cirrhosis of the liver;
- gastritis (inflammation of the stomach lining);
- pancreatitis (inflammation of the pancreas);
- high blood pressure (increasing the risk of a stroke);
- certain types of cancer, including the mouth and throat;
- heart failure;
- brain damage;
- epilepsy;
- vitamin deficiency.

Functional Skills English Level 2 Summative Assessment Papers, Marking Scheme, and Tutors' Guide – ISBN: 978-1-9049955-5-5

Research seems to indicate that women develop liver disease at lower levels of drinking than men.

Binge drinking has also been known to result in the following problems:

- obesity;

- skin problems;

- infertility (in both males and females);

- muscle disease.

## WHAT SOCIAL PROBLEMS CAN RESULT FROM CONTINUED BINGE DRINKING?

An increased level of alcohol can lead to an increase in accidents and crime. If someone is "wasted", they are more likely to fall or step into moving traffic. Someone suffering the result of binge drinking will have poor judgement and might accept a lift in a car being driven by someone who is also guilty of binge drinking — this is a decision someone is unlikely to make if sober.

Binge drinking can bring a person into unexpected contact with crime. The binge drinker could be the victim of a crime or carry out a crime. In the UK it is estimated that one third of burglaries and half of street crimes are the result of someone who has been binge drinking.

The clear message is that binge drinking damages you both in the short- and long-term, can lead to your involvement in crime and possibly death. Don't binge drink — it's not cool and it can be a killer.

So, the next time you binge drink and feel unwell the following day, or days, remember that no matter how unpleasant you feel, if you continue to damage your body that feeling of unpleasantness will increase in the long term, and you may even do damage which cannot be reversed.

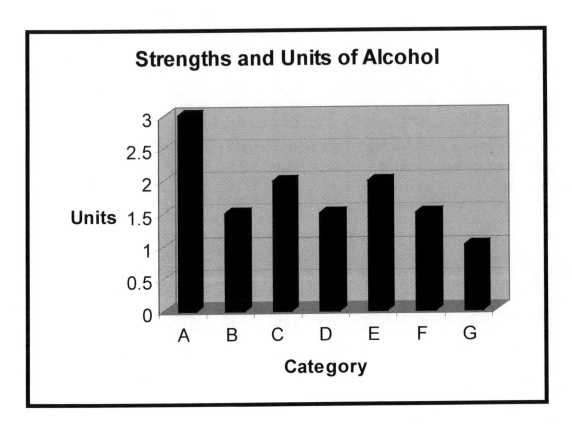

**Category Key**

| | | |
|---|---|---|
| A | 1 pint of strong lager or cider | 5% volume |
| B | Half-pint strong lager or cider | 5% volume |
| C | 1 pint standard strength lager | 5.5% volume |
| D | 275ml bottle of alcopop | 5.5% volume |
| E | 175ml glass wine (standard size) | 12% volume |
| F | 125ml glass wine (small size) | 12% volume |
| G | 25ml spirits (one measure) | |

Note that the number of units may vary according to **brand** and whether you are male or female.

Recommended daily unit intake:

Men        3 or 4

Women     2 or 3

Functional Skills English Level 2  Summative Assessment Papers, Marking Scheme,  and Tutors' Guide – ISBN: 978-1-9049955-5-5

## DOCUMENT 3

<u>**BINGE DRINKING IN YOUNG PEOPLE**</u>

A recent survey in the UK asked more than 14,000 students in Years 7 — 11 in secondary education, to assess their involvement in alcohol abuse.

Under-age drinking was common and more than four out of every ten students in Years 10 and 11 admitted to "binge drinking" because they consumed five or more alcoholic drinks in one session.

Six out of ten boys and 50 per cent of girls in Year 7 said they had tried at least one alcoholic drink.

Eight out of ten students in Year 11, of both sexes, said they had drunk alcohol in the four weeks before the survey was conducted.

More than a quarter of students, of both sexes, in Year 11 reported three or more alcohol "binge sessions" in the month before the survey.

The survey results seem to support the belief that there is a growing culture of intoxication amongst young people in the UK. Thirty-six per cent of men and 77 per cent of women aged 16–24 admit to binge drinking sessions at least once a week.

<u>How to avoid binge drinking</u>

As drinking large amounts of alcohol, on a regular basis, can lead to severe health problems in the short- and long-term, knowing how to avoid becoming a binge drinker is important.

Here are some tips:

1       Go out **later**, so you start drinking later.

2       Drink water **before** you go out so you are less thirsty.

3       Eat before you go out, or whilst you are drinking, as this slows down alcohol absorption into the blood stream.

4       Alternate an alcoholic drink with a soft drink.

5       Know what a **unit** is so you **do not** exceed the daily recommended unit count.

6       Have at least two alcohol-free days each week.

7       When you are drinking **set yourself a limit within the daily unit guide** and **stick to it**.

Functional Skills English Level 2  Summative Assessment Papers, Marking Scheme, and Tutors' Guide – ISBN:  978-1-9049955-5-5

## Functional Skills English Level 2 Assessment Paper

| Student's Name | | | |
|---|---|---|---|

| Paper's Title | **5-A-DAY** | Date Set | |
|---|---|---|---|
| | | Hand-in Date | |

| Activity | Possible Marks | | Marks Awarded | Totals |
|---|---|---|---|---|
| 1   Reading and Writing | Q1 | 2 | | |
| | Q2 | 4 | | |
| | Q3 | 3 | | |
| | Q4 | 1 | | |
| | Q5 | 1 | | |
| | Q6 | 6 | | |
| | | | Activity 1 | |
| 2   Reading and Writing | Q1 | 3 | | |
| | Q2 | 2 | | |
| | Q3 | 2 | | |
| | Q4 | 6 | | |
| | Q5 | 1 | | |
| | | | Activity 2 | |
| 3   Researching and Writing | Q1 | 12 | | |
| | Q2 | 7 | | |
| | | | Activity 3 | |
| | | | PAPER TOTAL | |
| | | | **PERCENTAGE** | |

| **Result** | | **PASS** |
|---|---|---|
| Circle the appropriate result | | **FAIL** |

Assessor's Signature ................................................................... Date ...........................

Functional Skills English Level 2  Summative Assessment Papers, Marking Scheme,  and Tutors' Guide – ISBN: 978-1-9049955-5-5

# 5-A-DAY

## Assessor's Comments

| Activity | Comments |
|---|---|
| 1 | |
| 2 | |
| 3 | |

# 5-A-DAY

This paper has **3** sections:

Sections 1 and 2    involve reading and writing

Section 3            involves reading, researching and writing a newsletter and a memo

There are **two** documents for you to read.

Read the documents **before** you begin to answer the questions and keep referring to them when you work through the sections.

You are reminded that clear written English and correct spelling and punctuation are important, together with presenting work neatly and making sure it is suitable for the purpose and the audience.

Functional Skills English Level 2  Summative Assessment Papers, Marking Scheme, and Tutors' Guide – ISBN: 978-1-9049955-5-5

# 5-A-DAY

ACTIVITY 1 — Reading and Writing

You will be assessed on the following:

— reading, finding and summarising information and ideas from different types of document;

— presenting your work and ideas clearly and logically;

— using a range of sentence structures, including complex sentences;

— using spelling, grammar and punctuation accurately and correctly.

Read **Document 1**, which includes a bar chart, then answer the following questions.

You should spend no longer than 25 minutes on questions 1 — 6.


For questions 4 and 5 choose one answer, A, B, C or D and put a ✓ (tick) in the box.

1 mark is awarded for the correct answer.


1    Explain the relationship between 80g of weight and the recommended daily intake of 400g a day.  **2 marks**

_____

_____

_____

_____


2    Which foods, other than fruit and vegetables, can be counted in the recommended daily intake ?  **4 marks**

_____

_____

_____

Functional Skills English Level 2  Summative Assessment Papers, Marking Scheme, and Tutors' Guide – ISBN: 978-1-9049955-5-5

3    Name three of the benefits of eating 400g of the recommended foods per day.
     **3 marks**

     _____

     _____

     _____

4    It's advisable to have a varied diet to make up the recommended daily intake.
     Which of the following combination of foods equals a recommended daily intake
     of five portions?

     A    7 cherry tomatoes, 1 satsuma, 3 glasses of fruit juice          ☐

     B    1 glass of vegetable juice, 1 glass of fruit juice, a bowl       ☐
          of lettuce

     C    3 tablespoons of fruit salad, a glass of vegetable              ☐
          juice, 3 heaped tablespoons of butter beans, 14 cherry
          tomatoes

     D    14 cherry tomatoes, 1 large grapefruit                          ☐

5    According to the information, how can the National Diet and Nutrition Survey
     results best be described?

     A    13% of men eat fewer than five portions a day but 15%           ☐
          of women eat more than five portions a day

     B    Men and women tend to eat the recommended portions              ☐
          but people between 19 and 54 eat only three portions a
          day

     C    More men than women consume the minimum of five                 ☐
          portions a day and the ages of these men are between
          19 and 54

     D    Whilst those aged 19–54 eat less than the daily                 ☐
          recommended intake, a greater percentage of women
          than men eat five or more portions a day

Functional Skills English Level 2 Summative Assessment Papers, Marking Scheme, and Tutors' Guide – ISBN: 978-1-9049955-5-5

6    Interpreting the chart, write an explanation of no more than 75 words, to explain the weekly trend over the four years, in the consumption of fruit and vegetables.
**6 marks**

_____

_____

_____

_____

_____

_____

_____

_____

_____

_____

_____

_____

_____

_____

## 5-A-DAY

ACTIVITY 2 — Reading and Writing

You will be assessed on the following:

— reading, finding and summarising information and ideas from different types of document;

— presenting your work and ideas clearly and logically;

— using a range of sentence structures, including complex sentences;

— using spelling, grammar and punctuation accurately and correctly.

**Document 2** contains draft notes which will be the basis of a school newsletter to parents. It includes a line graph, and text, related to the "School Fruit and Vegetable Scheme" (SFVS). Study the document then answer the following questions.

You should spend no longer than 25 minutes on questions 1 — 5.

1    Explain when the national SFVS began, its funding and how that funding arrangement changed.   **3 marks**

_____

_____

_____

_____

_____

_____

_____

Functional Skills English Level 2 Summative Assessment Papers, Marking Scheme, and Tutors' Guide – ISBN: 978-1-9049955-5-5

2     Explain how frequently the participating schools get their fruit and vegetable deliveries and their impression of the system?   **2 marks**

_____

_____

_____

_____

_____

_____

_____

3     Whilst the majority of pupils expressed positive opinions about the national scheme, give details of two more positive outcomes, not directly concerned with the service or the quality of the produce?   **2 marks**

_____

_____

_____

_____

_____

_____

Functional Skills English Level 2   Summative Assessment Papers, Marking Scheme, and Tutors' Guide – ISBN: 978-1-9049955-5-5

4    Explain the result of the Ward Nelson school survey as indicated in the graph.
     **6 marks**

_____

_____

_____

_____

_____

_____

_____

_____

5    What is the significance of advising mums to select fruit and vegetables of
     different colours each day?   **1 mark**

_____

_____

_____

_____

_____

Functional Skills English Level 2  Summative Assessment Papers, Marking Scheme, and Tutors' Guide – ISBN: 978-1-9049955-5-5

| 5-A-DAY |
| --- |

ACTIVITY 3 – Researching and Writing

## Producing a Newsletter and writing a Memo

You will be assessed on the following:

— locating relevant information from research;

— summarising research documents and the information and ideas they contain;

— adapting researched information to prepare documents;

— producing work which is suitable for the audience;

— presenting your work and information and ideas clearly and persuasively;

— using a range of writing styles for different purposes;

— using a range of sentence structures;

— using spelling, grammar and punctuation accurately and correctly.

**There are no suggested timings for this activity.**

## Scenario

The school Head, Brian Rhodes, wants you to put together a newsletter which will be sent to all parents during the final term of the academic year.

He has begun to put some thoughts together and these are shown in draft form in **Document 2**. However, they are not in a very sensible order, moving from the results of the school's findings to what the national scheme is all about and its findings, then back to matters relating to the school. Therefore, the notes need reorganising, amending, etc.

The Head has told you he wants his pupils' mums to have some help with menu planning so that at home they can continue the good work the school is doing on a daily basis. He thinks a few menus will also encourage those parents who are not yet actively involved in the scheme.

## Researching the topic

Carry out some research into the topics of "5-A-Day" and "Schools Fruit and Vegetable Scheme" to see if there is any other, brief, information you can add to the Newsletter. Additionally you need to find some recipes so parents can see how easy it is to incorporate fresh vegetables and fruit into the home's daily menus. A good starting point might be the website mentioned in Document 2.

Keep copies of your research documents to hand in with your work.

If you wish to do so, you can plan your work on the blank pages your tutor will hand you.

Functional Skills English Level 2 Summative Assessment Papers, Marking Scheme, and Tutors' Guide – ISBN: 978-1-9049955-5-5

# Research Notes

Functional Skills English Level 2  Summative Assessment Papers, Marking Scheme,  and Tutors' Guide – ISBN:  978-1-9049955-5-5

# 1    Newsletter   12 marks

The newsletter will be from the Head of the school, so his name and title must appear on it, together with that of the school.  The aim of the newsletter is to include the key facts and summaries from Document 2, but in a logical order.  You might need to add further information about the importance of 5-a-day and you must include at least two recipes which can be easily produced at home to encourage children to eat fruit and vegetables.  Make them simple because busy mums will not want to become involved if they think they won't have time!

You will need to incorporate the information from Document 2 and your tutor may allow you to cut and paste this information around what you write.

Your newsletter should contain no fewer than 500 words.

If you wish to do so, you can plan your newsletter and/or make rough notes on the following blank pages.

# 2    Memo   7 marks

When you have finished your newsletter, write a memo from yourself to the Head, dating it today and using the heading **Amended Newsletter for your Consideration**.

Say you have done as he requested and attach the newsletter for his consideration. You have included additional information ............. (describe it) because ................... Finish by saying you look forward to his comments and are happy to make any amendments he wishes.

Don't forget to sign it.

When you are ready to write your memo, ask your tutor for the blank memo sheet.

If you wish to do so, you can plan your memo and/or make rough notes on the blank pages your tutor will hand you.

Functional Skills English Level 2  Summative Assessment Papers, Marking Scheme, and Tutors' Guide – ISBN: 978-1-9049955-5-5

# Newsletter Plan

Functional Skills English Level 2  Summative Assessment Papers, Marking Scheme,  and Tutors' Guide – ISBN:  978-1-9049955-5-5

# Memo Plan

Functional Skills English Level 2  Summative Assessment Papers, Marking Scheme,  and Tutors' Guide – ISBN: 978-1-9049955-5-5

# MEMORANDUM

**To** _____     **From** _____

**Date** _____

**Re** _____

# WHY 5-A-DAY?

The advice to eat a minimum of 400g* of fruit and vegetables every day came from the World Health Organisation (WHO) in 1991.

The benefits of eating this daily recommendation include:

- fruit and vegetables are low in calories;

- fruit and vegetables are low in fat;

- fruit and vegetables are full of minerals;

- fruit and vegetables are an excellent, natural source of fibre;

- fruit and vegetables provide vitamins such as vitamin C and folate;

- fruit and vegetables contain phytochemicals which help to protect against a number of diseases such as heart disease and cancer.

5-a-day does not just include fruit and vegetables, other important health-giving foods are included on the recommended list. The other commodities include juice, dried fruit, pulses and beans. The five recommended portions per day does not include potatoes.

### EACH OF THE FOODS EQUALS ONE PORTION

| Fruit | Dried fruit | Vegetables | Juice | Pulses and beans |
|---|---|---|---|---|
| 1 medium banana<br><br>3 tablespoons fruit salad<br><br>2 satsumas<br><br>½ large grapefruit | 3 dried apricots<br><br>1 tablespoon of raisins<br><br>2 dried figs<br><br>4 dried apple rings | 2 tablespoons of peas<br><br>2 spears of broccoli<br><br>1 cereal bowl of lettuce<br><br>7 cherry tomatoes | 1 glass of 100% fruit or vegetable juice.<br><br>But you can only count juice as 1 portion a day however much you drink.<br><br>This is because juice contains very little fibre. | 3 heaped tablespoons of baked beans, haricot beans, kidney beans, cannelloni beans, butter beans or chick peas.<br><br>Remember that beans and pulses count, but only as 1 of the 5 portions, no matter how much you eat |

* 1 portion of fruit and vegetables equals 80g, so 5 portions equals 400g

Functional Skills English Level 2 Summative Assessment Papers, Marking Scheme, and Tutors' Guide – ISBN: 978-1-9049955-5-5

## HOW DOES THE 5-A-DAY RECOMMENDATION COMPARE WITH WHAT PEOPLE ARE EATING?

The National Diet and Nutrition Survey shows that the average consumption of fruit and vegetables per day is as follows:

- age group 19 – 64: less than three portions;

- only 13 per cent of men consume five or more portions;

- only 15 per cent of women consume five or more portions.

A recent survey revealed the gram consumption of fruit and vegetables per week, per person. The results are shown in the chart below.

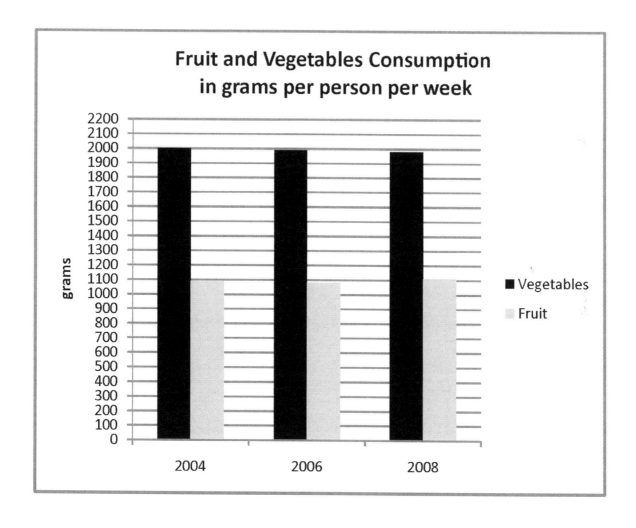

Functional Skills English Level 2  Summative Assessment Papers, Marking Scheme, and Tutors' Guide – ISBN:  978-1-9049955-5-5

### DRAFT NOTES FOR WARD NELSON JUNIOR SCHOOL'S
### REVIEWS OF ITS
### "SCHOOL FRUIT AND VEGETABLE SCHEME"

We launched, in September 2008, our **5-A-DAY SCHOOL FRUIT AND VEGETABLE SCHEME** programme designed to increase fruit and vegetable consumption.

The school's 7 to 11 year old pupils are entitled to a **free piece of fruit or vegetable.** (This is on every school day, every day of the academic year).

According to season, these are apples, pears, bananas, tangerines, strawberries and raspberries, mini-cucumbers, carrots and cherry tomatoes, radishes and sweetc.orn and butter beans, spinach and beetroot, cauliflower, courgettes, and turnips.

### THE RESULTS OF OUR PARENTS' SURVEY
### AT THE END OF TERM TWO

The Head, Brian Rhodes, met the parents at the end of the academic year in 2008 to say the school would be taking part in the **SCHOOL FRUIT AND VEGETABLE SCHEME** and to explain what was involved.

At the end of term two, in April 2009, Mr Rhodes met the parents once more to review progress and to ask the parents for their comments and thoughts on the scheme. Five hundred and seventy three parents took part in the review.

The result of this survey is shown in the graph below:

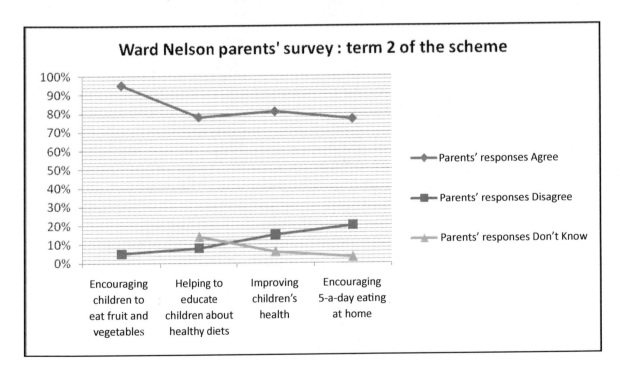

Functional Skills English Level 2 Summative Assessment Papers, Marking Scheme, and Tutors' Guide – ISBN: 978-1-9049955-5-5

## The National Scheme

The national "Schools Fruit and Vegetable Scheme" began in 2004 funded by 42 million pounds of lottery money. When, in 2005 the lottery money ran out, the Department of Health supported and financed the expansion of the scheme region by region.

Schools taking part in the Scheme in 2004 and 2005 reported the following:

- ninety-nine per cent of schools said the daily deliveries of fruit and vegetables were reliable or acceptable;
- ninety-three per cent of schools thought the quality of the produce was good;
- ninety-seven per cent of the schools regarded the scheme as a support to teaching and learning about healthy eating, particularly supporting the Government's 5-A-Day scheme;
- the majority of the pupils were positive about the scheme;
- the staff considered the scheme an excellent way of improving children's health and encouraging a healthy diet.

## Findings from a national pupil questionnaire

Girls tried more fruits and vegetables than boys.

More girls than boys were reported to like the fruit and vegetables scheme.

Only one-third of the children surveyed had been previously aware of the 5-A-Day scheme.

The children surveyed, who liked the scheme, were encouraged to try fruit and vegetables previously unfamiliar to them.

## Results from Ward Nelson's pupil questionnaire

On the whole the girls tended to try more fruit and vegetables and liked more fruit than the boys.

There was an increase in fruit and dried fruit contained in the children's lunch boxes and those who had school dinners tended to select more vegetables with their meals than had previously occurred.

A greater number of girls than boys chose fruit as their dessert at the end of the school lunch meal.

## TIPS FOR OUR MUMS

Eating 5-A-Day sets kids up for a healthy lifestyle. Fruit and vegetables of different colours provide a different range of vitamins, minerals, fibre and healthy antioxidants, which can help to protect the body throughout life.

Research has shown that eating five or more a day can help to maintain a healthier diet. Looking to our children's future, people who eat lots of fruit and vegetables can have a lower risk of heart disease, high blood pressure, strokes and some cancers.

To get the best benefit from the nutrients packed into fruit and vegetables, everyone should aim for a variety of different types and colours every day.

Recipe information and details of the fruit and vegetables in season each month of the year can be found at: www.5aday.nhs.uk/toptips/default.html

Functional Skills English Level 2  Summative Assessment Papers, Marking Scheme, and Tutors' Guide – ISBN: 978-1-9049955-5-5

# Functional Skills English Level 2 Assessment Paper

Student's Name

Paper's Title

**NO MESSIN'**

Date Set

Hand-in Date

| Activity | Possible Marks | | Marks Awarded | Totals |
|---|---|---|---|---|
| 1  Reading and Writing | Q1 | 3 | | |
| | Q2 | 2 | | |
| | Q3 | 2 | | |
| | Q4 | 3 | | |
| | Q5 | 1 | | |
| | | Activity 1 | | |
| 2  Reading and Writing | Q1 | 1 | | |
| | Q2 | 6 | | |
| | Q3 | 1 | | |
| | Q4 | 2 | | |
| | Q5 | 4 | | |
| | | Activity 2 | | |
| 3  Reading and Writing | Q1 | 5 | | |
| | Q2 | 2 | | |
| | Q3 | 3 | | |
| | | Activity 3 | | |
| 4  Researching and Writing | Q1 | 15 | | |
| | | Activity 4 | | |
| | | PAPER TOTAL | | |
| | | **PERCENTAGE** | | |

| Result | | PASS |
|---|---|---|
| Circle the appropriate result | | FAIL |

Assessor's Signature ................................................................ Date ...........................

Functional Skills English Level 2  Summative Assessment Papers, Marking Scheme,  and Tutors' Guide – ISBN: 978-1-9049955-5-5

# NO MESSIN'

## Assessor's Comments

| Activity | Comments |
|---|---|
| 1 | |
| 2 | |
| 3 | |
| 4 | |

# NO MESSIN'

This paper has **4** sections

Sections 1 to 3     involve reading and writing

Section 4          involves researching  and writing a brochure

There are **three** documents for you to read.

Read the documents **before** you begin to answer the questions and keep referring to them when you work through the sections.

You are reminded that clear written English and correct spelling and punctuation are important, together with presenting work neatly and making sure it is suitable for the purpose and the audience.

Functional Skills English Level 2 Summative Assessment Papers, Marking Scheme, and Tutors' Guide – ISBN: 978-1-9049955-5-5

## NO MESSIN'

ACTIVITY 1 — Reading and Writing

You will be assessed on the following:

— reading, finding and summarising information and ideas from text;

— presenting your work and ideas clearly and logically;

— using a range of sentence structures, including complex sentences;

— using spelling, grammar and punctuation accurately and correctly.

Read **Document 1,** then answer the following questions.

You should spend no longer than 25 minutes on questions 1 — 5.

1    According to the document, which parts of the railway property can people use which are not regarded as trespassing?  **3 marks**

_____

_____

_____

_____

_____

_____

2    Describe the two categories of people who trespass on the railway?  **2 marks**

_____

_____

_____

_____

3    Describe the difference between trespass and vandalism.  **2 marks**

_____

_____

_____

_____

4    Graffiti is seen as one form of vandalism.  Name three other activities which are regarded in the same way.  **3 marks**

_____

_____

_____

_____

5    Which crime could result in a prison sentence?  **1 mark**

_____

_____

_____

_____

Functional Skills English Level 2 Summative Assessment Papers, Marking Scheme, and Tutors' Guide – ISBN: 978-1-9049955-5-5

## NO MESSIN'

ACTIVITY 2 — Reading and Writing

The questions in this section assess your reading and writing skills.

You will be assessed on the following:

— reading, finding and summarising information and ideas from text;

— presenting your work and ideas clearly and logically;

— identifying the purpose and tone of the document;

— using a range of sentence structures, including complex sentences;

— using spelling, grammar and punctuation accurately and correctly.

Read **Document 2,** then answer the following questions.

You should spend no longer than 25 minutes on questions 1 — 5.

Question 2 requires you to choose one answer, A, B, C or D and put a ✓ (tick) in the box.

1 mark is awarded for the correct answer.

1      According to the document how many children have died on, or near, railway lines in the last five years? **1 mark**

_____

_____

2      Describe the type of company Network Rail is, its purpose, and the responsibility it has. **6 marks**

_____

_____

_____

_____

_____

_____

Functional Skills English Level 2  Summative Assessment Papers, Marking Scheme, and Tutors' Guide – ISBN:  978-1-9049955-5-5

3     What is the tone of the document?

    A     shocking                                                     ☐

    B     informative                                                ☐

    C     informative and factual                        ☐

    D     complaining                                           ☐

4     Vandalising railway property occurs most often when? **2 marks**

_____

_____

_____

_____

5     Understanding that vandalism and trespass are dangerous activities, what is Network Rail doing to try to change attitudes towards these offences, and who is it trying to re-educate or provide with information?     **4 marks**

_____

_____

_____

_____

_____

_____

230

# NO MESSIN'

ACTIVITY 3 — Reading and Writing

You will be assessed on the following:

— reading, finding and summarising information and ideas from different types of document;

— presenting your work and ideas clearly and logically;

— presenting your work and information on complex subjects, clearly;

— using a range of sentence structures, including complex sentences;

— using spelling, grammar and punctuation accurately and correctly.

Read **Document 3**, which includes graphs and charts, then answer the following questions.

You should spend no longer than 25 minutes on questions 1 — 3.

1    Write a summary, of no fewer than 70 words, of the chart entitled "Incidents as a result of vandalism 2003-2007" taking care to describe the trend of each incident. **5 marks**

_____

_____

_____

_____

_____

_____

_____

2    Looking at the chart related to Missile Damage to Train Windows, name the three counties with the highest and the five counties with the fewest number of incidents.  **2 marks**

_____

_____

_____

_____

3    The document states that vandalism and trespass increases the cost of rail travel.  Explain this statement.  **3 marks**

_____

_____

_____

_____

_____

_____

_____

_____

_____

Functional Skills English Level 2  Summative Assessment Papers, Marking Scheme,  and Tutors' Guide – ISBN: 978-1-9049955-5-5

| NO MESSIN' |
| --- |

ACTIVITY 4 – Researching and Writing

## Writing an Information Booklet

You will be assessed on the following:

— locating relevant information from research;

— summarising the research documents and the information/ideas they contain;

— adapting researched information to prepare documents;

— producing work which is suitable for the audience;

— presenting your work, information and ideas clearly and persuasively;

— using a range of writing styles for different purposes;

— using a range of complex sentence structures;

— using spelling, grammar and punctuation accurately and correctly.

**There are no suggested timings for this activity.**

## Scenario

Your former secondary school, with whom you maintain links, has asked if you would be interested in promoting the **No Messin'** campaign with its after-school club.

You decide you want to become involved and now have to do some research into the campaign so you can put together an informative booklet, the aim of which is to give facts and encourage membership of the school's No Messin' club.

## 1    Researching the topic

Carry out some research into the **No Messin'** campaign with a view to finding what the campaign is about, who is already involved, and the types of activities which are included.  Read the details in Task 2 to discover some of information you need to find in your research.

Keep copies of your research documents to hand in with your work.

If you wish to do so, you can plan your work on the blank pages your tutor will hand you.

# Research Notes

---

Functional Skills English Level 2 Summative Assessment Papers, Marking Scheme, and Tutors' Guide – ISBN: 978-1-9049955-5-5

## 2    Information Booklet    15 marks

Put together an information booklet, containing two or three pages.  The purpose is to provide some information on vandalism and trespassing, the dangers and its consequences, **then** to describe Network Rail's No Messin' campaign, its purpose, what and who is involved (or who has been involved),  and its success in recent years.

Looking at the information from your research on the type of activities offered by those already involved in the No Messin' campaign, decide upon some activities that you will recommend be offered in the after-school club.  Include these details, and any others you consider appropriate, in your booklet to **encourage membership** of the No Messin' Club.  You can assume that the school will approve of your recommendations and include these activities.

Don't forget to include the name of the school in the booklet and perhaps contact details for those interested in joining the Club.  If you use images, make sure these serve to enhance the meaning, or message, of the text.

If you wish to do so, you can plan your Information Booklet on the pages your tutor will hand you.

# Information Booklet Plan

Functional Skills English Level 2  Summative Assessment Papers, Marking Scheme, and Tutors' Guide – ISBN: 978-1-9049955-5-5

# RAILWAY TRESPASS AND VANDALISM ARE CRIMINAL ACTIVITIES

Each year, people are killed and injured because they trespass on, or vandalise the railway.

There are more than 28 million occurrences of trespass on the railway each year. A shocking 11 million of these events are committed by people under the age of 16. An average of 60 people are killed and many, many more suffer terrible injuries each year.

## What is trespassing on the railway?

Members of the public can use the railway stations, the platforms and the bridges and other safe crossing places such as underpasses and level crossings.  People are trespassing if they go onto any of the railway tracks, the embankments or any of the other railways areas at any time.

Adults who use the railway tracks as a shortcut are another group which commits trespass on railway property.

Remember: trespassing puts your life, and the life of others, in danger.

## What is vandalism on the railway?

You are committing vandalism if you deliberately damage railway property. Vandalism includes such things as graffiti, leaving litter, fly-tipping, breaking railway property (including fences), damaging railway property (including fences, bridges, tracks and railway signs).

The majority of vandalism has been found to be carried out by boys aged from 8 to 16 years. Shockingly some children as young as 5 have been found vandalising railway property.

> **Trespassing or vandalism of the railways is a criminal offence and carry fines of up to £1000. Graffiti is a crime that carries a prison sentence.**

Functional Skills English Level 2  Summative Assessment Papers, Marking Scheme, and Tutors' Guide – ISBN: 978-1-9049955-5-5

# The No Messin' Campaign
## begun by Network Rail

**Network Rail**, which is a private company responsible for maintaining and operating Britain's rail network, has approximately 33,000 employees nationally who take care of the 22,000 miles of track, 2,500 stations and 5,000,000 line-side neighbours such as embankments and all the other land between stations.

As over 60 children in the last five years have lost their lives on, or near, railway lines, Network Rail has begun a **No Messin'** programme. The aim of this is to provide fun, safe and healthy alternatives to playing on railway property.

Some young people regard the railway as a playground. Such behaviour puts in danger the safety of people living near the railway and Network Rail believes that providing structured, fun and safe alternatives is the way forward.

The main time for vandalism, such as throwing stones, putting objects on the tracks and playing "chicken", is between 4pm and 8pm. The majority of incidents occur in the school holidays, involve children and lead to the death of around 25 per cent of children aged between the years of 8 and 17.

The **No Messin'** campaign seeks to address both the anti-social and criminal behaviour which costs Network Rail upwards of £250m a year. The campaign works with youth groups, those in education, young offenders, those involved in after-school events and community police teams.

Network Rail has adopted an approach comprising three strands:

1    An education programme which has created "rail ambassadors" within schools. These representatives promote rail safety and advise on the safe use of leisure time.

2    Encouraging restorative work, especially aimed at young offenders. This restorative work involves cleaning up railway graffiti and providing "art spaces" on railway bridges.

3    Providing and supporting alternative activities in local communities and sponsoring and promoting local sports, dance and DJ clubs.

During the summer months Network Rail runs events held in some of the country's most deprived areas. It sees these events as important not only to raise awareness of the dangers and illegalities of trespassing and vandalising the railways, but to show young people alternative activities which are provided for them locally.

**No Messin'** has proved important in reducing death and injury on the railways as well as encouraging young people to spend their free time constructively and legally in their community.

Functional Skills English Level 2 Summative Assessment Papers, Marking Scheme, and Tutors' Guide – ISBN: 978-1-9049955-5-5

Network Rail reports that the number of train incidents, including damage from missiles, train fires and trains hitting obstructions, fell significantly from 2003 to 2007 as is shown in the chart below.

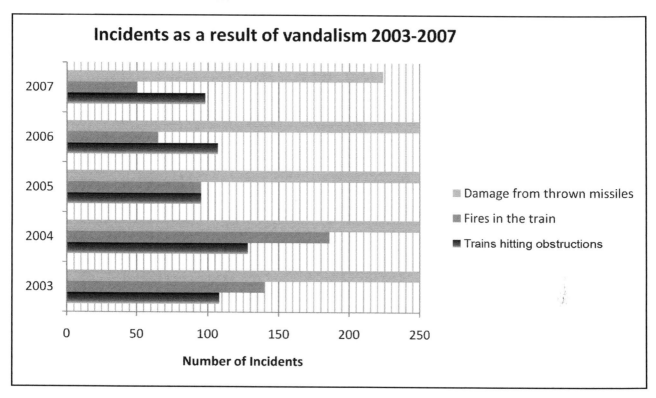

The total number of incidents as a result of vandalism in the five years were as follows:

| Year | Total number of incidents* |
| --- | --- |
| 2003 | 611 |
| 2004 | 642 |
| 2005 | 452 |
| 2006 | 438 |
| 2007 | 375 |

\* The incidents include: collisions, derailments, hitting obstructions on the line, fires in the trains and damage from thrown missiles.

In 2007 Network Rail reported incidents involving damage to train windows as a result of missiles being thrown at moving trains **and** trains running into obstructions on the line. An extract of the analysis, on an English county basis, is shown in the graph included on the following page.

Every incident is actually or potentially dangerous and costs the railway operators money in putting right the damage. This in turn increases the cost of rail travel and often results in delays to the schedules.

Clearly vandalism and trespassing on the railway network is dangerous, affects everyone, and can end in death; it is something which Network Rail takes seriously and is trying to combat.

Functional Skills English Level 2 Summative Assessment Papers, Marking Scheme, and Tutors' Guide – ISBN: 978-1-9049955-5-5

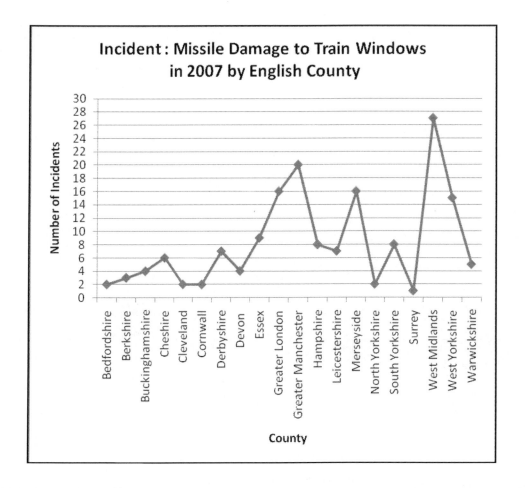

**ARTICLE FROM *THE MIDLAND GAZETTE* 1 JULY 2009**

A freight train driver was inches from serious injury after a concrete slab was thrown off a foot-bridge between York and Peterborough *reports a spokesman from* the newspaper. On June 30th the 45-year-old driver, Todd Linquist, was driving the train when the windscreen shattered and fell inwards pinning him to the seat. He suffered cuts to his face and hands caused by flying shards of broken glass.

The British Transport police have launched an investigation. If the people who committed this act are found, they will be charged with attempted murder.

Less than a week before this attack, two Virgin trains were stoned, one incident cracking a windscreen.

On 4 June two trains were damaged near Lancaster by objects suspended from a bridge. Although there were no injuries, both trains were taken out of service for repairs. CCTV cameras have now been fitted along this stretc.h of the line.

In Leicester the British Transport Police are investigating cases of concrete slabs or stones being thrown off bridges at passing trains.

Functional Skills English Level 2 Summative Assessment Papers, Marking Scheme, and Tutors' Guide – ISBN: 978-1-9049955-5-5

# Functional Skills English Level 2 Assessment Paper

Student's Name

Paper's Title

**THE COST OF BEING A FOOTBALL FAN**

Date Set

Hand-in Date

| Activity | Possible Marks | | Marks Awarded | Totals |
|---|---|---|---|---|
| 1  Reading | Q1 | 1 | | |
| | Q2 | 1 | | |
| | Q3 | 1 | | |
| | Q4 | 1 | | |
| | Q5 | 1 | | |
| | Q6 | 1 | | |
| | Q7 | 1 | | |
| | Q8 | 1 | | |
| | Q9 | 1 | | |
| | | | Activity 1 | |
| 2  Reading and Writing | Q1 | 3 | | |
| | Q2 | 2 | | |
| | Q3 | 3 | | |
| | Q4 | 2 | | |
| | Q5 | 1 | | |
| | Q6 | 1 | | |
| | Q7 | 2 | | |
| | Q8 | 5 | | |
| | | | Activity 2 | |
| 3  Researching, Writing and Making a Presentation | Q1 | 12 | | |
| | Q2 | 10 | | |
| | | | Activity 3 | |
| | | | PAPER TOTAL | |
| | | | PERCENTAGE | |

| Result | | PASS |
|---|---|---|
| Circle the appropriate result | | FAIL |

Assessor's Signature ................................................................... Date ...............................

Functional Skills English Level 2  Summative Assessment Papers, Marking Scheme,  and Tutors' Guide – ISBN: 978-1-9049955-5-5

# THE COST OF BEING A FOOTBALL FAN

## Assessor's Comments

| Activity | Comments |
|---|---|
| 1 | |
| 2 | |
| 3 | See also my comments on the Speaking and Listening Observation Sheet |

Functional Skills English Level 2 Summative Assessment Papers, Marking Scheme, and Tutors' Guide – ISBN: 978-1-9049955-5-5

# THE COST OF BEING A FOOTBALL FAN

This paper has **3** sections:

Section 1    involves reading

Section 2    involves reading and writing

Section 3    involves researching, writing a summary sheet and making a presentation

There are **two** documents for you to read.

Read both documents **before** you begin to answer the questions and keep referring to them when you work through the Sections.

You are reminded that clear written and spoken English and correct spelling and punctuation are important, together with presenting work neatly and making sure it is suitable for the purpose and the audience.

Functional Skills English Level 2  Summative Assessment Papers, Marking Scheme, and Tutors' Guide – ISBN: 978-1-9049955-5-5

# THE COST OF BEING A FOOTBALL FAN

ACTIVITY 1 – Reading

You will be assessed on the following:

— reading, finding and summarising information and ideas from different types of document.

Read **Document 1,** which contains text, a chart and a table, then answer the following questions.

You should spend no longer than 20 minutes on questions 1 — 9.

For each question choose one answer, A, B, C or D and put a ✓ (tick) in the box.

1 mark is awarded for each correct answer.

1 What is the document about?

  A figures related to money that football supporters ☐
    borrow

  B the rising cost that football supporters have to pay in a ☐
    season

  C how the cost of being a football supporter has risen ☐
    and the money some fans need to borrow in a season

  D the rising cost of season tickets at the Premier League ☐
    football teams

2 By how much is it suggested that the cost of a ticket has risen since the 2006—
  2007 season?

  A 33% ☐

  B 20% ☐

  C 15% ☐

  D 30% ☐

Functional Skills English Level 2 Summative Assessment Papers, Marking Scheme, and Tutors' Guide – ISBN: 978-1-9049955-5-5

3   Why does the document suggest some fans might find buying a season ticket especially difficult?

   A   because of rising prices   ☐

   B   because it coincides with when holidays have to be paid for   ☐

   C   because club's refuse to offer a "deferred payment" scheme   ☐

   D   because most football fans are in debt   ☐

4   What is the average price of a football shirt in team colours?

   A   £690   ☐

   B   £78   ☐

   C   £101   ☐

   D   £60   ☐

5   Looking at the chart, which club in the 2009–2010 Premier League has the cheapest season ticket?

   A   Aston Villa   ☐

   B   Blackburn   ☐

   C   Bolton   ☐

   D   Wigan   ☐

6   Looking at the chart, how many clubs in the 2009–2010 Premier League have tickets costing more than £650 for the season?

   A   8   ☐

   B   11   ☐

   C   10   ☐

   D   7   ☐

7   Looking at the table, the supporters of which club borrow the most money?

   A   Liverpool   ☐

   B   Manchester United   ☐

   C   Chelsea   ☐

   D   Arsenal   ☐

8    Looking at the chart and the table which of the following statements is true?

    A    the supporters of Manchester United borrow the least ☐
        amount of money

    B    the supporters of the club charging the least for a ☐
        season ticket borrow the least amount of money

    C    the club charging the third highest ticket prices has ☐
        fans who borrow the third highest amount of money

    D    the supporters of only three clubs borrow less than ☐
        £600 and the cheapest season tickets for each of
        these clubs are less than £450

9    What is seen as a possible disadvantage of some clubs allowing fans to buy season
tickets under a deferred payment scheme?

    A    the fan cannot attend matches until payment is made in ☐
        full

    B    there are high interest charges to be paid ☐

    C    the cost increases the amount of money the supporter ☐
        has to borrow

    D    some fans still cannot afford to buy season tickets ☐

Functional Skills English Level 2  Summative Assessment Papers, Marking Scheme, and Tutors' Guide – ISBN: 978-1-9049955-5-5

# THE COST OF BEING A FOOTBALL FAN

ACTIVITY 2 – Reading and Writing

You will be assessed on the following:

— reading, finding and summarising information and ideas from text;

— presenting your work and ideas clearly and logically;

— identifying the purpose of text;

— using a range of sentence structures, including complex sentences;

— using spelling, grammar and punctuation accurately and correctly.

Read **Document 2,** then answer the following questions.

You should spend no longer than 30 minutes on questions 1 — 8.

1 In the first paragraph of the document is the phrase "club regalia". The second paragraph mentions "merchandising". Explain how this phrase and word are linked. **3 marks**

_____

_____

_____

_____

2 Name two things, other than ticket prices, for which fans have to pay as a consequence of supporting their favourite team? **2 marks**

_____

_____

Functional Skills English Level 2 Summative Assessment Papers, Marking Scheme, and Tutors' Guide – ISBN: 978-1-9049955-5-5

3    Why might a fan be interested in having a club credit card and what benefit(s) might there be to the fan in having such a card?  **3 marks**

_____

_____

_____

_____

_____

4    Having a savings account linked to your club might not be the best financial step a fan could take.  Explain this statement.  **2 marks**

_____

_____

_____

_____

_____

5    The fans of which club are the most keen supporters?  **1 mark**

_____

6    How many days and hours does the article suggest a football fan spends following their team each season?  **1 mark**

_____

Functional Skills English Level 2  Summative Assessment Papers, Marking Scheme, and Tutors' Guide – ISBN: 978-1-9049955-5-5

7    Apart from going to matches, name two other ways in which fans spend time
     "following" their team?  **2 marks**

     _____

     _____


8    Summarise the message of the document using a minimum of 80 words and a
     maximum of 120 words.  **5 marks**

     _____

     _____

     _____

     _____

     _____

     _____

     _____

     _____

     _____

     _____

     _____

     _____

     _____

     _____

Functional Skills English Level 2  Summative Assessment Papers, Marking Scheme,  and Tutors' Guide – ISBN:  978-1-9049955-5-5

# THE COST OF BEING A FOOTBALL FAN

ACTIVITY 3 – Researching, Writing a Summary and Making a Presentation

## Producing a Summary Sheet and Making a Presentation

You will be assessed on the following:

— locating relevant information from research;

— summarising research documents and the information and ideas they contain;

— adapting researched information to prepare documents;

— presenting your work clearly, including appropriate illustration(s);

— using a range of writing and presentation styles for different purposes;

— making a presentation suitable for the audience and the situation;

— presenting your ideas clearly and persuasively to the audience.

**There are no suggested timings for this activity.**

## Scenario and Research details

You are going to research the cost of a range of goods sold in the shops of two teams and prepare a summary sheet and a presentation.

You will need to take into account the following:

— investigate one Premier League team and one team from a lower division;

— compare the prices of a minimum of eight similar items and a maximum of ten;

— the items must include clothing for adults and children and general items for the household.

You will assume that you support one of the two clubs whose merchandise you are comparing and that you have £100 to spend this season. This £100 will include not only an item for yourself but for a cousin/sister/brother/nephew/niece aged ten who began last season to support the same team and for whom you want to buy a present.

Keep copies of your research documents to hand in with your work.

If you wish to do so, you can plan your work on the blank pages your tutor will hand you.

Functional Skills English Level 2 Summative Assessment Papers, Marking Scheme, and Tutors' Guide – ISBN: 978-1-9049955-5-5

# Research Notes

Functional Skills English Level 2 Summative Assessment Papers, Marking Scheme, and Tutors' Guide – ISBN: 978-1-9049955-5-5

## 1    Summary Sheet    12 marks

The first aim of this sheet is to summarise, possibly in table form, the items you have chosen for the price comparison. You might wish to include illustration(s).

You must also write some information about both the clubs – perhaps mentioning their history, their recent successes (if any!), their current place in their league table, etc.

Your summary sheet must contain no fewer than 250 words.

If you wish to do so, you can plan your Summary Sheet on the blank pages your tutor will hand you.

Functional Skills English Level 2  Summative Assessment Papers, Marking Scheme, and Tutors' Guide – ISBN: 978-1-9049955-5-5

# Summary Sheet Plan

Functional Skills English Level 2 Summative Assessment Papers, Marking Scheme, and Tutors' Guide – ISBN: 978-1-9049955-5-5

## 2    Presentation    10 Marks

You must make a presentation to an audience, whom you can assume know little or nothing about the football club of your choice.

The purpose of the presentation will be to give them some brief background of the club you support, then say your relative (sister, nephew, etc.) and yourself attend most home matches and you have £100 to spend on club regalia this season.   You will need to give the audience some information about the relative's age.

Say what you have chosen to purchase for yourself and your relative, stating the cost of the items and giving reasons for your choices.

When you have put together your presentation notes you will make your presentation. You can illustrate your presentation if you so wish.

Your talk should last no fewer than four minutes and no longer than eight minutes.

You should encourage, and respond to, a few questions from the audience.

If you wish to do so, you can plan your work on the blank pages your tutor will hand you.

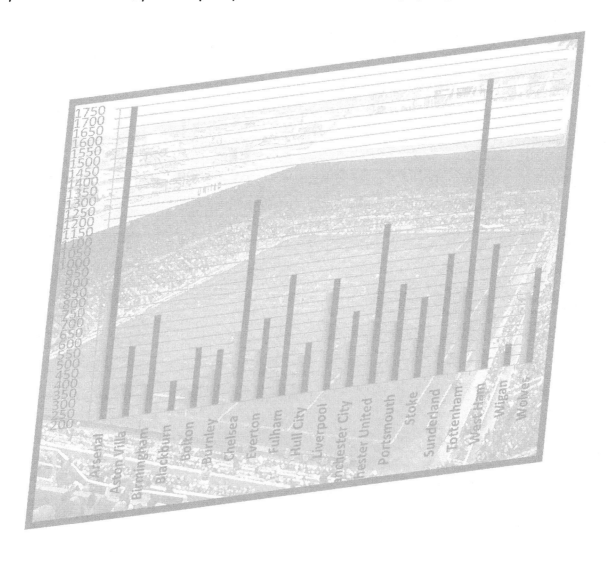

Functional Skills English Level 2  Summative Assessment Papers, Marking Scheme, and Tutors' Guide – ISBN: 978-1-9049955-5-5

# Presentation Notes/Plan

Functional Skills English Level 2 Summative Assessment Papers, Marking Scheme, and Tutors' Guide – ISBN: 978-1-9049955-5-5

# ARE FOOTBALL FANS BEING FORCED INTO DEBT?

Shockingly, it has been estimated that one in five footballs fans have gone into debt in order to fund the growing cost of following their football team.

In these days of rising costs, following a football team involves increased costs and many fans are struggling to meet the cost of attending matches and are opting to watch their favourite team from home.

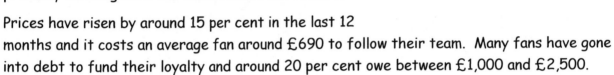

## What costs are involved?

Being a football supporter will involve spending money on tickets, including season tickets, travel, food, drink and probably clothing with the team's name and colours.

Prices have risen by around 15 per cent in the last 12 months and it costs an average fan around £690 to follow their team. Many fans have gone into debt to fund their loyalty and around 20 per cent owe between £1,000 and £2,500.

## Fans decide to cut back

The number of supporters, who have declared their intention to cut back on attendances at live matches next season, has been reported as one-third. More surprisingly, those fans who have already gone into debt through following their team in the previous season, intend to follow a less expensive lower league club in order to ensure they can afford to attend live games.

If clubs wonder why attendance at their games is decreasing it is because ticket costs have risen on average nearly 30 per cent since the start of the 2006-2007 season and the cost of a football shirt in the team's colours has risen from an average of £78 to £101.

Ticket costs have risen as Premier League clubs put up prices regardless of the ability of their fans to pay while the cost of season tickets requires a huge outlay of money at a time when some fans are also having to pay for a holiday for themselves and their relatives. Some clubs have recognised this and now offer a "deferred payment scheme" but the disadvantage is such schemes entail high interest charges.

Clearly it is time for football clubs to see what they can do to help ensure their fans can afford to attend matches without the extra worry about how they can afford to support their favourite team.

Functional Skills English Level 2 Summative Assessment Papers, Marking Scheme, and Tutors' Guide – ISBN: 978-1-9049955-5-5

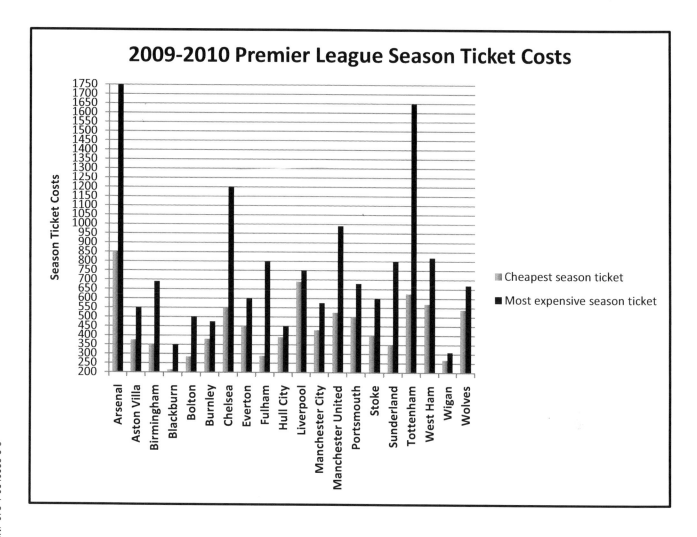

## TABLE OF AVERAGE SUM OF MONEY BORROWED BY CLUB SUPPORTERS TO FINANCE 2009-2010 SEASON'S FOOTBALL EXPENSES

| Club | Average figure borrowed by fans | Club | Average figure borrowed by fans |
|---|---|---|---|
| Arsenal | £1,300 | Liverpool | £1,195 |
| Aston Villa | £800 | Manchester City | £520 |
| Birmingham | £650 | Manchester United | £1,270 |
| Blackburn | £835 | Portsmouth | £700 |
| Bolton | £720 | Stoke | £915 |
| Burnley | £509 | Sunderland | £800 |
| Chelsea | £1,080 | Tottenham | £1,175 |
| Everton | £915 | West Ham | £1,000 |
| Fulham | £745 | Wigan | £500 |
| Hull City | £605 | Wolves | £605 |

Functional Skills English Level 2  Summative Assessment Papers, Marking Scheme, and Tutors' Guide – ISBN: 978-1-9049955-5-5

# FOOTBALL WEEKLY

## for the latest football news and views

### BEING A FOOTBALL FAN IS EXPENSIVE?

An average football fan spends almost 800 hours a season and travels over 2,000 miles following their favourite team. The costs of this dedication can include petrol, vehicle hire, train tickets, match tickets, food, alcohol and club regalia.

Just focusing on rising ticket and season ticket prices is only part of the equation. Programme costs, food expenses, merchandising and increased fuel bills have all contributed to spiralling costs for the avid football supporter.

With around 26 per cent of supporters declaring they will have to reduce the number of games they attend, some clubs have come up with a way to help because they are beginning to realise that all this dedication costs money. Many clubs now offer a club credit card and savings account. Supporters can sign up for credit cards or savings accounts linked to the team they support. A club credit card is usually in the club's colours and bears the club's logo and a percentage of what the user spends is given to the club or a charity linked to the club.

> **Burnley fans are the most dedicated with Tottenham fans coming second in that particular league table.**
>
> **Being a supporter adds up to an average of 33 days a season for a dedicated fan and this includes time spent travelling to and from matches, watching matches on television, using the Internet to search for details on the game and exchanging views with other supporters.**

For the smaller clubs such schemes as this make a much needed difference to their income.

For the card holder there are likely to be some benefits not given to fans who don't have a card and these benefits can include a small number of free tickets each season and a discount in the club's shop.

However, account holders are not usually offered competitive rates of interest so saving with a football club might not be the best method of trying to get the best return for your hard-earned cash.

Functional Skills English Level 2 Summative Assessment Papers, Marking Scheme, and Tutors' Guide – ISBN: 978-1-9049955-5-5

# Functional Skills English Level 2 Assessment Paper

Student's Name

Paper's Title

**TRAVEL SAFELY ABROAD**

Date Set

Hand-in Date

| Activity | Possible Marks | | Marks Awarded | Totals |
|---|---|---|---|---|
| 1   Reading and Writing | Q1 | 1 | | |
| | Q2 | 1 | | |
| | Q3 | 2 | | |
| | Q4 | 2 | | |
| | Q5 | 5 | | |
| | Q6 | 2 | | |
| | | | Activity 1 | |
| 2   Reading and Writing | Q1 | 6 | | |
| | Q2 | 3 | | |
| | Q3 | 10 | | |
| | | | Activity 2 | |
| 3   Researching and Writing | Q1 | 18 | | |
| | | | Activity 3 | |
| | | | PAPER TOTAL | |
| | | | **PERCENTAGE** | |

**Result**

Circle the appropriate result

**PASS**

**FAIL**

Assessor's Signature ................................................................ Date ...........................

Functional Skills English Level 2  Summative Assessment Papers, Marking Scheme, and Tutors' Guide – ISBN: 978-1-9049955-5-5

# TRAVEL SAFELY ABROAD

## Assessor's Comments

| Activity | Comments |
|----------|----------|
| 1 | |
| 2 | |
| 3 | |

Functional Skills English Level 2 Summative Assessment Papers, Marking Scheme, and Tutors' Guide – ISBN: 978-1-9049955-5-5

# TRAVEL SAFELY ABROAD

This paper has **3** sections:

Sections 1 and 2          involve reading and writing

Section 3          involves researching and writing a personal letter to a friend

There are **two** documents for you to read.

Read both documents **before** you begin to answer the questions and keep referring to them when you work through the sections.

You are reminded that clear written English and correct spelling and punctuation are important, together with presenting work neatly and making sure it is suitable for the purpose and the audience.

Functional Skills English Level 2  Summative Assessment Papers, Marking Scheme, and Tutors' Guide – ISBN:  978-1-9049955-5-5

# TRAVEL SAFELY ABROAD

ACTIVITY 1 — Reading and Writing

You will be assessed on the following:

— reading, finding and summarising information and ideas from text;

— presenting your work and ideas clearly and logically;

— identifying the purpose and tone of text;

— using a range of sentence structures, including complex sentences;

— using spelling, grammar and punctuation accurately and correctly.

Read **Document 1** then answer the following questions.

You should spend no longer than 25 minutes on questions 1 — 6.

Questions 1 and 2 are multiple-choice questions. For each question choose one answer, A, B, C or D and put a ✓ (tick) in the box.

1 mark is awarded for each correct answer.

1    Which **best** describes the main purpose of Document 1?

   A    to persuade                                    ☐

   B    to inform                                       ☐

   C    to encourage behaviour and inform              ☐

   D    to complain                                     ☐


2    Where might you need a visa?

   A    Switzerland                                     ☐

   B    Europe                                          ☐

   C    Europe and Switzerland                          ☐

   D    Non-European countries                          ☐

Functional Skills English Level 2 Summative Assessment Papers, Marking Scheme, and Tutors' Guide – ISBN: 978-1-9049955-5-5

Referring to the text, answer the following questions

3    Identify two actions you should take related to your money.    **2 marks**

_____

_____

_____

_____

_____

4    Explain what is needed when travelling to Europe, and **where** and **why** saying that
     you have health insurance is not necessarily a guarantee of medical treatment.
     **2 marks**

_____

_____

_____

_____

5    Explain why you should inform your bank or credit card company that you are
     going abroad and might be using your cards.    **5 marks**

_____

_____

_____

_____

6    What safety measures can you take so that someone in the UK knows where you will be at any given time during your trip abroad?  **2 marks**

_____

_____

_____

_____

_____

_____

Functional Skills English Level 2  Summative Assessment Papers, Marking Scheme, and Tutors' Guide – ISBN: 978-1-9049955-5-5

## TRAVEL SAFELY ABROAD

ACTIVITY 2 — Reading and Writing

You will be assessed on the following:

— reading, finding and summarising information and ideas from text;

— identifying the purpose and effectiveness of texts;

— presenting your work clearly and logically;

— using a range of sentence structures, including complex sentences;

— using spelling, grammar and punctuation accurately and correctly.

**Document 2** has been written by a young traveller who has visited many large cities in Europe and South America. The article appeared recently in a magazine called "Young Traveller Be Aware".

Read the document and answer the following questions.

You should spend no longer than 15 minutes on questions 1 — 3.

1       "The article seems to be trying to put people off visiting large cities."   Consider this statement and write your response, giving reasons for what you write.  You should write no fewer than 100 words.  **6 marks**

_____

_____

_____

_____

_____

_____

_____

Functional Skills English Level 2  Summative Assessment Papers, Marking Scheme, and Tutors' Guide – ISBN: 978-1-9049955-5-5

2    The article says that using a cash dispenser machine inside a bank is regarded as safer than using one outside.  Suggest three dangers a user might encounter when using a cash dispensing machine outside a bank.  **3 marks**

_____

_____

_____

_____

Considering both Document 1 and Document 2, answer the following question.

3    Consider if you were about to travel abroad with a group of friends, perhaps for the first time.  How helpful would you have found these two documents?  Give reasons for what you write.   You should write no fewer than 150 words in your answer. **10 marks**

_____

_____

_____

_____

_____

_____

_____

_____

_____

Functional Skills English Level 2  Summative Assessment Papers, Marking Scheme, and Tutors' Guide – ISBN:  978-1-9049955-5-5

# TRAVEL SAFELY ABROAD

ACTIVITY 3 — Researching and Writing

## Writing a Letter to a friend

You will be assessed on the following:

— locating relevant information from research;

— summarising research documents and the information and ideas they contain;

— adapting researched information to prepare documents;

— producing work which is suitable for the audience;

— presenting your work and ideas clearly and logically;

— using a range of sentence structures, including complex sentences;

— using a range of writing styles and sentence structures for different purposes;

— using spelling, grammar and punctuation accurately and correctly.

**There are no suggested timings for this activity.**

## Scenario

You and a friend are going on holiday and visiting two European destinations.  You have read the information contained in Documents 1 and 2 and know there are more details of which you should be aware. For instance vaccinations are necessary for certain countries; there might be particular health or security warnings related to the country/area you plan to visit (the Department of Health's website has up-to-date recommendations and warnings).  You have also heard that losing, or having had stolen, a UK passport abroad causes tremendous problems and that UK passports are particularly targeted for theft.

Accordingly you decide to research more aspects of your holiday and write to your friend with the information, advice and warnings you find.

## Researching the topics and writing your letter

A useful starting point is to decide which two destinations you will visit and carry out some research related to temperatures,  health requirements and advice, any special warnings the UK Government or other travellers have mentioned, etc.

Don't forget you should find information on some of the points mentioned in Documents 1 and 2.

Functional Skills English Level 2  Summative Assessment Papers, Marking Scheme, and Tutors' Guide – ISBN:  978-1-9049955-5-5

The website, www.direct.gov.uk has valuable travel information, **particularly** related to stolen or lost UK passports.  Include advice on keeping your documents and money safe and what to do if your passport is stolen or lost whilst abroad.

Keep copies of your research documents to hand in with your work.

If you wish to do so, you can plan your work on the blank pages your tutor will hand to you.

Functional Skills English Level 2  Summative Assessment Papers, Marking Scheme,  and Tutors' Guide – ISBN:  978-1-9049655-5-5

# Research Notes

Functional Skills English Level 2  Summative Assessment Papers, Marking Scheme,  and Tutors' Guide – ISBN:  978-1-9049955-5-5

# Writing your letter    18 marks

Write your letter to your friend.  Remember it is a personal letter so your address (or one you decide to make up) will appear at the top of the first page, along with the date you write the letter.  You don't need to put your friend's name and address under the date but you do need to begin with a suitable salutation.  You can end the letter informally with a phrase such as "Regards" or "Best Wishes".

The purpose of the letter is to pass on the information in a structured way, so side headings and bulleted or numbered points will probably be suitable.   Where appropriate, explain the comments you make.

Your letter should contain a minimum of 400 words and a maximum of 600 words.

Although the letter is informal you must use correct spelling, grammar and punctuation and complete sentences.

If you wish to do so, you can plan your letter on the blank pages your tutor will hand you.

Functional Skills English Level 2 Summative Assessment Papers, Marking Scheme, and Tutors' Guide – ISBN: 978-1-9049955-5-5

# Letter Plan

Functional Skills English Level 2  Summative Assessment Papers, Marking Scheme,  and Tutors' Guide – ISBN:  978-1-9049955-5-5

# TRAVEL CHECKLIST – BEFORE YOU GO

**It is always better to be safe than sorry. These tips are designed to help you stay safe when travelling abroad.**

☑ Find out about the country and area you are visiting. Check the Foreign and Commonwealth Office's Travel Checklists.

☑ Check if you need a visa. Some countries outside Europe require you to have a visa. Check the Connexions Youth Information website.

☑ Check you have adequate health insurance. In some countries if you need treatment you must prove you have insurance before you will be treated. In the USA sometimes even health insurance will not guarantee you emergency treatment. If you are travelling in Europe or Switzerland you are strongly advised to also have a European Health Insurance Card which is available from the Department of Health.

☑ Let people know where you are going and staying and if you are moving around let them know your itinerary.

☑ If you are able to do so, phone home on a regular basis to let someone in the UK know you are safe and healthy. This is especially important if you are planning to move around rather than stay in the same place or country.

☑ Take photocopies of your passport and visas and leave them with someone back in the UK.

☑ Remember to take your travel insurance documentation.

☑ If you are planning to use a bank or credit card whilst abroad, tell your bank or credit card company so they know to expect movement on your account outside the UK. This information will help the bank or credit card company to identify and authorise any of your transactions abroad as genuine because they know you are out of the UK and where you are.

☑ Keep your passport, traveller's cheques and currency safe and out of view at all times. All these items are difficult to replace if stolen or lost.

Functional Skills English Level 2 Summative Assessment Papers, Marking Scheme, and Tutors' Guide – ISBN: 978-1-9049955-5-5

# BE SMART IN THE CITY

**Travelling** to a big city is exciting and challenging but cities can also be dangerous places for the unwary.

**Here** are some travelling tips for big cities.

1   Walk as much as possible along major roads and through areas where there are lots of people and lots of traffic.  Avoid frequenting deserted streets, parks and other areas of any city, especially at night.

2   Be alert at all times.  As a tourist you will be more likely than most to stand and stare.  This singles you out as a tourist and you are then easily targetted by pickpockets and muggers. Remain alert to your surroundings, where you are, who is near, what others are doing in your vicinity, and always be aware of what is going on around you.

3   Use the cash machines **inside** banks, not on the outside.  You are more of a target when using those on the outside.

4   Keep your valuables, and cash and passport, in a very safe place. Pickpockets are expert in what they do – you won't feel anything and the first you will know is when you go for your wallet or valuables and find them missing.

5   If you suspect you are being followed, step into a store (remember you are keeping to busy areas of the city).  Check to see if the person, or people, has stopped following you, or ask the shop assistant for help.  When you step out into the street again have a quick look round to see if the person following you has really given up.

6   Keep hold of your bag(s), camera, and other belongings at all times. When you stop for a coffee or just to rest your feet, never leave your belongings next to you or on the table in front of you.  Keep these things on your lap or on the ground with their straps wrapped around your ankle.

7   If you are unfortunate enough to have something stolen, report it to the Police as soon as you know.  If you don't take this step you may not be able to claim on your insurance when you get home – you have got insurance haven't you?   The Police will give you an Incident or Report Number which you will need for your subsequent claim as proof you have reported the theft or loss.

Functional Skills English Level 2  Summative Assessment Papers, Marking Scheme, and Tutors' Guide – ISBN:  978-1-9049955-5-5

## Functional Skills English Level 2 Assessment Paper

Student's Name

Paper's Title

**SUNBED SAFETY**

Date Set

Hand-in Date

| Activity | Possible Marks | | Marks Awarded | Totals |
|---|---|---|---|---|
| 1  Reading and Writing | Q1 | 5 | | |
| | Q2 | 8 | | |
| | Q3 | 10 | | |
| | | | Activity 1 | |
| 2  Reading and Writing | Q1 | 1 | | |
| | Q2 | 1 | | |
| | Q3 | 1 | | |
| | Q4 | 2 | | |
| | Q5 | 2 | | |
| | Q6 | 1 | | |
| | Q7 | 2 | | |
| | | | Activity 2 | |
| 3  Researching  and Writing | Q1 | 17 | | |
| | | | Activity 3 | |
| | | | PAPER TOTAL | |
| | | | **PERCENTAGE** | |

**Result**

Circle the appropriate result

**PASS**

**FAIL**

Assessor's Signature ................................................................... Date ............................

Functional Skills English Level 2  Summative Assessment Papers, Marking Scheme, and Tutors' Guide – ISBN:  978-1-9049955-5-5

# SUNBED SAFETY

## Assessor's Comments

| Activity | Comments |
|---|---|
| 1 | |
| 2 | |
| 3 | |

## SUNBED SAFETY

This paper has **3** sections:

Sections 1 and 2    involve reading and writing

Section 3    involves researching and writing an information booklet

There are **two** documents for you to read.

Read both documents **before** you begin to answer the questions and keep referring to them when you work through the sections.

You are reminded that clear written English and correct spelling and punctuation are important, together with presenting work neatly and making sure it is suitable for the purpose and the audience.

Functional Skills English Level 2  Summative Assessment Papers, Marking Scheme, and Tutors' Guide – ISBN: 978-1-9049955-5-5

## SUNBED SAFETY

ACTIVITY 1 — Reading and Writing

You will be assessed on the following:

— reading, finding and summarising information and ideas from text;

— identifying the purpose and effectiveness of texts and distinguishing between opinion and fact;

— presenting your work and ideas clearly and logically;

— using a range of sentence structures, including complex sentences;

— using spelling, grammar and punctuation accurately and correctly.

Read **Document 1** then answer the following questions.

You should spend no longer than 30 minutes on questions 1 — 3.

1    You have a friend who uses sunbeds five times a week, sometimes twice a day and have heard this friend say most of the things in the "Opinion" column of the table. Describe what you think the information in the whole table is designed to do for someone such as your friend and say how effective you think it is. You should write no fewer than 50 words.   **5 marks**

_____

_____

_____

_____

_____

_____

_____

_____

2   The second part of the document discusses the latest proposals for regulating sunbed use in England.  Would you describe this information as opinion or fact? Explain your answer in no fewer than 75 words.   **8 marks**

_____

_____

_____

_____

_____

_____

3   The Sunbed Association operates on "voluntary guidelines" which means the Association sets its own standards. The Government is being asked to set legal guidelines such as those established in Scotland.  Discuss whether you think this would be an advantage to the sunbed user, given the facts outlined in the table. Give reasons for what you write.  You should write no fewer than 175 words. **10 marks**

_____

_____

_____

_____

_____

_____

Functional Skills English Level 2 Summative Assessment Papers, Marking Scheme, and Tutors' Guide – ISBN: 978-1-9049955-5-5

## SUNBED SAFETY

ACTIVITY 2 — Reading and Writing

You will be assessed on the following:

— reading, finding and summarising information and ideas from different types of document;

— presenting your work and ideas clearly and logically;

— using a range of sentence structures, including complex sentences;

— using spelling, grammar and punctuation accurately and correctly.

Read **Document 2**, which contains charts, and answer the following questions;

You should spend no longer than 20 minutes on questions 1 — 7.

1    Which is the most common form of cancer for one-third of people aged over 14 and under 35 years of age?    **1 mark**

_____

2    According to the document, what proportion of those over 70 years of age die from malignant melanoma?    **1 mark**

_____

3    Looking at the first chart, which part of the body for which gender is malignant melanoma mostly found?    **1 mark**

_____

4    Looking at the first two charts, which gender, and in what ratio, suffers most from malignant melanoma?    **2 marks**

_____

Functional Skills English Level 2 Summative Assessment Papers, Marking Scheme, and Tutors' Guide – ISBN: 978-1-9049955-5-5

5       According to the final chart, in 2006 which age group and which gender had the most number of reported cases of malignant melanoma?  **2 marks**

_____

6       According to the final chart, in which age group were the third highest, female, number of reported cases?  **1 mark**

_____

7       Whilst survival rates for patients with malignant melanoma can be said to have increased in the last five years, upon what does the chance of survival mostly depend?  **2 marks**

_____

_____

Functional Skills English Level 2 Summative Assessment Papers, Marking Scheme, and Tutors' Guide – ISBN: 978-1-9049955-5-5

## SUNBED SAFETY

ACTIVITY 3 — Researching and Writing

# Writing an Information Booklet

You will be assessed on the following:

— locating relevant information from research;

— summarising research documents and the information and ideas they contain;

— adapting researched information to prepare documents;

— producing work which is suitable for the audience;

— presenting your work and ideas clearly and logically;

— using a range of sentence structures, including complex sentences;

— using a range of writing styles and sentence structures for different purposes;

— using spelling, grammar and punctuation accurately and correctly.

**There are no suggested timings for this activity.**

## Scenario

You use a sunbed in your local salon "Sun Kissed". It operates safe tanning policies. As your friend, described earlier, is not in the care of a responsible salon owner, you aim to persuade them to change their behaviour.

You decide to do some research to add to the information you will put together for your friend. You want to mention the health benefits of safe sunbed use before you add details on the two types of cancer and their related symptoms/appearances, so the reader has an effective way of knowing if they already have a problem. You should also offer advice on where to go for help.

It is not your aim to frighten but to provide facts in a structured and logical way.

## Researching the topics

As well as some of the information in Documents 1 and 2, useful websites to visit would be www.sunbedassociation.org.uk and http://news.bbc.co.uk/1/hi/health/8172690.stm but there will be other sources you will use and other information you will seek.

Keep copies of your research documents to hand in with your work.

If you wish to do so, you can plan your work on the blank pages your tutor will hand to you.

Functional Skills English Level 2  Summative Assessment Papers, Marking Scheme, and Tutors' Guide – ISBN: 978-1-9049955-5-5

# Research Notes

---

Functional Skills English Level 2  Summative Assessment Papers, Marking Scheme,  and Tutors' Guide — ISBN:  978-1-9049955-5-5

## Writing your Information Booklet   17 marks

Write your Information Booklet.

Remember also to advise your friend on the benefits of safe sunbed use and stress that there are salons which operate safely and responsibly and whose practices would not need to change if the proposed regulation was to be introduced.

Include information from your research, expressed as far as possible in your own words. Add the key facts and summaries from Documents 1 and 2 in a logical order, expanding the information as appropriate.

Your information booklet should contain no fewer than 500 words and you can include relevant illustrations if you so wish.

If you wish to do so, you can plan your Information Booklet and/or make rough notes on the blank pages your tutor will hand you.

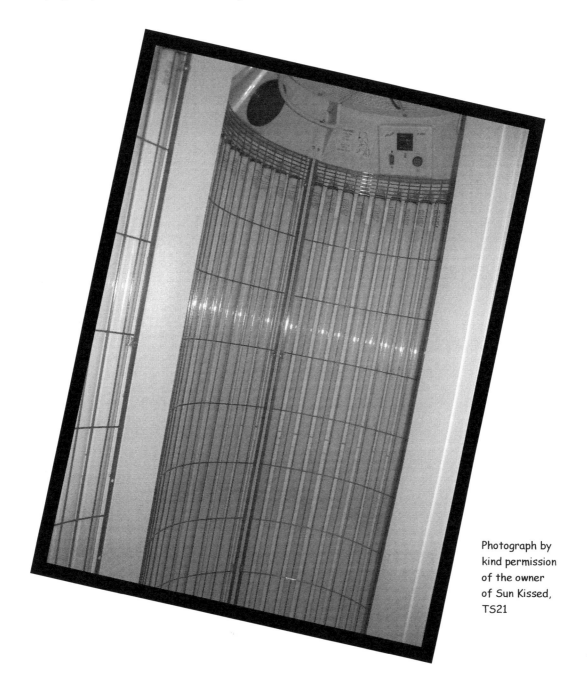

Photograph by kind permission of the owner of Sun Kissed, TS21

Functional Skills English Level 2 Summative Assessment Papers, Marking Scheme, and Tutors' Guide – ISBN: 978-1-9049955-5-5

# Information Booklet Plan

Functional Skills English Level 2 Summative Assessment Papers, Marking Scheme, and Tutors' Guide – ISBN: 978-1-9049955-5-5

# SUNBEDS AND SKIN CANCER – What's the truth?
## What's the latest news?

| OPINION | FACT |
|---|---|
| Sunbeds are safer than sunbathing. | Sunbeds are not a safe alternative to soaking up the sun. |
| Sunbeds don't have harmful rays. | Just like the sun, sunbeds emit harmful UV rays that damage the DNA in our skin cells and the damage can cause skin cancer. |
| The more you use a sunbed the more your skin gets used to it and there is no danger. | The more you use a sunbed the greater the risk of skin cancer. |
| Using a sunbed each month poses no danger. | Using a sunbed each month can increase your risk of skin cancer by more than half. |
| When the tan fades any damage has gone. | When the tan fades the damage remains. |
| Sunbeds stop the ageing process. | Using sunbeds can cause premature skin ageing, just like the sun. |
| It's OK to use a sunbed as a teenager. | Using sunbeds before the age of 35 increases the risk of developing melanoma skin cancer by 75 per cent. |
| If I get skin cancer it can be removed without leaving a scar. | Surgical treatment for skin cancer can result in serious scarring. |
| I know I should wear goggles when using a sunbed but there is no real danger. | Not wearing goggles whilst using a sunbed can result in irritation, conjunctivitis and even eye cancer. |

## HOT OFF THE SUNBED PRESS

The Government is being urged to adopt new controls which will see the use of sunbeds restricted in England and allow England to follow the restrictions already in operation in Scotland.

Experts are advising that unmanned sunbeds should be banned and that all sunbeds should be restricted to those over 18 years of age.

It is thought that in the UK around 100 deaths from skin cancer every year can be linked to the use of sunbeds.

**What has The Sunbed Association said to these proposals?**

Although The Sunbed Association has consistently denied there is proof that skin cancer is linked to the use of sunbeds, they stress that members of The Sunbed Association receive correct advice and operate responsibly and the 8,000 tanning salons abide by voluntary guidelines which the sunbed industry has drawn up.

# NUMBER OF CASES OF NON-MELANOMA SKIN CANCER IN THE UK INCREASES TO OVER 81,000

There are two main types of skin cancer:

1    non-melanoma skin cancer; and

2    malignant melanoma.

The first type is very common and the second type is less common but much more serious.

In 2006 more than 81,600 cases of the first type of skin cancer were reported but it is thought that the actual number was more likely to have been more than 100,000 cases and that this figure is the number which occurs in the UK each year.

Although skin cancer increases with age, malignant melanoma is very high in younger people with almost one-third of all cases of this form of skin cancer reported in people under 50 years of age.  It is the most common form of cancer in adults between the ages of 15 and 34.

Worryingly, in the UK over the last 25 years the rate of malignant melanoma has risen faster than any other form of more common cancer.

**How many people die from skin cancer?**

More than 2,600 people die each year and of those people more than 2,000 have malignant melanoma.

Non-melanoma skin cancer tends to be the skin cancer which affects those over 70 years of age whilst more than half of people who die from malignant melanoma are younger than 70 years of age.

**Who is most at risk from skin cancer?**

There are a number of factors, other than exposure to sun or sun beds, which influence the development of skin cancer.

Check it out – do you fit into any of these categories?
-    People with light eyes or hair who **sunburn easily** or who do not tan
-    People with a lot of moles which are unusually shaped or large
-    People with a lot of freckles
-    People with a history of sunburn because this doubles the risk of developing melanoma and increases the risk of non-melanoma skin cancer
-    Young people who use sunbeds (regularly or irregularly)
-    People with a previous history of non-melanoma skin cancer
-    People with a close relative (parent or sibling) diagnosed with skin cancer.

Functional Skills English Level 2 Summative Assessment Papers, Marking Scheme, and Tutors' Guide – ISBN: 978-1-9049955-5-5

**Does gender affect where the skin cancer appears?**

The distribution of malignant melanoma on parts of the body differs from male to female, as this chart illustrates.

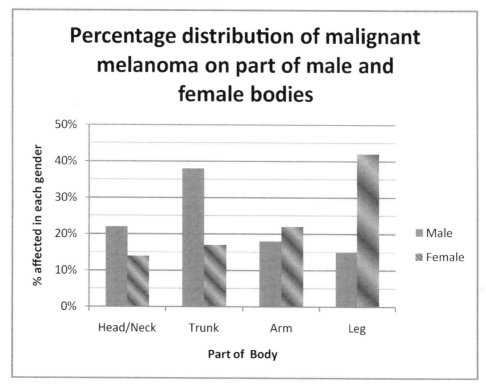

**Which gender most suffers malignant melanoma?**

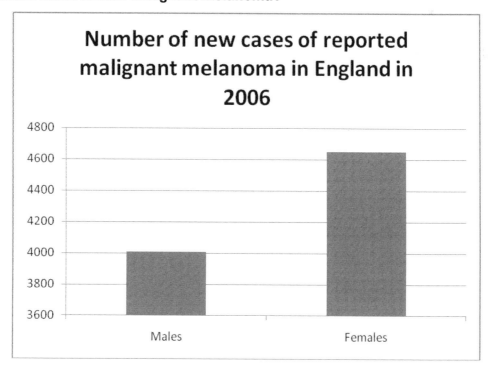

The male:female ratio is 4:5. In 2006 it was the sixth most common cancer in females and the eighth in males.

Functional Skills English Level 2 Summative Assessment Papers, Marking Scheme, and Tutors' Guide – ISBN: 978-1-9049955-5-5

**What was the 2006 age distribution of malignant melanoma patients?**

**HOW MANY PEOPLE SURVIVE SKIN CANCER?**

Although non-melanoma skin cancer is very common, in the majority of cases if it is detected sufficiently early, it is not life-threatening.  The survival rates of malignant melanoma have been improving over the last 25 years and this type of cancer now has the highest survival rate of any other type of cancer.

Around 78 per cent of men and 91 per cent of women are alive five years after they were diagnosed.

It is true to say that malignant melanoma survival rates are greatest for people diagnosed early with the smallest and thinnest of skin tumours.

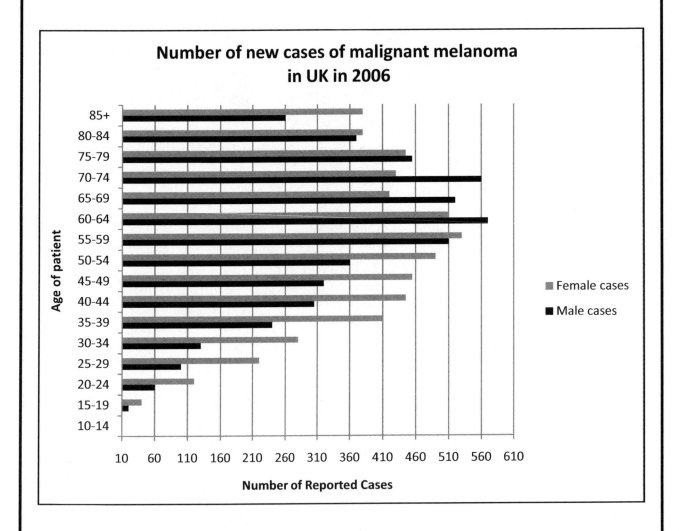

Functional Skills English Level 2  Summative Assessment Papers, Marking Scheme,  and Tutors' Guide – ISBN:  978-1-9049955-5-5

# Functional Skills English Level 2 Assessment Paper

Student's Name

Paper's Title

**WASTE BATTERY RECYCLING AND DISPOSAL**

Date Set

Hand-in Date

| Activity | Possible Marks | | Marks Awarded | Totals |
|---|---|---|---|---|
| 1   Reading and Writing | Q1 | 1 | | |
| | Q2 | 1 | | |
| | Q3 | 2 | | |
| | Q4 | 2 | | |
| | Q5 | 4 | | |
| | | | Activity 1 | |
| 2   Reading and Writing | Q1 | 2 | | |
| | Q2 | 3 | | |
| | Q3 | 2 | | |
| | Q4 | 2 | | |
| | Q5 | 5 | | |
| | Q6 | 1 | | |
| | Q7 | 1 | | |
| | | | Activity 2 | |
| 3   Researching and Writing | Q1 | 12 | | |
| | Q2 | 12 | | |
| | | | Activity 3 | |
| | | | PAPER TOTAL | |
| | | | **PERCENTAGE** | |

**Result**

Circle the appropriate result

**PASS**

**FAIL**

Assessor's Signature ........................................................................ Date ...............................

Functional Skills English Level 2  Summative Assessment Papers, Marking Scheme, and Tutors' Guide – ISBN: 978-1-9049955-5-5

# WASTE BATTERY RECYCLING AND DISPOSAL

## Assessor's Comments

| Activity | Comments |
|---|---|
| 1 | |
| 2 | |
| 3 | |

290

Functional Skills English Level 2  Summative Assessment Papers, Marking Scheme, and Tutors' Guide – ISBN: 978-1-9049955-5-5

# WASTE BATTERY RECYCLING AND DISPOSAL

This paper has **3** sections:

Sections 1 and 2     involve reading and writing

Section 3          involves researching, designing a poster and writing a memo

There are **three** documents for you to read.

Read each document **before** you begin to answer the questions and keep referring to them when you work through the sections.

You are reminded that clear written English and correct spelling and punctuation are important, together with presenting work neatly and making sure it is suitable for the purpose and the audience.

# WASTE BATTERY RECYCLING AND DISPOSAL

ACTIVITY 1 — Reading and Writing

You will be assessed on the following:

— reading, finding and summarising information and ideas from text;

— identifying the purpose and effectiveness of texts and distinguishing between opinion and fact;

— presenting your work and ideas clearly and logically;

— using a range of sentence structures, including complex sentences;

— using spelling, grammar and punctuation accurately and correctly.

Read **Document 1** then answer the following questions.

Questions 1 and 2 are multiple-choice questions. For each question choose one answer, A, B, C or D and put a ✓ (tick) in the box.

1 mark is awarded for each correct answer.

1 Which option **best** describes the main purpose of Document 1?

   A   to inform                          ☐

   B   to encourage actions               ☐

   C   to persuade                        ☐

   D   to frighten                        ☐

2 The document states that 45 per cent of portable batteries must be recycled by the year 2016. How many batteries represent this percentage?

   A   634 million                        ☐

   B   2010 batteries per household, per year   ☐

   C   500 million                        ☐

   D   25 million                         ☐

Functional Skills English Level 2 Summative Assessment Papers, Marking Scheme, and Tutors' Guide – ISBN: 978-1-9049955-5-5

You should spend no longer than 20 minutes on questions 3 — 5.

3    The article is about recycling portable batteries. Describe the batteries which fit into this category.    **2 marks**

_____

_____

4    Only some retailers have to provide a free battery collection service. Explain the minimum criteria which has to be met before a retailer has to include this service.   **2 marks**

_____

_____

_____

5    What are the two categories of retailer who must provide the free battery collection service and what must each do to ensure customers know about the service? **4 marks**

_____

_____

_____

_____

_____

_____

## WASTE BATTERY RECYCLING AND DISPOSAL

ACTIVITY 2 — Reading and Writing

You will be assessed on the following:

— reading, finding and summarising information and ideas from text;

— identifying the purpose and effectiveness of texts and distinguishing between opinion and fact;

— presenting your work and ideas clearly and logically;

— using a range of sentence structures, including complex sentences;

— using spelling, grammar and punctuation accurately and correctly.

Read Documents 2 and 3 then answer the following questions.

You should spend no longer than 25 minutes on questions 1 — 7.

1    According to **Document 2** which categories of people will have to comply with the new Regulations?  **2 marks**

_____

_____

2    Name the three types of battery mentioned in **Document 2**.   **3 marks**

_____

_____

_____

3    Name two pieces of equipment, mentioned in **Document 2**, which might have batteries containing zinc carbon.   **2 marks**

_____

_____

Functional Skills English Level 2 Summative Assessment Papers, Marking Scheme, and Tutors' Guide – ISBN: 978-1-9049955-5-5

4    According to **Document 3**, how did Royal Mail transport the batteries which consumers wished to recycle?    **2 marks**

_____

_____

5    Summarise the purpose of **Figure 1**, and the figures and information it displays. **5 marks**

_____

_____

_____

_____

_____

6    According to the information contained in **Figure 2**, in which areas of the country were consumers given the opportunity to recycle portable batteries as part of the community scheme **and** via the Royal Mail?    **1 mark**

_____

7    According to **Figure 2**, which areas, of more than 60,000 households, took part in the community drop off scheme?  **1 mark**

_____

_____

_____

Functional Skills English Level 2  Summative Assessment Papers, Marking Scheme, and Tutors' Guide – ISBN:  978-1-9049955-5-5

## WASTE BATTERY RECYCLING AND DISPOSAL

ACTIVITY 3 — Researching and Writing

## Researching, Designing a Poster and Writing a Memo

You will be assessed on the following:

— locating relevant information from research;

— summarising research documents and the information and ideas they contain;

— adapting researched information to prepare documents;

— producing work which is suitable for the audience;

— presenting your work and ideas clearly and logically;

— using a range of sentence structures, including complex sentences;

— using a range of writing styles and sentence structures for different purposes;

— using spelling, grammar and punctuation accurately and correctly.

**There are no suggested timings for this activity.**

## Scenario

Your school, college or firm has decided to take part in the battery recycling scheme by providing a number of collection points throughout its building. Accordingly, you have been asked by your tutor/supervisor to design a poster which will advertise this service.

Once your poster has been approved it will be printed professionally and displayed in numerous parts of the building.

The aim of the poster is to inform people when the Regulations came into effect, why batteries should be recycled rather than thrown away in domestic rubbish, what kind of batteries are included and that there will be recycling points in the organisation with effect from the eighth of next month.

After you have designed the poster you will write a Memo to your tutor/supervisor which will ask for his/her approval of your poster's content and design.

Functional Skills English Level 2 Summative Assessment Papers, Marking Scheme, and Tutors' Guide – ISBN: 978-1-9049955-5-5

## Researching the topic

You will probably want to include some information from Documents 1 and 2 but may also want to research the topic further so you have up-to-date facts for your poster.

Mark the information in Documents 1 and 2 which you plan to use on your poster.  If you plan to find additional information useful websites to visit might be:

www.batteryback.org

**and**

www.defra.gov.uk/environment/waste/producer/batteries/index.htm.

There will probably be other sources you will use.

Keep copies of your research documents to hand in with your work.

If you wish to do so, you can plan your work on the blank pages your tutor will hand you.

Functional Skills English Level 2  Summative Assessment Papers, Marking Scheme,  and Tutors' Guide – ISBN:  978-1-9049955-5-5

# Research Notes

---

Functional Skills English Level 2  Summative Assessment Papers, Marking Scheme, and Tutors' Guide – ISBN: 978-1-9049955-5-5

# 1    Designing your Poster    12 marks

Design your poster, including at least one appropriate image.

Remember you want to attract attention to your poster, inform those who stop to read it, and encourage them to take part in the scheme.

Include the information in a logical order, remembering to list the places where there will be collection points and the date on which the scheme starts.

Your poster should contain no fewer than 150 words.

If you wish to do so, you can plan your poster and/or make rough notes on the blank pages your tutor will hand you.

Functional Skills English Level 2  Summative Assessment Papers, Marking Scheme, and Tutors' Guide – ISBN: 978-1-9049955-5-5

# Poster Plan

Functional Skills English Level 2  Summative Assessment Papers, Marking Scheme, and Tutors' Guide – ISBN:  978-1-9049955-5-5

## 2   Writing the Memo   12 marks

Write a memo, dated with today's date, to your tutor/supervisor saying that you are attaching your poster for his/her approval.

Assuming the poster's design and content is approved you want to know some details about printing the poster.  For instance, the name and address of the printer who will be doing the work, the size the printed poster needs to be, how many posters are required and the date the finished posters must be received by your tutor/supervisor.

Your memo must contain no fewer than 200 words.

If you wish to do so, you can plan your memo on the blank pages your tutor will hand you.

Write your memo on the sheet your tutor will give you.

# Memo Plan

Functional Skills English Level 2  Summative Assessment Papers, Marking Scheme, and Tutors' Guide – ISBN: 978-1-9049955-5-5

# MEMORANDUM

To:                                          From:

Date:                                        Subject:

Functional Skills English Level 2  Summative Assessment Papers, Marking Scheme,  and Tutors' Guide – ISBN:  978-1-9049955-5-5

## Fewer than 3 per cent of portable\* batteries in the UK are recycled. In the UK about 634 million batteries are sold annually.

New regulations which came into force on the 5th May 2009 require recycling levels of batteries to rise to 45 per cent by 2016. Forty-five per cent means over 500 million batteries must be recycled. The target by 2012 is that 25 per cent of waste portable batteries must be recycled.

From 1st February 2010 any retailer selling over 32kg\*\* of batteries must by law provide free battery collection by placing collecting bins in their store. Consumers can recycle batteries in any store's collecting bins, even if they did not purchase the battery, or any other equipment, from that store.

This requirement also applies to distance sellers.

Retailers and distributors must also provide information at their sales points which informs customers about the details of their take-back arrangements. If you are a distance seller you must make it clear on your website, or in your catalogue or brochures, what arrangements you have made for the take-back facility.

It will cost nothing for consumers to dispose of batteries in this way, but manufacturers might increase their prices by a few pence per battery in order to cover their costs.

The aim of the regulations is to reduce the number of used batteries, which contain hazardous materials such as cadmium and lead, going into landfill.

**\* rechargeable batteries from hearing aids, mobile phones and laptops**

**\*\* selling one pack of four AA batteries a day**

Functional Skills English Level 2 Summative Assessment Papers, Marking Scheme, and Tutors' Guide – ISBN: 978-1-9049955-5-5

# THE EU WASTE BATTERIES AND ACCUMULATORS REGULATIONS

**These regulations will affect:**

- companies that import, manufacture, distribute or sell portable batteries;

- the way in which consumers can recycle used household portable batteries.

## Why is it important to recycle batteries?

Batteries can contain chemicals such as lead, mercury or cadmium.

If they are included in a household's rubbish, they will end up in landfill where the chemicals they contain may leak into the ground. These chemicals can pollute the soil and water and may even harm human health.

## Portable battery types

Portable batteries range from AAA cells, to mobile phone batteries, to button cells used in hearing aids and watches.

If a battery is available for purchase by the general public or a business, then it is likely to be portable, that is, it can be carried by hand.

Other products which use portable batteries include cameras, laptops, cordless power tools, toys and household appliances such as electric toothbrushes, razors and hand-held vacuum cleaners. Portable batteries can be of mixed sizes and contain a range of chemicals, such as alkaline, lithium, nickel cadmium and nickel metal hydride.

The most common **types** of household battery are the **dry-cell non-rechargeable.** They are used in such appliances as:

- torches, clocks, shavers and radios – these contain **zinc carbon and/or zine chlorine;**
- personal stereos, radio-cassette players – these contain **alkaline manganese.**


Another battery **type** is a **button cell battery.** These are to be found in such things as:

- hearing aids, pacemakers, radio pagers and photographic equipment and can contain **mercuric oxide and zinc air;**
- electronic watches, photographic equipment and calculators can contain **silver oxide and lithium.**

The **dry-cell rechargeable battery** type is used generally as a rechargeable battery and can contain **nickel cadmium** and **nickel metal hydride.**

Functional Skills English Level 2 Summative Assessment Papers, Marking Scheme, and Tutors' Guide – ISBN: 978-1-9049955-5-5

Since 2008, prior to the **EU Waste Batteries and Accumulators Regulations** coming into force, a number of organisations chose to take part in Battery Collection Trials.

These organisations included local authorities collecting them as part of their kerb-side recycling scheme; retailers' take-back scheme; community drop-off points in places such as local council offices, museums, libraries, sport centres and local shops where consumers could leave portable batteries for recycling; postal recycling where consumers, particularly those in rural communities, could post portable batteries to be recycled via the Royal Mail in pre-paid, polythene envelopes; the National Health Service and the Fire Service each with collection points on their premises.

**Fig 1** shows the costs incurred in 2008 (Year 1) and 2009 (Year 2). The cost included the initial cost of setting up the scheme (in Year 1), and the cost to the organisation of forwarding the batteries for recycling.

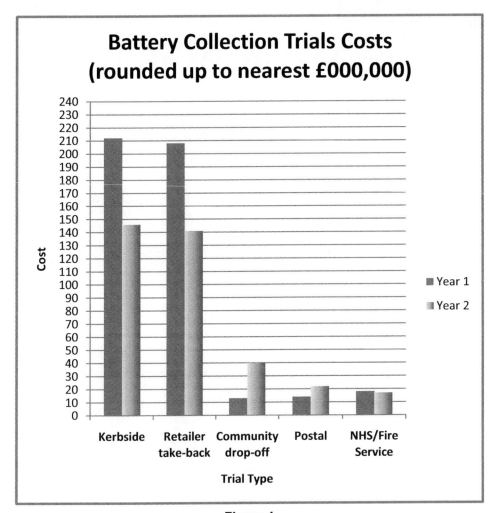

**Figure 1**

Functional Skills English Level 2 Summative Assessment Papers, Marking Scheme, and Tutors' Guide – ISBN: 978-1-9049955-5-5

The table in **Figure 2** gives details of which areas of England were involved in the Battery Collection Trials in the years 2008 and 2009. The purpose of the trials was to establish the most efficient and cost effective way to collect portable household waste batteries. The areas of the country were chosen at random and all those participating in each area did so voluntarily.

**Figure 2**

| Area | Trial Type | | | | | Participating household numbers in Area |
|---|---|---|---|---|---|---|
| | 1 | 2 | 3 | 4 | 5 | |
| Abingdon | ✓ | ✓ | | | | 80,000 |
| Cambridge | | ✓ | ✓ | ✓ | | 104,000 |
| Darlington | | ✓ | ✓ | | ✓ | 39,800 |
| Durham | ✓ | | ✓ | | ✓ | 53,000 |
| Eastleigh | ✓ | | ✓ | | | 48,000 |
| Harrow | | | ✓ | | ✓ | 64,500 |
| Ipswich | | | ✓ | ✓ | | 53,900 |
| Stockton on Tees | | | ✓ | | ✓ | 75,000 |
| Weston-super-Mare | | | ✓ | ✓ | | 52,800 |

Key

Trial Type

1       Local Authority Kerbside Collection

2       Retailer take-back

3       Community drop-off

4       Postal

5       NHS/Fire Service

Functional Skills English Level 2  Summative Assessment Papers, Marking Scheme, and Tutors' Guide – ISBN:  978-1-9049955-5-5

# Suggested Assessment Points

## PAPER 1: THE BLUE FLAG SCHEME

| Activity 1 | Total Marks Achievable: 12 | |
|---|---|---|
| **Question / Task** | **Marks** | **Answer / Must include** |
| 1 | 1 | B |
| 2 | 2 | Two from the following:<br><br>There is an introductory paragraph that describes the scheme — how it began and what it has now become.<br><br>Use of emboldening has emphasised part of the text which has been explained and enlarged upon.<br><br>There are individual paragraph headings which clearly indicate what is being written about.<br><br>Each of the four criteria has been further explained and it is clear which point they relate to because of the paragraph headings. |
| 3 | 2 | To award a Blue Flag, in France, if criteria had been met on:<br><br>sewage treatment, and<br><br>bathing water quality. |
| 4 | 2 | The scheme has been developed **internationally** to include:<br><br>Criteria 1–4 (these should be listed). |
| 5 | 2 | Beach Management Committee<br><br>In charge of environmental management and carries out regular environmental inspection of the beach(es) in its care. |
| 6 | 3 | Three from the following:<br><br>an adequate number of lifeguards/lifesaving equipment;<br><br>safe access to the beach;<br><br>the beach must be patrolled;<br><br>at least one beach in the Blue Flag area must have access and toilet facilities for disabled persons;<br><br>there must be a map indicating the facilities. |

## PAPER 1: THE BLUE FLAG SCHEME

| Activity 2 | Total Marks Achievable: 8 | |
|---|---|---|
| **Question / Task** | **Marks** | **Answer / Must include** |
| 1 | 1 | A |
| 2 | 2 | Because the facilities are better and monitored and as the Blue Flag Scheme means the beaches are clean and safe, tourists are more likely to visit the area, bringing money which they spend on the area, helping the local economy — shops, hotels, tourist attractions, transport, etc. |
| 3 | 1 | D |
| 4 | 1 | C |
| 5 | 1 | B |
| 6 | 1 | D |
| 7 | 1 | A |

Functional Skills English Level 2 Summative Assessment Papers, Marking Scheme, and Tutors' Guide – ISBN: 978-1-9049955-5-5

## PAPER 1: THE BLUE FLAG SCHEME

| Activity 3 | Total Marks Achievable: 10 Marks | |
|---|---|---|
| **Question / Task** | **Marks** | **Answer / Must include** |
| Business Letter | 2 | The student follows the standard conventions of layout and standard information to be included. Salutation and complimentary close match. |
| | 4 | All the requested information has been included and the tone of the letter is polite. |
| | 1 | As there are distinct topics within the letter the student has used a new paragraph for each topic. |
| | 2 | Spelling, grammar and punctuation and verb/tense/subject agreement are correct. |
| | 1 | There is probably a polite final paragraph requesting confirmation/information. |

## PAPER 1: THE BLUE FLAG SCHEME

| Activity 4 | Total Marks Achievable: 20 Marks | |
|---|---|---|
| **Question / Task** | **Marks** | **Answer / Must include** |
| 1 Handout | 1 | The student includes evidence of the research (source) documents. |
| | 3 | The handout shows a list with additional information for each of the four criteria. |
| | 2 | Spelling, grammar and punctuation and verb/tense/subject agreement are correct. |
| 2 Presentation | 14 | The student includes evidence of the research (source) documents.<br><br>The presentation content is suitable for the audience who knows nothing of the subject and may, or may not, include suitable image(s).<br><br>The student delivers the presentation with competence and confidence. |

## PAPER 2: NATIONAL BLOOD SERVICE

| Activity 1 | Total Marks Achievable: 10 Marks | |
|---|---|---|
| **Question / Task** | **Marks** | **Answer / Must include** |
| 1 | 1 | D |
| 2 | 1 | C |
| 3 | 1 | D |
| 4 | 1 | C |
| 5 | 1 | D |
| 6 | 1 | A |
| 7 | 1 | C |
| 8 | 1 | B |
| 9 | 1 | C |
| 10 | 1 | B |

## PAPER 2: NATIONAL BLOOD SERVICE

| Activity 2 | Total Marks Achievable: 15 Marks | |
|---|---|---|
| Question / Task | Marks | Answer / Must include |
| 1 Fact Sheet | 4 | The student includes information on each of the requested headings. |
| | 2 | The fact sheet is structured so the information on the whole sheet is in a logical order. |
| | 4 | There is evidence the student's inclusion is a minimum of 300 words. |
| | 2 | The student includes evidence of the research (source) documents. |
| | 3 | Spelling, grammar and punctuation and verb/tense/subject agreement are correct. |

## PAPER 2: NATIONAL BLOOD SERVICE

| Activity 3 | Total Marks Achievable: 25 Marks | |
|---|---|---|
| Question / Task | Marks | Answer / Must include |
| 1 Presentation | 25 | The student includes evidence of the research (source) documents. |
| | | The presentation content is suitable for the audience who knows nothing of the subject. |
| | | The presentation content and tone acknowledges the audience concerns/fears about the topic and seeks to reassure. |
| | | If illustrations are included, they are used to enhance/explain the topic. |
| | | The student delivers the presentation with competence and confidence. |

## PAPER 3: A HOLIDAY IN BUDAPEST

| Activity 1 | Total Marks Achievable: 13 Marks | |
|---|---|---|
| Question / Task | Marks | Answer / Must include |
| 1 | 1 | C |
| 2 | 1 | C |
| 3 | 1 | A |
| 4 | 1 | D |
| 5 | 1 | D |
| 6 | 1 | B |
| 7 | 1 | B |
| 8 | 1 | B |
| 9 | 1 | C |
| 10 | 1 | A |
| 11 | 1 | A |
| 12 | 1 | B |
| 13 | 1 | D |

Functional Skills English Level 2  Summative Assessment Papers, Marking Scheme, and Tutors' Guide – ISBN: 978-1-9049955-5-5

## PAPER 3: A HOLIDAY IN BUDAPEST

| Activity 2 | Total Marks Achievable: 12 Marks | |
|---|---|---|
| **Question / Task** | **Marks** | **Answer / Must include** |
| 1 Astoria Park Hotel | 4 | Description says ideal for families. Baby-sitting service and child minding (ideal for the three-year-old if parents want to do something not suited to that age-group).<br><br>Likely to be cheaper than the 4* hotels.<br><br>Tourist attractions are within walking distance.<br><br>Peaceful, so likely to be quiet for the three-year-old. |
| 2 Astoria Park Hotel | 3 | The location of the hotel — perhaps including a map with the hotel and the sites indicated.<br><br>Payment methods so the traveller knows if credit/debit cards are accepted.<br><br>Contact details of the hotel — address (to perhaps tell the taxi-driver taking them from airport to hotel), telephone number (if journey delayed) and email address to confirm booking etc. |
| 3 Astoria Park Hotel | 2 | The student should mention that the language is clear and easy to understand and describes the hotel and its facilities and seems to be "warm" and welcoming. |
| 4 Astoria Park Hotel | 3 | The student should mention a stay in the hotel is likely to be comfortable as it is newly built with modern facilities. These include a number of restaurants, leisure facilities and rooms with telephone and television and Wi-Fi facilities and air conditioning. The description gives the impression that guests will be looked after well as it specifically mentions the staff are efficient and aim to make guests' stay happy and memorable. |

## PAPER 3: A HOLIDAY IN BUDAPEST

| Activity 3 | Total Marks Achievable: 25 Marks | |
|---|---|---|
| **Question / Task** | **Marks** | **Answer / Must include** |
| 1 Telephone Call | 1 | The student follows the usual conventions of introduction and reason for call. |
| | 5 | The student clearly gives the information, and seeks the information, detailed on the task sheet. |
| | 4 | Exchange is clear and confident and student responds to the information given or asks further questions which are relevant to the task. |
| 2 Personal Letter | 3 | The student follows the standard conventions of a personal letter layout and the standard information is included. (Name is not included above the address line). |
| | 1 | Complimentary close and salutation match. |
| | 2 | Spelling, grammar and punctuation is accurate. Verb/subject/tense agreement is evident. |
| | 4 | All the information requested on the task sheet **and as a result of the telephone call** is included. |
| | 2 | All the information included is accurate. |
| | 3 | The student displays the information in a way which aids the reader's understanding — perhaps making use of bullet points, numbered lists, a tabular display. |

**Notes for the Tutor for the Telephone Call**

You will take the part of an employee from Cities and Flights so answer the telephone with this information, possibly giving your name.

Listen to the student and check that she/he is clear about giving you the details you need to book the holiday and flights, namely:

- dates of travel – outbound and return;
- number in party (ask for the names at an appropriate time, if the student offers them immediately, say "no" you will want these later in the call);
- airport of departure;
- flight times;
- hotel;
- accommodation requirements.

Question the student on any point not covered/offered.

You should confirm the arrangements are available and booked and perhaps ask the student to spell the names.

Read back the information you have, asking student if this is correct. **If the student is handling the call effectively and confidently, you could make a mistake with one item and expect him/her to correct you.**

## PAPER 4: BUYING SAFELY ONLINE

| Activity 1 | Total Marks Achievable: 5 Marks | |
|---|---|---|
| Question / Task | Marks | Answer / Must include |
| 1 | 1 | D |
| 2 | 1 | D |
| 3 | 1 | C |
| 4 | 1 | C |
| 5 | 1 | B |

## PAPER 4: BUYING SAFELY ONLINE

| Activity 2 | Total Marks Achievable: 11 Marks | | |
|---|---|---|---|
| Question / Task | Marks | Notes | Answer / Must include |
| 1 | 5 | 1 Mark for each point correctly detailed up to a maximum of 5 Marks | When goods cost **over one hundred pounds** and **turn out to be faulty,** under **the Consumer Credit Act the customer may be protected.** This means the **credit card company is also liable** and the **consumer can claim either from the seller or the credit card company.** |
| 2 | 3 | | The buyer has the right to cancel the purchase up to seven days after placing the order. |
| 3 | 3 | | Someone might be able to access the personal details you entered via the computer when making the transaction. |

## PAPER 4: BUYING SAFELY ONLINE

| Activity 3 | Total Marks Achievable: 11 Marks | | |
|---|---|---|---|
| Question / Task | Marks | Notes | Answer / Must include |
| 1 | 1 | | C |
| 2 | 1 | | B |
| 3 | 1 | | A |
| 4 | 8 | 1 mark for each point correctly detailed up to a maximum of 8 marks | What appears: **description of the goods offered; delivery arrangements; address and telephone company;** and **details of when contact is available.** What does not appear but may do if an order is placed: **Cancellation rights.** Details of the **cooling-off period** (these details may be sent in an email after the order has been placed). **There must** be a **confirmation of the order** as it is being placed via the Internet. |

Functional Skills English Level 2 Summative Assessment Papers, Marking Scheme, and Tutors' Guide – ISBN: 978-1-9049955-5-5

## PAPER 4: BUYING SAFELY ONLINE

| Activity 4 | Total Marks Achievable: 23 Marks | |
|---|---|---|
| Question / Task | Marks | Answer / Must include |
| 1 Fact Sheet | 5 | The student includes information which is relevant to the topic. |
| | 2 | The fact sheet is structured so the information is in a logical order. |
| | 2 | The fact sheet's tone is informative and aimed at an audience which knows little, or nothing, about the topic. |
| | 2 | Spelling, grammar and punctuation is accurate. Verb/subject/tense agreement is evident. |
| | 2 | There is evidence the student's document contains a minimum of 500 words. |
| | 1 | The student includes evidence of the research (source) documents. |
| 2 Personal Letter | 3 | The student follows the standard conventions of layout and standard information to be included.  Salutation and complimentary close match. |
| | 5 | The letter has an introductory paragraph/sentence explaining the topic of the Fact Sheet.<br><br>The student uses simple sentences with correct spelling, grammar and punctuation. Verb/tense/subject agreement is correct. |
| | 1 | There is a closing, polite paragraph. |

## PAPER 5: TRINITY HOUSE

| Activity 1 | Total Marks Achievable: 10 Marks | |
|---|---|---|
| Question / Task | Marks | Answer / Must include |
| 1 | 1 | C |
| 2 | 1 | D |
| 3 | 1 | B |
| 4 | 1 | C |
| 5 | 1 | D |
| 6 | 2 | Tabular Form.<br><br>Perhaps mentioning: (Table 1)  two columns Height and Name of Lighthouse arranged in alphabetical order or ascending/descending order.<br><br>(Table 2)  two columns  Light range and Name of Lighthouse, arranged in alphabetical order or ascending/descending order of light range.<br><br>Whilst some people find numbers in tables easy to follow, graphs are ideal for information which can be interpreted at a glance. |
| 7 | 3 | Any three of the bullet points, possibly including the fact that they are eliminating carbon emissions. |

## PAPER 5: TRINITY HOUSE

| Activity 2 | | Total Marks Achievable: 13 Marks |
|---|---|---|
| Question / Task | Marks | Answer / Must include |
| 1 | 1 | Different light signals. |
| | 1 | No regulations to control the brightness of the light. |
| | 1 | No regulations to control the position of the light. |
| | 1 | Most lights did not highlight the hazards to shipping. |
| 2 | 1 | All privately-owned lights in England, Wales and the Channel Islands were bought and became managed by Trinity House. |
| 3 | 3 | Stronger beams of light reflected from more powerful lenses **resulted in** the beam travelling further. <br><br> Such lights were also able to flash and rotate. |
| 4 | 1 | Flamborough. |
| 5 | 1 | Because they are not **in the sea** but sit on land, close to the sea, usually on a cliff. |
| 6 | 3 | As each lighthouse has individual light and sound patterns, mariners will have a guide to the light and fog horn patterns of each lighthouse, so in the dark and fog they will be able to recognise their geographical position. |

## PAPER 5: TRINITY HOUSE

| Activity 3 | | Total Marks Achievable: 27 Marks |
|---|---|---|
| Question / Task | Marks | Answer / Must include |
| 1 Fact Sheet/ Brochure | 15 | The student includes evidence of the research (source) documents. <br><br> The document contains details of the lighthouse location (extension of the first paragraph of Document 3 — perhaps including a map) and its history and is clearly presented as facts rather than opinions or ideas. <br><br> The student should use language that is clear and easy to understand and the tone of the document is suited to the purpose (to inform) and the audience (those with an interest in the lighthouse and its history) and who will welcome a commemorative Fact Sheet. <br><br> The fact sheet is structured so the information on the whole sheet is in a logical order. <br><br> The display of the document makes use of headings, side headings and perhaps bulleted or numbered points. <br><br> Spelling, grammar and punctuation is accurate. Verb/subject/tense agreement is evident. <br><br> There is evidence that the document contains a minimum of 500 words. <br><br> Where image(s) are included, these are relevant to the topic and enhance the document's appearance. |
| 2 Invitation | 12 | The requested information is included in the finished document: <br><br> — correct place and time and name of the event (ending at 5pm); <br> — afternoon tea is included; <br> — mention of the specially-designed cake; <br> — a line for the recipient's name; <br> — a RSVP line; <br> — the correct name and address of the person to whom the RSVP slip must be returned; <br> — the correct date (11th next month) by which the RSVP slip must be returned. <br><br> If an image is included, it is relevant to the topic and enhances the document's content and appearance. <br><br> Spelling, grammar and punctuation is accurate. Verb/subject/tense agreement is evident. <br><br> The tone of the Invitation is warm and welcoming. |

314

Functional Skills English Level 2  Summative Assessment Papers, Marking Scheme, and Tutors' Guide – ISBN: 978-1-9049955-5-5

## PAPER 6 : CLIMATE CHANGE

| Activity 1 | Total Marks Achievable: 9 Marks | |
|---|---|---|
| Question / Task | Marks | Answer / Must include |
| 1 | 2 | The average weather including the patterns of temperature, wind and rainfall occurring over a long period. |
| 2 | 2 | The number of days' skiing in that area is fewer than previously because either the snow is melting as the temperature is warmer, or it is not cold enough to snow for the number of days it used to do. |
| 3 | 2 | Because the heat is prevented from escaping into space by the greenhouse gas trapped in the atmosphere.<br><br>This means the heat cannot escape and increases the temperature of the Earth. |
| 4 | 1 | Methane. |
| 5 | 1 | Fossil fuels. |
| 6 | 1 | Carbon Dioxide (or $CO_2$). |

## PAPER 6 : CLIMATE CHANGE

| Activity 2 | Total Marks Achievable: 9 Marks | |
|---|---|---|
| Question / Task | Marks | Answer / Must include |
| 1 | 2 | – A reputation which is not wanted.<br>– A title which Europe does not want to have.<br>– Europe does not want to be known as the biggest $CO_2$ emitter. |
| 2 | 1 | B |
| 3 | 1 | A |
| 4 | 1 | B |
| 5 | 1 | C |
| 6 | 1 | The title suggests that the text will explain what Europe is doing about trying to tackle Climate Change in the EU. |
| | 1 | The article begins by explaining that Europe is the biggest $CO_2$ polluter but says it is trying to tackle the problem. |
| | 1 | It then goes on to say how it is doing so by describing three courses of action (Treaties) and within each one explaining what it covers and what is being done. |

## PAPER 6 : CLIMATE CHANGE

| Activity 3 | Total Marks Achievable: 16 Marks | |
|---|---|---|
| Question / Task | Marks | Answer / Must include |
| 1 Writing an Article | 1 | The student includes evidence of the research (source) documents. |
| | 4 | Each article is structured so the information is in a logical order. |
| | 2 | The content of each article is directed towards the reader bearing in mind the reader is likely to be a householder and a business person. |
| | 1 | The tone of each should be informative and persuasive and provide facts, not opinions, and where possible these facts should be supported with examples. |
| | 1 | If illustrations are included these are relevant and appropriate. |
| | 2 | The display of the articles makes use of headings, side headings and perhaps bulleted or numbered points. |
| | 2 | Spelling, grammar and punctuation is correct. |
| | 1 | There is verb/tense/subject agreement. |
| | 2 | There is evidence that the student's documents each contain a minimum of 400 words. |

## PAPER 6 : CLIMATE CHANGE

| Activity 4 | Total Marks Achievable: 16 Marks | |
|---|---|---|
| Question / Task | Marks | Answer / Must include |
| 1 Presentation | 16 | The student includes evidence of the research (source) documents. |
| | | The presentation content is suitable for the audience who may be interested, or antagonistic, and it may, or may not, include suitable image(s). |
| | | If illustrations are included, they are used to enhance/explain the topic. |
| | | The student delivers the presentation with competence and confidence. |
| | | The questions from the audience are handled politely and answered satisfactorily. |

## PAPER 7 : THE YORKSHIRE THREE PEAKS CHALLENGE WALK

| Activity 1 | Total Marks Achievable: 12 Marks | |
|---|---|---|
| Question / Task | Marks | Answer / Must include |
| 1 | 1 | C |
| 2 | 1 | D |
| 3 | 1 | C |
| 4 | 1 | B |
| 5 | 1 | C |
| 6 | 1 | C |
| 7 | 1 | D |
| 8 | 1 | B |
| 9 | 1 | D |
| 10 | 1 | B |
| 11 | 1 | D |
| 12 | 1 | C |

Functional Skills English Level 2 Summative Assessment Papers, Marking Scheme, and Tutors' Guide – ISBN: 978-1-9049955-5-5

## PAPER 7 : THE YORKSHIRE THREE PEAKS CHALLENGE WALK

| Activity 2 | Total Marks Achievable: 15 Marks | | |
|---|---|---|---|
| Question / Task | Marks | Notes | Answer / Must include |
| 1 | 1 | | D |
| 2 | 1 | | B |
| 3 | 4 | | Moss Grove Inn, High Birkwith. It describes where the village is situated. It names some main towns and says where they are located in relation to the village of High Birkwith. |
| 4 | 5 | If all three hotels are mentioned, and the quotations | Golden Lion — ideal for those doing the Three Peaks Challenge Walk. Moss Grove Inn — perfectly situated base for the Yorkshire Three Peaks Challenge Walk. White Swan — mentions the Whernside Peak outside the village which is one of the peaks on the Three Peaks Challenge Walk. |
| 5 | 1 | | It is now a heated indoor swimming pool and Jacuzzi area. |
| 6 | 3 | | Situated **on the Helwith Park Estate** which is **1 mile east and 2 miles south** of the **village of Helwith Bridge.** |

## PAPER 7 : THE YORKSHIRE THREE PEAKS CHALLENGE WALK

| Activity 3 | Total Marks Achievable: 10 Marks | | |
|---|---|---|---|
| Question / Task | Marks | Notes | Answer / Must include |
| 1 Telephone Call | 1 | | The student follows the usual conventions of introduction and reason for call and ends the call. |
| | 4 | | The student clearly gives the information in points 1–4 on the task sheet. |
| | 1 | | The student gives an appropriate reason for having selected the accommodation. |
| | 3 | | The student asks for, establishes, the additional information set out on the task sheet. |
| | 1 | | Exchange is clear and confident and student responds to the information given or asks further questions if the information is not what was requested. |

Notes for the Tutor for the Telephone Call

You will take the part of the chosen hotel's employee so answer the phone with the name of the hotel, possibly giving your name.

Listen to the student and check if s/he is clear about all details you will need to know about the intended reservation:

- dates reflect Friday to Monday (leaving Tuesday) – 2nd week of next month's dates;
- the surname of the two men in the party will be the same – whether student opts for Mr and Mrs X, or two Mr Xs and Ms/Miss (different surnames) is acceptable;
- the booking will be for two double rooms;
- student will ask room/breakfast rate;
- student may not tell you their time of arrival so you must ask for this;
- the student will specifically ask about tourist attractions in the area (making it clear the ladies will have use of a car) and will ask to be sent some details.

By the end of the call you will know that the two men are doing the Three Peaks Challenge Walk.

Question the student directly on any point which she/he has not covered.

The student should end the call as the person who placed the call.

Functional Skills English Level 2 Summative Assessment Papers, Marking Scheme, and Tutors' Guide – ISBN: 978-1-9049955-5-5

## PAPER 7 : THE YORKSHIRE THREE PEAKS CHALLENGE WALK

| Activity 4 | Total Marks Achievable: 13 Marks | | |
|---|---|---|---|
| Question / Task | Marks | Notes | Answer / Must include |
| 2 Business Letter | 1 | | The student includes evidence of the research (source) documents. |
| | 3 | | The student follows the standard conventions of business letter layout and standard information to be included.  Salutation and complimentary close match and the letter is to be signed by the manager/proprietor. |
| | 9 | | The information from the telephone call is confirmed in the letter and the student demonstrates the standard conventions of correct sentence structure, spelling, grammar and punctuation.  Verb/tense/subject agreement is evident. |
| | | | There is information from the research about  four or five attractions. |

## PAPER 8: SWIM BETTER — FEEL FITTER

| Activity 1 | Total Marks Achievable: 10 Marks | |
|---|---|---|
| Question / Task | Marks | Answer / Must include |
| 1 | 1 | D |
| 2 | 1 | B |
| 3 | 1 | D |
| 4 | 1 | D |
| 5 | 1 | B |
| 6 | 1 | Strengthens the back. |
| | 1 | Tones arms and legs. |
| | 1 | Increases mobility of shoulders and hips. |
| | 1 | Improves cardiovascular fitness. |
| 7 | 1 | Check with reception the timetable for the classes, then book the session. |

## PAPER 8: SWIM BETTER — FEEL FITTER

| Activity 2 | Total Marks Achievable: 10 Marks | |
|---|---|---|
| Question / Task | Marks | Answer / Must include |
| 1 | 1 | C |
| 2 | 1 | The Government is providing funding for people aged 60+   to swim free outside school holidays. |
| | 1 | Some local authorities have extended this scheme to provide 60+ free swimming all year round. |
| | 1 | In some local authority pools the times the 60+ can swim free will not be restricted. |
| 3 | 1 | 6–22 year old scheme "Fit for the Future". |
| | 1 | Because this initiative involves the fitness industry of which First Steps to Fitness is a member. |
| 4 | 4 | **16 is the youngest age** because **they have just left school where they took part in a weekly physical education programme** which has **ended now they have left school.** |
| | | This initiative will **allow them to continue their fitness regime** if they wish to continue with it. |

Functional Skills English Level 2  Summative Assessment Papers, Marking Scheme, and Tutors' Guide – ISBN: 978-1-9049955-5-5

## PAPER 8: SWIM BETTER — FEEL FITTER

| Activity 3 | Total Marks Achievable: 30 Marks | |
|---|---|---|
| Question / Task | Marks | Answer / Must include |
| 1 Report | 1 | There is evidence of research (source) documents on four local councils. |
| | 4 | The report includes the information and headings requested. |
| | 2 | The student has compared the findings for all four councils and displayed in a logical, easy-to-read way. Possibly in table form. |
| | 2 | The student has made use of side headings/bullet points/numbered or lettered headings to emphasise the content. |
| | 8 | The sentence structure is complex with spelling, grammar and punctuation correct. Verb/tense/subject agreement is evident. |
| | 13 | The student has offered a logical, plausible way in which the company could be involved in the scheme, correctly interpreting the information from the graphs and using common sense. |

## PAPER 9: THINK ABOUT RECYCLING

| Activity 1 | Total Marks Achievable: 15 Marks | | |
|---|---|---|---|
| Question / Task | Marks | Notes | Answer / Must include |
| 1 | 1 | | B |
| 2 | 1 | | C |
| 3 | 1 | | B |
| 4 | 1 | | C |
| 5 | 1 | | D |
| 6 | 2 | 1 mark for each valid point (up to a maximum of 2 marks). | To make the point that whilst householders are recycling, they have to include lots of packaging which comes with the goods they buy.<br><br>To inform the reader that householders are targeted by the Government and encouraged to recycle but that manufacturers and retailers should be encouraged to reduce packaging.<br><br>To give the householder advice on what they can do to encourage manufacturers and retailers to reduce the amount of packaging on the goods they sell. |
| 7 | 4 | 1 mark for each valid, explained point (up to a maximum of 4 marks). | If customers get used to buying foods which are "loose" and not heavily packaged, or packaged at all, **they will realise packaging is not always essential and continue to buy goods in this way** because **it is kinder to the environment** and **they don't have to add the packaging to their recycling boxes**. Buying from elsewhere will mean **retailers might notice a change in their sales figures** and **together with the letters from customers** understand excess packaging is not wanted. |
| 8 | 4 | 2 marks for each valid, explained point (up to a maximum of 4 marks). | To protect delicate goods, such as electrical equipment, small or large. Packaging can protect the equipment and stop the goods from moving in their box at the risk of being damaged or broken.<br><br>To protect food from spilling, for instance, cereal needs to be contained in a box which is less likely to be crushed or damaged, and the cereal within in a packet to keep it fresh once the box is opened. |

Functional Skills English Level 2 Summative Assessment Papers, Marking Scheme, and Tutors' Guide – ISBN: 978-1-9049955-5-5

## PAPER 9: THINK ABOUT RECYCLING

| Activity 2 | | Total Marks Achievable: 19 Marks | |
|---|---|---|---|
| Question / Task | Marks | Notes | Answer / Must include |
| 1 | 4 | Allocate 1 mark for each valid, supported, point, up to a maximum of 4 marks. | To **promote the products which Riverside Products (UK) Ltd sells** which help the householder to recycle.<br><br>This is evidenced by the **advertisements and prices of several products** of which the company give details **together with** giving details of how the reader can obtain a **catalogue of the products the company sells**, and **where the stores are situated.** |
| 2 | 3 | | The Kitchen-Compost Tidy.<br><br>The two sizes would cost: £6.49 and £11.49 on production of the advice sheet at a Riverside store.<br><br>The customer would have to take the advice sheet into the store. |
| 3 | 2 | | To **reduce the impact of packaging and packaging waste** on the environment. |
| | 1 | | It includes both **recovery** and **recycling** targets of packaging. |
| | 1 | | It encourages **reuse**. |
| 4 | 8 | Allocate 2 marks for each valid, supported, point, up to a maximum of 8 marks. | The student could put forward the following comments/arguments.<br><br>Yes – they would buy from the store **because the article indicates it cares about the environment** and has **already begun reducing its packaging.** It gives advice on what the householder can do to **recycle effectively. It has products which will help this process. It offers discounts on some of its products.**<br><br>Yes – the student **would be encouraged to recycle** because the **ways of doing so are clearly described** in the article.<br><br>The student could put forward an argument against being encouraged to recycle or to buy from the company. The points made must be valid. |

## PAPER 9: THINK ABOUT RECYCLING

| Activity 3 | | Total Marks Achievable: 5 Marks |
|---|---|---|
| Question / Task | Marks | Answer / Must include |
| 1 | 1 | C |
| 2 | 1 | D |
| 3 | 1 | C |
| 4 | 1 | D |
| 5 | 1 | D |

Functional Skills English Level 2 Summative Assessment Papers, Marking Scheme, and Tutors' Guide – ISBN: 978-1-9049955-5-5

## PAPER 9: THINK ABOUT RECYCLING

| Activity 4 | | Total Marks Achievable: 11 Marks |
|---|---|---|
| Question / Task | Marks | Answer / Must include |
| 1 | 1 | There is evidence of research (source) document(s) which give details about reusable, recyclable shopping bags. |
| | 2 | The student mentions the information required in the task (the information from Document 3). |
| | 4 | The student includes information on three or four different types of material which can be used for recyclable, reusable bags, and gives sufficient information on how it degrades, how long a bag made out of the material is expected to last, etc. It should be easy for the reader to compare like information in each description so look for consistency. |
| | 2 | The leaflet will usually be 1 side of an A4 sheet, but other sizes are acceptable as long as it contains all the information, it is attractively and consistently displayed, uses correct grammar, spelling and punctuation, and subject/verb/tense agreement and includes correct details from Document 3, and the image(s) is appropriate to the topic. |
| | 2 | The purpose of the leaflet is to educate and persuade. |

## PAPER 10: BINGE DRINKING

| Activity 1 | | | Total Marks Achievable: 19 Marks |
|---|---|---|---|
| Question / Task | Marks | Notes | Answer / Must include |
| 1 | 3 | Allocate 1 mark for each point, up to a maximum of 3 marks. | 1 heavy drinking; <br> 2 alcohol abuse; <br> 3 problem drinking; <br> 4 drinking too much, too often. |
| 2 | 1 | | C |
| 3 | 3 | Allocate 1 mark for each point, up to a maximum of 3 marks — expressed in own words. | A woman will **get drunk more quickly** because she has **less water in her body** than a man of **equal size and weight**. The recommended daily **units are reduced to allow for this**. |
| 4 | 1 | 1 mark for each valid point. | Poor judgement. |
| | 1 | | Loss of inhibitions. |
| 5 | 1 | | Increased risk of a stroke. |
| 6 | 3 | Allocate 1 mark for each valid point, up to a maximum of 3 marks — expressed in own words. | By falling or stepping into moving traffic. By agreeing to be a passenger in a car driven by someone under the influence of alcohol — something they are not necessarily aware of as they are drunk themselves. Had they not been drunk they would be unlikely to agree to get into a car driven by someone who had been drinking heavily. |
| 7 | 6 | Allocate 1 mark for each valid point, up to a maximum of 6 marks — expressed in own words. | Binge drinkers can find themselves **unexpectedly associated with crime**, whether the **victim of a crime** because they are **vulnerable to attack and unaware of the danger**, or **carrying out a crime**. <br> The estimate is that up to **one-third of burglaries** are carried out by **people under the influence of alcohol**, and up to **half of street crimes** are **carried out by a binge drinker**. |

Functional Skills English Level 2  Summative Assessment Papers, Marking Scheme, and Tutors' Guide – ISBN: 978-1-9049955-5-5

## PAPER 10: BINGE DRINKING

| Activity 2 | | Total Marks Achievable: 4 Marks |
|---|---|---|
| Question / Task | Marks | Answer / Must include |
| 1 | 1 | D |
| 2 | 1 | C |
| 3 | 1 | C |
| 4 | 1 | B |

## PAPER 10: BINGE DRINKING

| Activity 3 | | | Total Marks Achievable: 10 Marks |
|---|---|---|---|
| Question / Task | Marks | Notes | Answer / Must include |
| 1 | 8 | Allocate 1 mark for each valid point, up to a maximum of 8 marks — expressed in own words. | **Four out of every ten students** in Year 11 were **involved in binge drinking** because this number admitted to having had **five or more alcoholic drinks in any one session of drinking.** <br><br> **Eight out of ten students (80 per cent)** both **male and female**, had **drunk alcohol in the four weeks prior to taking part in the survey.** <br><br> **More than a quarter of the Year 11 students, of both sexes, admitted to having** had three, or more, binge sessions **in the month before taking part in the survey.** |
| 2 | 2 | Allocate 1 mark for each idea and reason to support that idea, up to a maximum of 2 marks. | Factual because it summaries the result of a survey. <br><br> Giving advice because it gives some tips about how to avoid becoming a binge drinker. <br><br> Helpful because it states facts and gives advice. <br><br> A mixture of fact and opinion because the first paragraphs are the result of a survey, the numbered paragraphs give opinions about how to avoid becoming a binge drinker but cannot be described as facts as each person's approach to avoidance is likely to be different. |

## PAPER 10: BINGE DRINKING

| Activity 4 | | Total Marks Achievable: 17 Marks |
|---|---|---|
| Question / Task | Marks | Answer / Must include |
| 1 Report | 2 | There is evidence of research (source) documents. |
| | 2 | The Report includes the information and headings requested. |
| | 8 | The information included is displayed in a logical, easy-to-read way. |
| | 2 | The student has made use of side headings/bullet points/numbered or lettered headings to emphasise the content. |
| | 3 | The sentence structure is complex with spelling, grammar and punctuation correct. Verb/tense/subject agreement is evident. |

Functional Skills English Level 2 Summative Assessment Papers, Marking Scheme, and Tutors' Guide – ISBN: 978-1-9049955-5-5

## PAPER 11: 5-A-DAY

| Activity 1 | Total Marks Achievable: 17 Marks | | |
|---|---|---|---|
| **Question / Task** | **Marks** | **Notes** | **Answer / Must include** |
| 1 | 1 | | 80g equals 1 portion of the recommended daily intake. |
| | 1 | | 5 portions equals 80g x 5 = 400g. |
| 2 | 1 | | Dried fruit. |
| | 1 | | Juice. |
| | 1 | | Pulses. |
| | 1 | | Beans. |
| 3 | 1 | | Low in calories; low in fat; full of minerals(particularly C and folate). |
| | 1 | | Excellent and natural source of fibre. |
| | 1 | | Contain phytochemicals which help protect against such diseases as heart disease and cancer. |
| 4 | 1 | | C |
| 5 | 1 | | D |
| 6 | 1 | Allocate 1 mark for each correct point. | The chart plots the course of fruit and vegetables consumed, in grams, per person, per week. (*Explanation of chart title and content*) |
| | 1 | | It shows that the consumption of vegetables dropped in each year. |
| | 1 | | Although only by a small amount, say from approximately 2000g to 1980g. |
| | 1 | | However the consumption of fruit dropped between 2004 and 2006 but rose in 2008. |
| | 1 | | In 2008 the consumption was greater than in 2004. |
| | 1 | | Approximate figures are 950, 1700 and 1150. |

## PAPER 11: 5-A-DAY

| Activity 2 | Total Marks Achievable: 14 Marks | | |
|---|---|---|---|
| **Question / Task** | **Marks** | **Notes** | **Answer / Must include** |
| 1 | 1 | Allocate 1 mark for each correct point. | It began in 2004 with £42m of funding from lottery money. |
| | 1 | | In 2005 the Department of Health financed the scheme when the lottery money ran out. |
| | 1 | | The DoH expanded the Scheme, region by region. |
| 2 | 1 | Allocate 1 mark for each correct point. | Fruit and vegetables are delivered daily. |
| | 1 | | 99% said the system was reliable and acceptable. |
| | 1 | Allocate 1 mark for each correct point. | The scheme supported teaching and learning about healthy eating. |
| | 1 | | The scheme was considered by staff as an excellent way of improving the children's health and encouraging a healthy diet. |

| Activity 2 | | Total Marks Achievable: 14 Marks | |
|---|---|---|---|
| Question / Task | Marks | Notes | Answer / Must include |
| 4 | 6 | Allocate 1 mark for each correct point up to a maximum of 6 marks from this range of answers. | The survey was related to the parents' thoughts on the scheme after two terms. |
| | | | The categories of responses were: "Agree", "Disagree", "Don't Know". |
| | | | The categories on which opinions were sought were: Encouraging children to eat fruit and vegetables, Helping to educate children about healthy diets, Improving children's health, and Encouraging 5-a-day eating at home. |
| | | | Most parents agreed with each of the four categories. |
| | | | On Helping to educate children about healthy diets, although most parents agreed, the second most popular response was "Don't Know". |
| | | | "Don't Know" was the lowest response in the categories Improving Children's Health and Encouraging 5-a-day eating at home. No one responded with "Don't Know" in the Encouraging children to eat fruit and vegetables category. |
| | | | 96 per cent of parents thought the scheme encouraged children to eat fruit and vegetables; 86 per cent thought the scheme helped to educate children about healthy diets; 82 per cent thought the scheme improved children's health and 76 per cent thought it encouraged 5-a-day at home (these figures are approximate as the graph may be a little small to determine accuracy). Students might also compare and contrast the "Agree" and "Disagree" figures. |
| 5 | 1 | | Different colours provide different vitamins, minerals, fibres and antioxidants. |

## PAPER 11: 5-A-DAY

| Activity 3 | | Total Marks Achievable: 19 Marks |
|---|---|---|
| Question / Task | Marks | Answer / Must include |
| 1 Newsletter | 2 | The Newsletter content is logical. |
| | 2 | The key facts from Document 2 have been included. |
| | 2 | The name of the school and the head is included. |
| | 2 | The information included is displayed in a logical, easy-to-read way and that the original document and the research document(s) have, **to some extent,** been changed into the student's own words. |
| | 1 | Suggested recipes have been included in the Newsletter and this is evidence of research. |
| | 1 | The student has made use of side headings/bullet points/numbered or lettered headings to emphasise the content. |
| | 1 | The sentence structure is complex with spelling, grammar and punctuation correct. Verb/tense/subject agreement is evident. |
| | 1 | There is evidence of research (source) documents – perhaps some additional information related to the 5-a-day scheme or the School's Fruit and Vegetables Scheme. |
| 2 Memo | 2 | The memo is addressed to Mr Brian Rhodes, Head, and is from the student, dated today (dd/mm/yyyy) and has the requested heading. |
| | 2 | The spelling, grammar and punctuation is correct and there is verb/tense/subject agreement. Paragraphs are present and logically ordered. |
| | 2 | All the requested information is included, along with the descriptions requested. |
| | 1 | The student has signed the memo. |

Functional Skills English Level 2 Summative Assessment Papers, Marking Scheme, and Tutors' Guide – ISBN: 978-1-9049955-5-5

## PAPER 12: NO MESSIN'

| Activity 1 | Total Marks Achievable: 11 Marks | | |
|---|---|---|---|
| Question / Task | Marks | Notes | Answer / Must include |
| 1 | 3 | All five categories to be included in the answer. If any point is missing award 2 marks only. | Stations; Platforms; Bridges; Underpasses; Level crossings. |
| 2 | 1 | Allocate 1 Mark for each correct category. | Adults. |
| | 1 | | People under 16 years of age. |
| 3 | 1 | Allocate 1 Mark for each correct answer. | Trespass: unauthorised people in unauthorised sections of railway property. |
| | 1 | | Vandalism: anyone deliberately damaging railway property. |
| 4 | 3 | Student may combine breaking/ damaging railway property. | Leaving litter; Fly-tipping; Breaking railway property; Damaging railway property; |
| 5 | 1 | | Graffiti. |

## PAPER 12: NO MESSIN'

| Activity 2 | Total Marks Achievable: 14 Marks | | |
|---|---|---|---|
| Question / Task | Marks | Notes | Answer / Must include |
| 1 | 1 | | Over 60. |
| 2 | 6 | Award one mark for each response up to a maximum of 6 marks. | It is a private company. It maintains Britain's rail network. It employs approximately 33,000 people who take care of the track, stations and such things as embankments, and the land between the stations. |
| 3 | 1 | | C |
| 4 | 1 | Allocate 1 mark for each correct answer. | In school holidays. |
| | 1 | | Between 4pm and 8pm. |
| 5 | 4 | Allocate 1 mark for each correct category included. | It has set up a No Messin' campaign. To address anti-social and criminal behaviour (at a cost of £250m + a year). It is aimed at those in education, young offenders and those involved in after-school activities. It is intended to inform community policy teams. |

## PAPER 12: NO MESSIN'

| Activity 3 | Total Marks Achievable: 10 Marks | | |
|---|---|---|---|
| Question / Task | Marks | Notes | Answer / Must include |
| 1 | 5 | Award 1 mark for each set of figures correctly chosen and described (student preferably quotes the figures). | In each year of the five years from 2003–2007 the highest number of incidents recorded related to damage from thrown missiles, although in 2007 the previous four years' recording of 250 had reduced to around 225.<br><br>The number of fires in trains peaked in 2004 to around 185 and in 2007 this figure was 50.<br><br>The Hitting Obstructions category also peaked in 2004 to around 155, decreasing in 2005 to around 95 but rising in 2006 to 115 before falling in 2007 to around 98.<br><br>Of all the categories reported only the Hitting Obstructions category reflected the least decrease in the number of incidents.<br><br>The student describes the trend for each incident in a logical way, summarising the meaning of the figures in relation to increasing or decreasing incidents over the period of time.<br><br>Ideally the student includes a summary, either about the whole chart's figures or just (as in the sample answer) summarises the figures for one incident. |
| 2 | 2 | | Highest: Greater London, Merseyside, West Midlands.<br><br>Lowest: Bedfordshire, Cleveland, Cornwall, North Yorkshire, Surrey. |
| 3 | 3 | Award the 3 marks to a response which is logical and complete. If any "steps" are missing award only 1 or 2 marks. | Damage has to be repaired. Repairs cost. Cost of installing CCTV cameras. Costs come out of budget/profit. Companies operate on profit-making basis so need to get the money back. Puts up cost of tickets to passengers.<br><br>**The response should be logical and reflect the steps in this sequence.** |

## PAPER 12: NO MESSIN'

| Activity 4 | Total Marks Achievable: 15 Marks | |
|---|---|---|
| Question / Task | Marks | Answer / Must include |
| | 1 | There is evidence of research (source) documents. |
| | 2 | The student has incorporated relevant factual information from the 3 documents included in the assessment. |
| | 3 | The information selected from the researched document(s) is relevant and has been used to describe planned activities in the brochure. |
| | 3 | The information included is incorporated in a logical, easy-to-read way. |
| | 3 | The student has adopted a number of consistent ways in which to emphasise the content. If image(s) are included they serve to enhance the meaning of the text and are placed appropriately. |
| | 3 | The sentence structure is complex with spelling, grammar and punctuation correct. Verb/tense/subject agreement is evident. |

Functional Skills English Level 2 Summative Assessment Papers, Marking Scheme, and Tutors' Guide – ISBN: 978-1-9049955-5-5

## PAPER 13: THE COST OF BEING A FOOTBALL FAN

| Activity 1 | | Total Marks Achievable: 9 Marks |
|---|---|---|
| Question / Task | Marks | Answer / Must include |
| 1 | 1 | C |
| 2 | 1 | D |
| 3 | 1 | B |
| 4 | 1 | C |
| 5 | 1 | B |
| 6 | 1 | B |
| 7 | 1 | D |
| 8 | 1 | D |
| 9 | 1 | B |

## PAPER 13: THE COST OF BEING A FOOTBALL FAN

| Activity 2 | | | Total Marks Achievable: 19 Marks |
|---|---|---|---|
| Question / Task | Marks | Notes | Answer / Must include |
| 1 | 3 | Allocate 1 mark for the definition linking the word and phrase. Allocate 1 mark (to a maximum of 2 marks) for items suggested as "regalia". | Club regalia relates to anything with the club's logo/name on used for merchandising (promoting the club – selling the club's name). The club regalia can include current season team strips for adults and children, videos of past successes, household goods such as tea towels, clocks, table mats, calendars, diaries, personal items such as pens, pencils, pencil cases, badges, etc. |
| 2 | 2 | Award 1 mark for each item, up to a maximum of 2 marks. | Programme costs; Travelling costs (including vehicle hire and petrol); Team regalia; Food; Alcohol. |
| 3 | 3 | Award 1 mark for each valid and relevant point. | It will have on it the club's name and probably colours and logo, thus identifying them with their club. Having a credit card might offer them some advantages not on offer to those without a card. For instance, discounts in the club's shop or a number of free tickets each season. |
| 4 | 1 | Award 1 mark for each valid and relevant point. | Whilst credit cards might give some advantages, the interest paid on club's savings accounts is usually lower than could be obtained for other types of savings accounts. |
| | 1 | | Consequently as a means of making money work for the account holder, club savings accounts are not the best choice. |
| 5 | 1 | | Burnley. |
| 6 | 1 | | 800 hours and 33 days. |

Functional Skills English Level 2 Summative Assessment Papers, Marking Scheme, and Tutors' Guide – ISBN: 978-1-9049955-5-5

| Activity 2 | Total Marks Achievable: 19 Marks | | |
|---|---|---|---|
| Question / Task | Marks | Notes | Answer / Must include |
| 7 | 2 | Allocate 1 mark for each item mentioned to a maximum of 2 marks. | Watching matches on television. Searching for information on the Internet. Exchanging views with other supporters on the Internet. |
| 8 | 5 | Allocate 1 mark for each main "theme", to a maximum of 3 marks. (The student might not mention the Internet research and chat so do not penalise if this is not included.) Award 2 marks for sentence structure which reflects their own words and correct spelling, grammar and punctuation. | The cost of being a football fan is rising – because of increased costs of tickets, fuel (which increases travel costs whether car, train or hire vehicle), cost of goods for sale in the club's shops. Around 26 per cent of supporters are having to reduce the number of live games they attend because they can no longer afford the increased prices. Some clubs have realised the reason their fans are not able to pay the higher prices and are offering some incentives such as a club credit card which will provide some discounts in a season, and a club savings account. The idea is that the fans will benefit and the club will have extra money at its disposal. The dedicated football fan spends more time following their team than just attending matches, such as researching and exchanging information on the Internet. |

## PAPER 13: THE COST OF BEING A FOOTBALL FAN

| Activity 3 | Total Marks Achievable: 22 Marks | | |
|---|---|---|---|
| Question / Task | Marks | Notes | Answer / Must include |
| 1 Summary Sheet | 1 | | The student includes evidence of the research (source) documents. |
| | 2 | | All information is structured, using side headings and perhaps bulleted or numbered points, so the information is in a logical order. |
| | 1 | | The tone is informative. |
| | 2 | | The comparison of the products chosen is clear and presented, possibly in a table. |
| | 1 | | If illustrations are included these are relevant and appropriate. |
| | 2 | | Spelling, grammar and punctuation is correct. |
| | 1 | | There is verb/tense/subject agreement. |
| | 2 | | There is evidence the student's inclusion is a minimum of 250 words per sheet. |
| 2 Presentation | 1 | | The student includes evidence of the research (source) documents. |
| | 1 | | The presentation content is suitable for the audience who know little or nothing of the subject. |
| | 3 | | The presentation includes some details of the chosen club, together with details of the relative. |

328

| Activity 3 | Total Marks Achievable: 22 Marks | | |
|---|---|---|---|
| Question / Task | Marks | Notes | Answer / Must include |
| | 1 | | If illustrations are included, they are used to enhance/explain the topic. |
| | 2 | | The student delivers the presentation with competence and confidence. |
| | 2 | | The sum of £100 has been allocated and the reasons for the purchases have been explained. |

## PAPER 14: TRAVEL SAFELY ABROAD

| Activity 1 | Total Marks Achievable: 13 Marks | | |
|---|---|---|---|
| Question / Task | Marks | Notes | Answer / Must include |
| 1 | 1 | | C |
| 2 | 1 | | D |
| 3 | 1 | | Tell your bank and/or credit card company if you are going abroad, where you will be and when. |
| | 1 | | Keep traveller's cheques and currency safe and out of view. |
| 4 | 1 | | It is advisable to have a Health Insurance Card in Europe and Switzerland together with adequate health insurance. |
| | 1 | | In some countries, such as USA, health insurance does not guarantee emergency health cover. |
| 5 | 3 | Student's response should show they have understood the text and thought out, and expressed, the "consequences" in their own words. If this is not the case deduct 1 mark for each unsupported response. | If you plan to use a credit or a debit card abroad tell your credit card company or bank. In this way they will know that any purchase made using these cards abroad is "expected" and they can link the use to the information you gave them about being in a certain country on a certain date. If they don't have this information they will not necessarily know the attempted use was genuinely made by the card holder and they might reject the use. |
| | 2 | | Keep your money and traveller's cheques safe and out of view. If you lose your money, or have it stolen, it will be difficult to replace it or continue without it. |
| 6 | 1 | | Leave a copy of your travel itinerary with someone in the UK. |
| | 1 | | Phone home regularly to let someone know you are safe and well. |

## PAPER 14: TRAVEL SAFELY ABROAD

| Activity 2 | | Total Marks Achievable: 19 Marks | |
|---|---|---|---|
| Question / Task | Marks | Notes | Answer / Must include |
| 1 | 6 | The student should have disagreed with the statement in the question and justified that opinion by mentioning the useful hints the article includes.<br><br>It might be that the student has responded using a more "personal" approach such as "I found the tip on ...to be very helpful." | The article is not trying to put people off visiting large cities. It is saying how exciting and challenging visiting a large city can be and that the traveller should be aware of problems which might arise in cities and how to avoid being involved in such problems.<br><br>It offers 7 points of advice related to important things such as never walking alone in quiet areas, particularly in the dark and always to be alert to what is going on around you that could become a problem.<br><br>There is useful information related to if you think you are being followed and how to take care of your valuables when you are relaxing.<br><br>It also mentions what to do if you are a victim of theft. |
| 2 | 3 | Award 1 mark for each valid point up to a maximum of 3 marks. | The student's answer will demonstrate that she/he has thought out the reasons behind the statement in Point 3 in the document. Some possible responses are:<br><br>In the street there is more likely to be someone watching with a view to stealing your money, your card or your pin number.<br><br>In the street there is more likely to be someone to jostle you to steal the money you take out or your card.<br><br>Machines in the street are more likely to have been tampered with so your card is "lost" in the machine and they can then take the card and use it, having watched you enter your pin number.<br><br>In the bank the machines are not likely to have been tampered with.<br><br>In the bank it is unlikely anyone will steal your money from you (although they may do so once you are in the street).<br><br>There are likely to be security cameras in the bank so the possibility of theft or foul play is minimal.<br><br>In the bank you are less likely to be "crowded" at the machine (thieves crowd to gain information and steal). |

Functional Skills English Level 2  Summative Assessment Papers, Marking Scheme, and Tutors' Guide – ISBN: 978-1-9049955-5-5

| Activity 2 | | Total Marks Achievable: 19 Marks | |
|---|---|---|---|
| Question / Task | Marks | Notes | Answer / Must include |
| 3 | 10 | Allocate 2 marks for each relevant comment, expanded to show their understanding, up to a maximum of 7 marks.<br><br>Allocate 3 marks for correct sentence structure, spelling and grammar. | The student answers that she/he would have found the articles useful and perhaps mentions the following:<br><br>Document 1 mentions where to look for additional information;<br><br>The information about the need to have visas outside Europe is useful (some first time travellers will head outside the EU);<br><br>The information about telling a bank or credit card company is particularly important (the instances of pin number theft are high and this is a sensible precaution to know about);<br><br>Having an itinerary, giving someone in the UK a copy of it, and regularly phoning home are useful pieces of information and students should be aware of people who go missing abroad;<br><br>Document 2 gives reasons why doing "touristy" things, such as standing around to look/take photographs/study a map, etc. are likely to highlight the traveller as a tourist and alert pickpockets etc.;<br><br>There is useful information on not leaving crowded areas (but being aware of the problems within a crowded area);<br><br>The information related to reporting something lost or stolen to the local police is very useful and there is a reason beyond hoping to get your property back (that related to a subsequent insurance claim);<br><br>Students should have written complete sentences, selected useful tips, expanded on some of them, and put things into their own words. |

## PAPER 14: TRAVEL SAFELY ABROAD

| Activity 3 | | Total Marks Achievable: 18 Marks | |
|---|---|---|---|
| Question / Task | Marks | Notes | Answer / Must include |
| 1 Personal Letter | 3 | | There is evidence of research (source) documents on the chosen European destinations together with the additional information requested in the Scenario. |
| | 2 | | The personal letter includes the standard information requested. |
| | 2 | | The sentence structure is complex with spelling, grammar and punctuation correct. Verb/tense/subject agreement is evident. |
| | 3 | | The student has made use of side headings/bullet points/numbered or lettered headings to emphasise the content. |
| | 6 | | The student has offered the information in a logical way. Perhaps the letter begins with the facts (about the destinations) then progresses to the advice (related to health and passport safety). |
| | 2 | | The letter meets the purpose which is to inform and give facts. |

Functional Skills English Level 2 Summative Assessment Papers, Marking Scheme, and Tutors' Guide – ISBN: 978-1-9049955-5-5

## PAPER 15: SUNBED SAFETY

| Activity 1 | Total Marks Achievable: 23 Marks | | |
|---|---|---|---|
| **Question / Task** | **Marks** | **Notes** | **Answer / Must include** |
| 1 | 5 | Award a maximum of 5 marks.<br><br>Deduct 2 marks if the standard of written English does not meet the stated requirements. | The information in the table aims to challenge the commonly held beliefs held by many people, particularly those who use sunbeds.<br><br>Because it quotes those beliefs then goes on to give the facts related to each belief, it is an effective way of communicating the facts.<br><br>Hopefully this will make sunbed users aware of the risks and they might then think about the health risks involved in sunbed use.<br><br>The student mentions similar points, perhaps using the first person in his or her responses — "I think".<br><br>**The response should contain correct grammar, spelling, punctuation and subject/verb agreement and be in the student's own words.** |
| 2 | 8 | There are 4 facts and 1 opinion enabling you to award 1 mark for each point, up to a maximum of 5 marks with the additional 3 awarded to the standard of English.<br><br>Deduct 3 marks if the standard of written English does not meet the stated requirements. | It is a combination of fact and opinion.<br><br>The facts are:<br><br>The Government is being urged to adopt new sunbed restrictions in England in line with those already in operation in Scotland.<br><br>The advice is that sunbeds should not be allowed to be used by anyone under 18 years of age.<br><br>The Sunbed Authority says there is no proof yet that skin cancer is linked to sunbed use (it may be an opinion but it is a fact the Sunbed Authority has made the statement).<br><br>The Sunbed Authority says that its 8,000 tanning salons already operate under the voluntary guidelines drawn up by the sunbed industry.<br><br>It is opinion that the approximate figure of 100 deaths which occur each year from skin cancer are related to sunbed use. The phrase "It is thought" make this an opinion not a provable fact.<br><br>**The student mentions similar points and the response is in their own words and contains correct spelling, grammar and punctuation and subject/verb agreement.** |

Functional Skills English Level 2 Summative Assessment Papers, Marking Scheme, and Tutors' Guide – ISBN: 978-1-9049955-5-5

| Activity 1 | | Total Marks Achievable: 23 Marks | |
|---|---|---|---|
| Question / Task | Marks | Notes | Answer / Must include |
| 3 | 10 | Deduct 3 marks if the standard of English does not meet the stated requirements. | If the Government of England draws up laws related to the use of sunbeds it will, presumably, take into account the facts which have been established.<br><br>The current voluntary code set up by the Sunbed Association does not necessarily protect the sunbed user from skin cancer dangers.<br><br>Because the Sunbed Association does not accept that skin cancer is linked to the use of sunbeds, their voluntary code does not at the moment set out guidelines which acknowledge skin damage.<br><br>A law will limit the use of sunbeds, and as the law will be enforceable, sunbed operators will have to work safely and work within the restrictions which have been established to protect the health of the user.<br><br>If a law is established, as additional information is forthcoming on sunbed dangers, then the law can be changed and enforced.<br><br>If a law is established it will mean sunbed users will be protected more than they are currently, and prevented from using a sunbed with a frequency which is dangerous to their health and which encourages skin cancer.<br><br>Sunbed users would not be able to over-use sunbeds, as some perhaps do now, and in that way the law would be helping to protect them from skin cancer.<br><br>**The student mentions similar points and the response is in their own words, showing they have understood the topic and thought through their responses. Correct spelling, grammar, punctuation and subject/verb agreement is evident.** |

## PAPER 15: SUNBED SAFETY

| Activity 2 | | Total Marks Achievable: 10 Marks | |
|---|---|---|---|
| Question / Task | Marks | Notes | Answer / Must include |
| 1 | 1 | | Malignant melanoma. |
| 2 | 1 | | 50% — half. |
| 3 | 1 | | Leg: Female. |
| 4 | 2 | 1 mark for each correct answer. | Female: 5:4 ratio **(Note: the male female ratio is quoted at 4:5, hence the female ratio is 5:4).** |
| 5 | 1 | | Age group 60–64 |
| | 1 | | Gender Male. |
| 6 | 1 | | 50–54 |
| 7 | 1 | | People are diagnosed early. |
| | 1 | | People with small, thin skin tumours. |

## PAPER 15: SUNBED SAFETY

| Activity 3 | Total Marks Achievable: 17 Marks | | |
|---|---|---|---|
| Question / Task | Marks | Notes | Answer / Must include |
| Writing an Information Booklet | 17 | | The student includes evidence of the research (source) documents. |
| | | | There is evidence the information from the source documents has been put into the student's own words as far as is possible to do so. (For any technical information it is accepted that this will not be possible.) |
| | | | The booklet's content is structured so the information is in a logical order. |
| | | | The content of each article is directed towards the person who currently over-uses sunbeds and aims to explore the myths, the benefits and state the facts. |
| | | | The tone of each should be informative and persuasive and provide facts, not opinions. |
| | | | The explanation on the two types of cancer, and possibly the associated statistics of each, is clear and includes details of the symptoms (possibly the student has included a self-check list. |
| | | | If illustrations are included these are relevant and appropriate. |
| | | | The display of the booklet's information makes use of headings, side headings and perhaps bulleted or numbered points. |
| | | | Spelling, grammar and punctuation is correct. There is verb/tense/subject agreement. |
| | | | There is evidence the student's inclusion is a minimum of 500 words per article. |

## PAPER 16: WASTE BATTERY RECYCLING AND DISPOSAL

| Activity 1 | Total Marks Achievable: 10 Marks | | |
|---|---|---|---|
| Question / Task | Marks | Notes | Answer / Must include |
| 1 | 1 | | A |
| 2 | 1 | | C |
| 3 | 2 | Student should mention all three as these are included in the footnote explaining to the word "portable". | Batteries from hearing aids, mobile phones and laptops. |
| 4 | 1 | | The retailer must sell **over** 32kg of batteries (a day). |
| | 1 | | This weight equates to 1 pack of four AA batteries, **a day**. |
| 5 | 1 | | Category 1: retailers (shops)/ |
| | 1 | | Category 2: retailers (distance selling i.e. Internet selling, magazines, catalogues etc.). *Student does not have to qualify "Distance Selling".* |
| | 1 | | Category 1 (shops) must display details of the "take-back" arrangements at their **sales points**. |
| | 1 | | Category 2 (distance sellers) must include similar details on their website/in their catalogues. |

334

## PAPER 16: WASTE BATTERY RECYCLING AND DISPOSAL

| Activity 2 | | Total Marks Achievable: 16 Marks | |
|---|---|---|---|
| Question / Task | Marks | Notes | Answer / Must include |
| 1 | 1 | | Category 1: Companies which import, manufacture, distribute or sell portable batteries. |
| | 1 | | Category 2: Consumers. |
| 2 | 1 | | 1. Dry-cell non-rechargeable. |
| | 1 | | 2. Button cell. |
| | 1 | | 3. Dry-cell rechargeable. |
| 3 | 2 | Student selects 2 from the 4 mentioned. 1 mark for each correct answer. | 1. Batteries from torches 2. Clocks 3. Shavers 4. Radios. |
| 4 | 1 | | 1. Pre-paid. |
| | 1 | | 2. Polythene envelopes. |
| 5 | 1 | | The purpose of the bar chart is to illustrate the cost of each of the **5** methods of recycling involved in the Battery Collection Trials in the years 2008 and 2009. |
| | 1 | | <u>Summary possibilities</u><br><br>In 2008 the Kerbside scheme cost the most money (just over £210,000) but this cost dropped in Year 2 – 2009 to approximately £145,000.<br><br>This trend was echoed in the Retailer Take-Back category with the figures for years 1 and 2 being approximately £208,000 and £140,000 respectively. |
| | 3 | 1 mark each correct summary up to a maximum of 3 marks. | The NHS/Fire Service scheme also cost more in year 1 than in year 2 (£19,000 and £18,000 respectively).<br><br>The Community Drop-Off and the Postal scheme each cost more in Year 2 than in Year 1 (*Student might mention the figures*).<br><br>Those for the Community Drop-Off scheme cost considerably more in Year 2 than Year 1 (£40,000 and £12,000 approximately). |
| 6 | 1 | Award 1 mark only if both areas are correctly identified. | Ipswich **and** Weston-super-Mare. |
| 7 | 1 | Award 1 mark only if all three areas are correctly identified. | Cambridge, Harrow **and** Stockton-on-Tees. |

## PAPER 16: WASTE BATTERY RECYCLING AND DISPOSAL

| Activity 3 | Total Marks Achievable: 24 Marks | | |
|---|---|---|---|
| Question / Task | Marks | Notes | Answer / Must include |
| 1. Designing a Poster | 1 | | The student includes evidence of the research (source) documents. |
| | 2 | | The poster is structured and the information is presented in a logical order. |
| | 1 | | There is at least one, but not too many, appropriate image which enhances the purpose of the poster's message. |
| | 2 | | The tone should be informative and persuasive and provide facts, not opinions, and where possible these facts should be supported with examples. |
| | 2 | | The display makes use of such methods of emphasis as headings, side headings and perhaps bulleted or numbered points. |
| | 2 | | Spelling, grammar and punctuation is correct as is verb/tense/subject agreement where appropriate. |
| | 1 | | The information is accurate, including the date when the scheme begins. |
| | 1 | | There is evidence the student's inclusion is a minimum of 150 words. |
| 2 Memo | 4 | | The Memo, presented on the Memo paper provided, is from the student (inital[s]/first name and surname), addressed to the student's tutor/supervisor and includes that person's name and initial(s) and possibly a title. It is dated today (dd/mm/yyyy) and has a suitable heading. |
| | 3 | | The spelling, grammar and punctuation is correct and there is verb/tense/subject agreement. Paragraphs are present and logically ordered. |
| | 4 | | All the requested information is included and is accurate and there is evidence the document contains a minimum of 200 words. |
| | 1 | | The student signs the Memo. |

Functional Skills English Level 2 Summative Assessment Papers, Marking Scheme, and Tutors' Guide – ISBN: 978-1-9049955-5-5

Lightning Source UK Ltd.
Milton Keynes UK
23 August 2010